# ROUND THE CLOCK

Editor-in-Chief
**Austen Kark**

Managing Editor
**G.M.S. Scimone**

House Editors
**Leslie Sayers • S.M. Venuti**
**Rosemary Warne**

Ninth edition June 2001



---

British Library Cataloguing in Publication Data
A catalogue record for this book is available from the British Library
ISBN 0-907237-44-4

---

**Photography** Charles Love, Andrew O'Byrne

**Picture Research** Sue Folders

**Advertisement** Mark Simon

**Distribution** Peter Betts

**Design & Production** John Seabright, Steve Serowka

**Cartography** FWT Studios

**Printing** Waterside Press

---

**CPC GUIDEBOOKS** is an imprint of
Canal Publishing Co. Ltd, 23 Golden Square, London W1F 9JP
Tel. (020) 7439 8639 Fax. (020) 7437 0696
e-mail. mail@cpcguidebooks.co.uk

---



**Acknowledgements**

Canal Publishing/CPC Guidebooks gratefully acknowledge the help received from Merrill Lynch with this revised and expanded ninth edition and wishes to thank the many museums, archives, organizations, photographers and individuals who have given their help and made available copyright material for reproduction. Special thanks are due to: Bank of England; British Library; British Museum; BTA; Corporation of London; English Heritage; Foster and Partners; Historic Royal Palaces (Crown Copyright); National Gallery; National Portrait Gallery; National Trust; Board of Trustees of the Royal Armouries (Copyright Her Majesty the Queen); Science Museum; Tate; Victoria and Albert Museum (Crown Copyright); Wallace Collection (Crown Copyright); Dean and Chapter of Westminster.

**Front Cover:**
Wellington Arch, Hyde Park Corner

**Back Cover:**
A view of London looking north-east
with the Millennium Bridge in the foreground.

# CONTENTS

**How to use the guide**. The INDEX is the quickest way to locate an entry. It excludes places of entertainment and commercial concerns which are dealt with within their specialist sections.

'City' stands for the 'City of London', the area that is approximately within the boundaries of the original walled city. For addresses of London hotels and restaurants see "YELLOW PAGES" (pp.210-215). For opening times of places of interest see PRACTICAL HINTS.

The Area Telephone Code for London is (020). This is omitted throughout the guide. An asterisk (*) marks entries that are described more fully elsewhere in the text. In the chapter EXCURSIONS the Area Telephone Code is not repeated for places within the same area.

**Abbreviations & Symbols**. In the text these are kept to a minimum. Please also see those on the set of maps (pp. 218-219).

| | | | |
|---|---|---|---|
| bn | billion | km | kilometres |
| BTA | British Tourist Authority | LRT | London Regional Transport |
| C | Century | LTB | London Tourist Board |
| c | circa | m | metres or million |
| DLR | Docklands Light Railway | qv | quod vide (which see) |
| EU | European Union | St | Saint or Street |
| ha | hectares | TIC | Tourist Information Centre |
| Ho | House | UK | United Kingdom |

| | | | |
|---|---|---|---|
| ☛ | charge | ☺ | population |
| 🚘 | distance from London by road | £ | pound sterling |
| € | euro | ☎ | Telephone Number |
| ☞ | free entry | *i* | Tourist Information Centre's |
| ⇌ | National Rail Station | ⊖ | Underground Station |
| ✈ | nearest airport | $ | US dollar |

## Editorial Team

**Austen Kark**, CBE, MA (Oxon), Chairman and Editor-in-Chief of Canal Publishing Co Ltd (CPC Guidebooks) since 1987, was Managing Director of the BBC World Service.

**G.M.S. Scimone**, economist, journalist and former academic, has been Editorial Director of CPC since 1978.

**Leslie Sayers**, OBE, MA Cambridge (classics and history), worked for the British Council before joining CPC as Editorial Consultant and House Editor.

**Stefana M. Venuti**, Doctor of Literature (classics), has edited several books in English and other European languages for CPC.

**Rosemary Warne**, MBE, writer and researcher, spent several years in the Army after a spell as a teacher of modern history.

## Contributors

Peter Barber, Piero Bertolotti, Susan Capano, Miranda Carroll, Marjorie L. Caygill, James Dunseath, Jonathan Haslam, Peter Hill, Ben Luke, Jenny McLaughlin, Victor Rance, Jamin Smith, Antony Thorncroft.

# CONTENTS

# THE MICROCOSM

Britain's capital is one of the great cities of the world, with a distinguished and sometimes turbulent history. The first recorded description of Londinium as "a town of the highest repute and a busy emporium ..." occurs in the *Annals* of Tacitus compiled after the Roman conquest in AD 43. It has, in its time, been a centre of global and military power; a magnet for, and a creator of wealth; a beacon of hope, sanity and parliamentary democracy which has shone through storms of dictatorship and war elsewhere; and a cultural, artistic and aristocratic metropolis. It has evolved from a warren of Shakespearean alleys, stews and brothels, an abyss of Dickensian poverty, a hive of Trollopian snobbery and a concatenation of separate villages.

❑ **A NATION WITHIN A NATION.** As home for centuries to wave after wave of immigrants and refugees, London is perhaps the most ethnically mixed city in the world. It has a dozen daily newspapers, a large variety of theatres, hundreds of good and distinctive restaurants, shops and stores galore to suit every taste and old English pubs at most street corners. It is where the most long-lived monarchy exists, rich in its dramas of coronations, divorces, abdications, adulteries, ceremonies and tragedies. With an area of 1,580km$^2$, seven million inhabitants and in 1999 a Gross Domestic Product (£116bn), larger than that of Finland (£88bn), Greece (£86bn), Portugal (£74bn) or the Republic of Ireland (£48bn), London is now, and always has been, a city of unique substance and importance.

Wellington Arch, designed by Decimus Burton (1828); bronze quadriga by Adrian Jones (1912)

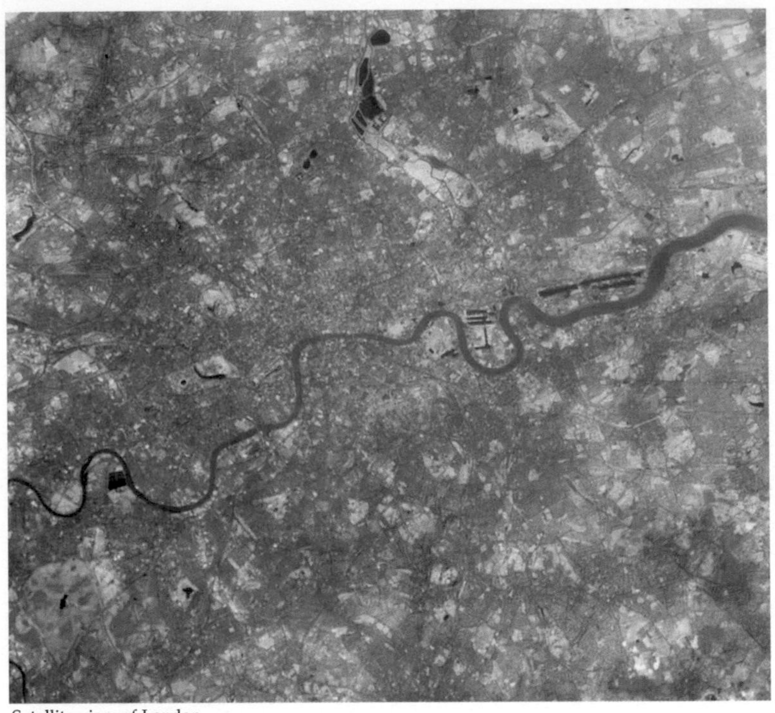
Satellite view of London

It encompasses Wembley Stadium for football, Wimbledon for tennis, Lord's for cricket and Twickenham for rugby. It is often crowded, traffic-choked, and rubbish-strewn but it has hectares of green parks, amidst the urban sprawl, and many streets and squares of elegant Georgian town houses which vary in degrees of affluence and style. It is a very handsome city, at its best, and contains one of the great global centres of finance, known as The City; the City of London, that is, as opposed to the City of Westminster where the Houses of Parliament and the West End, the centre for shopping, arts and entertainment, are to be found. It has wonderful churches and cathedrals and some of the world's greatest museums and art collections.

In addition to its 33 self-governing local authorities, Greater London has at last got its first elected mayor and General Assembly to launch

Traditionally the **East End** describes the stretch along the Thames east of Tower Bridge where especially in the 19thC groups of newcomers settled. The **West End** roughly corresponds to the south side of the City of Westminster where the greatest number of shops and places of entertainment are concentrated. Since the 17thC the word **Cockney** applies to Londoners born within the sound of the bells of the church of St Mary-le-Bow in the City.

Millenium Bridge

the first decade of the 2000s. Benjamin Disraeli, the great Victorian Prime Minister, described London as "a nation, not merely a city".

The throne, and the colourful pageantry which surrounds it, is the symbol of continuity, but the continuum against which the drama of history is played is the city itself. One year London is the 'coolest' place in the universe and a few years later it is thought unfashionable, expensive, criminal and untidy. But London remains as four-square as ever it was; a fine, tolerant, rumbustious mixture of peoples and cultures, enclosed within the elegant historic reminders of former centuries.

During the re-making of the South Bank, one building close to the river was found to have layers of older floors and entrances, rather like an inverted skyscraper. At the lowest basement, which must have been level with the Thames, was a Roman tessellated pavement. Much higher up, but again matching the contemporary level of the river, was a 19thC pawnbroker's shop, still used as a cellar by its successor, and above it, a variety of offices, merchants' stores and living space for another three floors. It was a paradigm and a palimpsest. The city changes: the city carries on.

The new millennium generated a vast programme of initiatives at public and private level, like the Dome at Greenwich and the London Eye, the world's largest Ferris wheel, near Westminster Bridge. The Millennium Bridge, a modern suspension foot-bridge across the Thames, links the area of St Paul's Cathedral to the Tate Modern at Bankside.

❑ **MILESTONES.** The capital began as a small settlement. Its initial growth was largely due to the enterprise of its Roman founders, 2,000 years ago.

• **The Roman Heritage**. The influence of Roman colonisation from 55 BC to the first part of the 5thC AD stretches far beyond the creation of Londinium as the large commercial centre and eventual premier city of Britannia. Latin still lingers on in modern English and sections of the roads built to serve the Roman legions still carry heavy traffic. Although evidence of the long Roman presence in London has been heavily overlaid by the invasions of Anglo-Saxons and Vikings, various artefacts survive. Parts of the 3rdC city wall still stand near Tower Hill and the Barbican. The layout of the *Roman Temple of Mithras**, uncovered during digging for the foundations of a modern building, can be seen in Queen Victoria Street (EC4).

Roman Wall (2ndC) and Statue probably of the Roman Emperor Trajan (AD 98-117), in Tower Gardens, Tower Hill

• **Norman Conquest** In 1066 the Norman defeat of Saxon King Harold at the Battle of Hastings led to the coronation of William the Conqueror as king of England. The new monarch set about planning fortifications, including the White Tower at the Tower of London with its Romanesque chapel of St John. The Normans compiled the comprehensive inventory of properties in England known as the *Domesday Book*; William II built *Westminster Hall* (qv Houses of Parliament) and in 1215 King John signed the document which is regarded as the basis of English liberties called *Magna Carta*. Four copies of the original survive, two in the British Library.

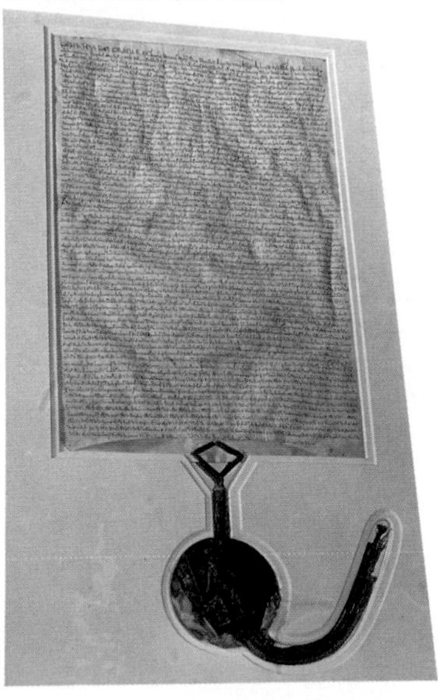

*Magna Carta*, British Library

• **Tudor Splendour.** The Tudor dynasty emerged after the defeat of Richard III by Henry Tudor at the Battle of Bosworth Field (1485). Henry VIII initiated the Reformation by breaking with the Pope and took steps to make England a great maritime power. The arts were encouraged while, in place of churches, royal and aristocratic buildings proliferated. The red-brick St James's Palace and Hampton Court Palace are fine examples of the architecture of this period. Under Elizabeth I, London enjoyed new prosperity based on the expansion of trade with the first overseas colonies, made possible by the resourcefulness of Francis Drake and other famous sea captains. Collegiate legal institutions like the Inner and Middle Temples evolved and the Shakespearean *Globe Theatre* flourished.

National Portrait Gallery: *Elizabeth I*, by or after George Gower, c1588

London from Southwark, c1650

• **The Stuarts and Cromwell.** King and Parliament were threatened by the Gunpowder Plot (1605). Charles I, who assembled a large collection of European art, was beheaded in 1649 outside Inigo Jones's Banqueting House following the fratricidal Civil War. Oliver Cromwell's Commonwealth lasted until 1660 when the monarchy was restored under Charles II. The *Great Plague* (1665) killed over 70,000 Londoners out of an estimated population of 460,000. After the *Great Fire* (1666), Christopher Wren rebuilt St Paul's Cathedral as a major baroque place of worship. He designed fifty other churches in the City including St Mary-le-Bow.

National Portrait Gallery: *Oliver Cromwell*, by Samuel Cooper, 1649

• **Georgian Classicism**. With the accession of the Hanoverian George I (1714), London became a major centre for international business, scientific achievement and art appreciation. Enterprises like the *East India Company* accumulated huge profits by dominating the trade in tea and spices from the Indian sub-continent and China. The Bank of England, founded in 1694, came to be decisive in financial transactions while Lloyd's and the Stock Exchange rose in importance. The Royal Institution, one of Europe's foremost learned scientific societies, was founded in 1799 by the physicist Benjamin Thompson. In architecture the Scottish-born Adam brothers left a lasting mark. John Nash created the magnificent Regent's Park Terraces and Regent Street while rebuilding Buckingham Palace.

Kenwood House: Library by Robert Adam

---

• **Victorian Grandeur**. London reached its mercantile zenith during the sixty-four years of Queen Victoria's reign (1837–1901). Constructed of glass and iron, the Great Exhibition of 1851 in Hyde Park owed much to the dynamism of Prince Albert, the Queen's Consort, and attracted almost 6m visitors.The rapid expansion of the railway and the erection of big stations like King's Cross (1852), Paddington (1854) and Liverpool Street (1881) enriched the image of the capital which also acquired one of the largest subway systems in the world (the Underground). The Metropolitan Police Force, with its headquarters at Scotland Yard, was established in 1829. The National Gallery opened in a neoclassical building in Trafalgar Square in the 1830s. For the Houses of Parliament, St Pancras Station and other public buildings, a neo-Gothic style was thought more appropriate.

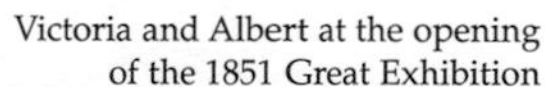

Victoria and Albert at the opening of the 1851 Great Exhibition

The Eurotunnel Link, completed in 1994, is one of the greatest engineering projects ever undertaken

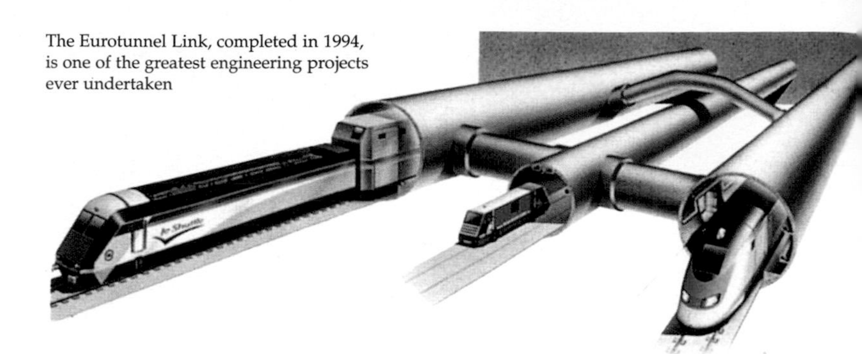

• **The 20th Century**. After the grim austerity of World War I London enjoyed one of its brightest decades only marred by massive unemployment in the 1930s. This upheaval did not prevent a rapid expansion of population to nearly 9m by 1939. Almost 1m new homes were built in Outer London, with the farmland beyond the Victorian suburbs being eaten up by housing. In central London new imposing buildings were erected. The City and the East End suffered greatly in the air raids (the 'Blitz') of World War II. The Olympic Games (1948), the Festival of Britain (1951) and the accession to the throne of Elizabeth II (1952) were the major events celebrated in post-war London. The 1960s, minis (skirts and cars), the Beatles and the Rolling Stones heralded the new carefree spirit of Carnaby Street and the King's Road 'Swinging London'. The 50km Eurotunnel twin rail link between Cheriton (Folkestone) and Fretun (Calais) was completed in 1994 with London's Waterloo Station becoming the first international terminus for trains to and from the Continent.

---

• **At the Dawn of the 21stC**. The freer business climate introduced by Margaret Thatcher and maintained by Tony Blair's New Labour government helped to give London a fresh face. The extension of the Underground Jubilee Line, linking the metropolis with the Port of London, will speed up the regeneration of the banks of the Thames. The skyline of the metropolis is bound to change dramatically following the development of a new district around Paddington Station which includes several buildings rising to 43 floors. When fully developed the site will radically transform an area the size of Soho. Other major projects include a massive skyscraper planned for the City and another by London Bridge. Here Renzo Piano, winner of the Pritzker Prize in 1998, is proposing to build a tower of glass and steel 66 storeys high which will be the sixth-highest habitable building in the world. About 10,000 would work there.

Paddington Basin Project

A

B

❑ **ARCHITECTURE.** The architecture of London embraces many styles and traditions. Construction and rebuilding during the course of the capital's history account for the juxtaposition of old and new: in the City, Wren churches shelter in the shadow of skyscrapers and, in the West End, leafy 18thC squares branch off from contemporary shopping thoroughfares. The principal architectural styles to be seen around London include:

**Norman** (11–12thC) is typified by round arches, massive columns and simple decoration of which the Chapel of St John at the Tower of London A and St Bartholomew-the-Great in Smithfield are good examples. **Gothic** (13–15thC) is represented by Westminster Abbey B with its pointed arches and traceried stained–glass windows. **Tudor** (15–16thC), an example of which is St James's Palace C, is characterised by red brick, flattened arches and fine timberwork. It gave way to a Jacobean variation and then to **English Baroque** (17–18thC) with its strong classical elements as in St Paul's Cathedral D. **Georgian** (18thC), inspired by the Palladian school with handsome door-cases

E

F

C

D

and finely proportioned windows, emerged with the arrival of the Hanoverian George I (1714) and remained in fashion for over a century. It was well-suited to the houses of the West End E. **Neoclassical** (18–19thC) refers to the revival of interest in antiquity and produced buildings with white painted façades, statuary, tall windows and Grecian decoration, such as the Terraces in Regent's Park F. The past was also echoed in the **Victorian** era (19thC), for example the Natural History Museum G and the Houses of Parliament. **Modern** architecture (20thC–21stC) encompasses a diversity of schools including Modernism, Brutalism, Hi-Tech and Post-Modernism. Current trends are represented in Embankment Place H, designed by Terry Farrell, an imposing new office building above Charing Cross Station facing the Thames half-way between Westminster and Waterloo Bridges, and in other buildings all over London. For a complete historical index, including photographs and drawings, on London's architectural heritage there is no better source than the ***National Monuments Record*** (55 Blandford St W1 ☎ 7208 8200 ⊖ Baker Street ☞).

G

H

❑ **CITIES & BOROUGHS**. London is a string of towns and villages which through the centuries have developed lives of their own. It is inevitable that visitors only identify the City, Westminster and the Royal Borough of Kensington and Chelsea with the capital. However, these areas make up but a small portion of London. They are the ancient core, the heart, as it were, but the body includes 30 other boroughs, some of which can claim a past going back several centuries.

A brief description is given of each of them with the exception of the City, Greenwich and Kensington & Chelsea. These are dealt with more fully under BUILDINGS AND LANDMARKS. Boroughs publish information on their attractions and provide facilities for tourists. To find out more, ring the borough switchboard.

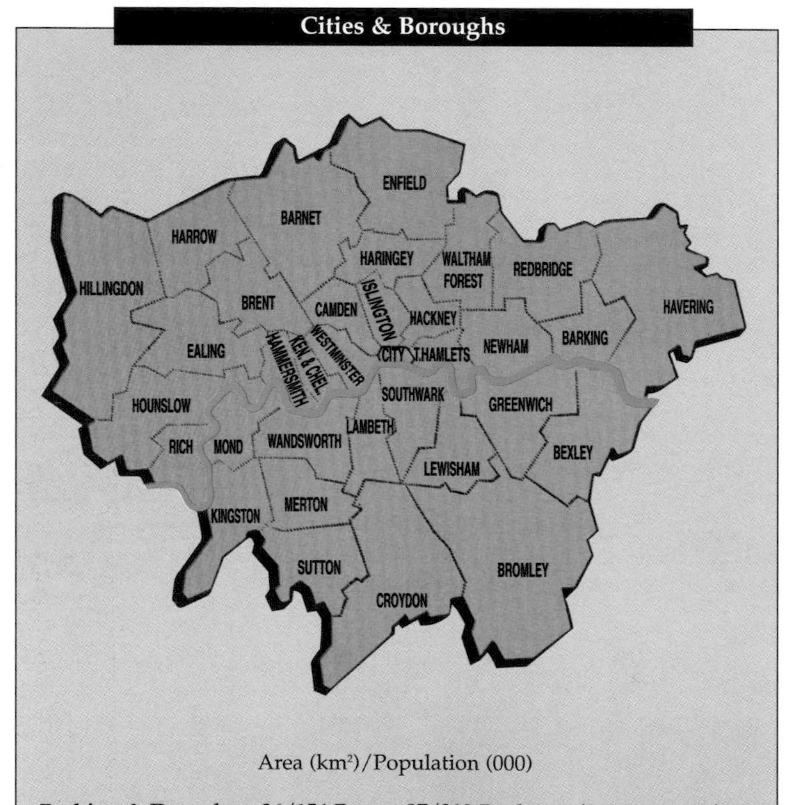


Area (km²)/Population (000)

**Barking & Dagenham** 36/154 **Barnet** 87/319 **Bexley** 61/219 **Brent** 44/244 **Bromley** 152/296 **Camden** 2/187 **City** 3/5 **Croydon** 91/327 **Ealing** 56/275 **Enfield** 81/260 **Greenwich** 50/208 **Hackney** 19/194 **Hammersmith & Fulham** 16/157 **Haringey** 30/212 **Harrow** 50/211 **Havering** 112/230 **Hillingdon** 116/232 **Hounslow** 59/204 **Islington** 15/165 **Kensington & Chelsea** 12/159 **Kingston-upon-Thames** 38/142 **Lambeth** 27/261 **Lewisham** 35/242 **Merton** 38/168 **Newham** 36/230 **Redbridge** 56/227 **Richmond-upon-Thames** 59/166 **Southwark** 29/236 **Sutton** 43/176 **Tower Hamlets** 20/178 **Waltham Forest** 40/220 **Wandsworth** 34/267 **Westminster** 22/204

**BARKING & DAGENHAM** (☎ 8592 4500), named after former fishing villages along the Thames, became industrialised with the arrival of the railway. Within the borough are the ancient ruins of Barking Abbey (7thC). In *St Margaret's Church* (13thC), Captain James Cook was married in 1762. The *Valence House Museum and Art Gallery* (Becontree Avenue, Dagenham ☎ 8595 8404 ☞), in a fine 17thC building, displays Stone and Bronze Age implements, Roman pottery, Saxon artefacts and portraits by Sir Peter Lely and other famous artists.

Major features of **BARNET** (☎ 8359 2000) are the *Hampstead Garden Suburb*, housing developments started in the 1920s, employing amongst its architects Sir Edwin Lutyens, and the Royal Air Force Museum*. The *Barnet Museum* (Wood St ☎ 8440 8066 ⊖ High Barnet ☞) and the *Church Farmhouse Museum* (Greyhound Hill NW4 ☎ 8203 0130 ⊖ Hendon Central ☞) display local history exhibits.

In **BEXLEY** (☎ 8303 7777), in the East of London, south of the Thames, *St Mary's* and *St Paulinus'* are two pre-Conquest churches with medieval remains. The *Red House* in

Crossness Pumping Station, Bexley

Bexleyheath was designed for the artist William Morris in 1860. The *Bexley Museum* (Hall Pl, Bourne Rd, Bexley ☎ (01322) 526574 ⇌ Bexley ☞) and the *Erith Museum* (Erith Library, Walnut Tree Rd, Erith ☎ (01332) 526574 ⇌ Erith ☞) are concerned with the geology, archaeology, natural history and social history of this area. The *Crossness Pumping Station* (Belvedere Rd SE2 ☎ 8311 3711 ⇌ Abbey Wood, by appointment ☛), built in the 1860s to treat sewage, is one of the finest examples of its kind in Britain.

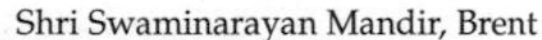

Shri Swaminarayan Mandir, Brent

Hampstead Heath

**BRENT** (☎ 8904 1244) fosters a rich diversity of cultures, including Europe's biggest *Irish Festival* and the *Hindu Navratri Festival*. The *Shri Swaminarayan Mandir* is the most intricate Hindu temple outside India. It took 27 months to build and used 2,828 tonnes of Bulgarian limestone, 2,000 tonnes of Indian and Italian marble and 127 tonnes of granite. No steel or iron was used. *Fryent Country Park* provides good views over central London. *Kensal Green Cemetery*, the first burial ground to be built outside London in the 19thC and still privately owned, contains the graves and memorials of many famous people, including the novelist Thackeray and the civil engineers Marc Isambard and his son Isambard Kingdom Brunel. *The Grange Museum of Community History* (Neasden Lane NW10 ☎ 8452 8311 ⊖ Neasden ☞) illustrates the different aspects of past life in the Wembley, Kingsbury and Willesden area.

The heritage of **BROMLEY** (☎ 8464 3333), London's largest municipality, includes Down House* where Charles Darwin lived from 1842 for 40 years until his death (1882). *Chislehurst Caves* are former chalk mines dating back to Roman times and extending for 34km. The writer H.G. Wells was born in the borough. The *Bromley Museum* (The Priory, Church Hill, Orpington ☎ (01689) 873826 ☞) explains the human development within the borough from prehistoric times to the present day. The story of the famous palace of glass, which in 1851 housed the Great Exhibition in Hyde Park and was re-erected on the present site, is displayed in the *Crystal Palace Museum* (Anerley Hill E19 ☎ 8676 0700 ⇌ Anerley Hill ☞) in the only part that survived the fire of 1936.

The area known as *Bloomsbury*, where the University of London has evolved and where the British Museum* stands, is in the south part of **CAMDEN** (☎ 7278 4444). The borough has a great number of other places of cultural and scientific interest and possesses a fine selection of Georgian, Victorian and Edwardian architecture. To the north-west is the village of *Hampstead*, surrounded by 324ha of heath. Open-air concerts take place at Kenwood. *Burgh House* (New End Sq NW3 ☎ 7431 0144 ⊖

Burgh House

Croydon Clocktower

Hampstead ☞), a Queen Anne building (1703), is a centre for local meetings and cultural activities. It houses the small *Hampstead Museum*.

Markets and fairs have flourished in **CROYDON** (☎ 8686 4433) from as early as the 13thC around the Old Palace, summer residence of the Archbishop of Canterbury until 1758. Now it is a busy town with a mini-Manhattan skyline. In 1915 *Croydon Airport* was opened as a military air base, becoming London's principal airport for thirty years. The Croydon Airport Society (☎ 8393 5226) has photographs and memorabilia of it. The *Croydon Clocktower* (Katherine St ☎ 8760 5400 ⇌ East Croydon ☛) is a new arts centre with library, cinema, concert hall and exhibition galleries.

The opening of the *Grand Union Canal* and the Great Western Railway transformed **EALING** (☎ 8579 2424) from forest and farmland into a residential area. Today *Southall* contains the biggest Indian retailing centre in Europe. *Pitshanger Manor* (Mattock Lane W5 ☎ 8567 1227 ⊖ Ealing Broadway ☞), now a museum, was the country retreat of Sir John Soane, the 18thC architect of the Bank of England and founder of Sir John Soane's Museum.

**ENFIELD** (☎ 8356 6565) boasts extensive parks. The *Enfield Chase* was a royal hunting ground in medieval and Tudor times. *Capel Manor Garden* has an 18thC house and 12ha planted with flowers and herbs of the Stuart period. *Forty Hall Museum* (Forty Hill ☎ 8363 8196 ⇌ Enfield Town ☞), in a 17thC house still retaining much of the original plasterwork and carved woodwork, exhibits collections on local history and art displays.

**HACKNEY** (☎ 8356 5000) became a sanctuary for refugees from Eastern Europe over 100 years ago when building development transformed the area from marshes and farmland. In *Shoreditch* the Elizabethan actor James Burbage established a playhouse called The Theatre before building The Globe in partnership with Shakespeare in Southwark. The church of *St Leonard* retains strong connections with actors. From the 16thC to the 18thC the nobility and rich merchants built their houses in Hackney. A fine example is the 16thC (with subsequent additions) *Sutton House* (2 & 4 Homerton High St E9 ☎ 8986 2264 ⇌ Hackney Central ☛). Set in a row of early 18thC alms-houses, the Geffrye Museum* has collections of furniture and decorative arts.

Pitshanger Manor Museum: Breakfast Room

*Fulham Palace* in **HAMMERSMITH & FULHAM** (☎ 8748 3020) was the home of the Bishops of London until recent times. Its history is told in the *Museum of Fulham Palace* (Bishops Avenue SW6 ☎ 7736 3233 ⊖ Putney Bridge ☛), based in a Georgian part of the building. Close by the Thames, the gardens are a delight. Items in the borough's archives date from 1484 and comprise paintings, prints, old photographs (over 60,000 of them), pottery and material relating to William Morris and A.P. Herbert.

The principal districts of **HARINGEY** (☎ 8975 9700) are Wood Green and Tottenham. *Alexandra Palace,* opened in 1862 as a recreational centre, was the setting for the first television transmission in 1936. A permanent exhibition covering the history of the borough is on display at the *Bruce Castle Museum* (Lordship Lane N17 ☎ 8808 8772 ⊖ Wood Green then Bus ☞).

**HARROW** (☎ 8863 5611), the only municipality to retain its Domesday boundaries, is dominated by a steep hill on top of which is *St Mary's* church, a landmark for centuries. Harrow is famous for its public school, founded in 1572, whose pupils included Lord Byron, Anthony Trollope and Sir Winston Churchill. *The Harrow School Old Speech Room Gallery* (High St, Harrow-on-the-Hill ☎ 8869 1205 ⊖ Harrow-on-the-Hill ☞) contains a varied collection of treasures: antiquities, paintings, books and mementoes of its famous pupils which include an oil of Venice by Sir Winston Churchill and a romantic portrait of Byron by W.E. West. The *Harrow Museum and Heritage Centre* (Headstone Manor Recreation Ground, ☎ 8861 2626 ⊖ North Harrow ☞), in a group of timber-framed listed buildings, displays domestic interiors and bygone agricultural implements.

**HAVERING** (☎ (01708) 434343) is situated along the great Roman road between London and Colchester. *Havering Country Park* has much to interest naturalists and a bridle path running to Hainault Forest. The chancel and nave in the church of *St Mary Magdalene* date from about 1170. Several memorials are dedicated to the Poyntz family, who for over 300 years were landlords in the area.

**HILLINGDON** (☎ (01895) 250111) accommodates *Heathrow,* the world's largest airport, and *Brunel University*, specialising in engineering. The borough has a number of interesting churches. *St Mary's* at Harmondsworth and *St Peter and St Paul's* at Harlington both have Norman doors with delicate carving.

Neighbouring **HOUNSLOW** (☎ 8570 7728) contains *Chiswick House* (Burlington Lane W4 ☎ 8995 0508 ⊖ Turnham Green ☛), one of the first and finest examples of English Palladian architecture, completed in 1729 for Lord Burlington and notable for its collection of classical statues; Hogarth's House*; Syon House*, London residence of the Duke of Northumberland; and *Osterley Park House* (Isleworth ☎ 8560 3918 ⊖ Osterley ☛), an Elizabethan mansion transformed into a grand neoclassical villa by Robert Adam in the 18thC.

Harrow School Old Speech Room Gallery: Greek vase collection

Osterley Park House

The *Gunnersbury Park Museum* (Gunnersbury Park W3 ☎ 8992 1612 ⊖ Acton Town ☞) occupies a former palatial mansion of the Rothschild family.

There is a large concentration of Georgian buildings in **ISLINGTON** (☎ 7226 1234), amongst which is the *Marx Memorial Library* (37a Clerkenwell Green EC1 Map 2Md ☎ 7253 1485 ⊖ Farringdon ☞) where Lenin edited 'Iskra' ('The Spark') during his stay in London (April 1902 to May 1903). Islington's nine theatres include Sadler's Wells, the Almeida and the King's Head in Upper Street. Among its street markets is Camden Passage for antiques and bric-à-brac.

In **KINGSTON-UPON-THAMES** (☎ 8546 2121), whose name means the King's enclosure, the most notable treasure is the *Coronation Stone*, on which several Saxon rulers are thought to have been crowned between 900–975. It is to these coronations and this stone that Kingston owes its ancient style of 'Royal Borough'. The heart of the town is the *Market*. In 1628 Charles I granted it a patent so that no other market could be established for seven miles around. Until 1750 the bridge was the first across the Thames after London Bridge. The history of Kingston is narrated at the *Kingston Museum and Heritage Service* (Wheatfield Way ☎ 8546 5386 ⇌ Kingston ☞).

Chiswick House

Within **LAMBETH** (☎ 7926 1000), almost opposite the Houses of Parliament, is *Lambeth Palace* (Lambeth Palace Rd SE1 ☎ 7928 6222 ⊖ Lambeth North), the London residence of the Archbishop of Canterbury. Architecturally the palace is a mixture: a late 12thC crypt still used as a Chapel; a Great Hall built in 1663 but modelled on a medieval banqueting hall and a massive mock Gothic wing of 1830. The Great Hall houses the Library with 200,000 printed books and 4,000 manuscripts as well as papers and diaries belonging to well known personalities of English history. Access to the Library (☎ 7928 6222) is by prior application only. From time to time the rest of the palace is open to the the public. Further down the river is South Bank*, a centre of London's cultural life. The borough is also home to the *Surrey County Cricket Club* with its *Kennington Oval* ground where international matches are played. Brixton has a large Afro-Caribbean population.

**LEWISHAM** (☎ 8314 6000) has a focus in Blackheath with its pleasant village life and a large green, where corpses were buried during the Black Death (1348). *St Paul's* in Deptford High Street is an eccentric example of Baroque architecture.

In Wimbledon, part of **MERTON** (☎ 8543 2222), the *All England Lawn Tennis and Croquet Club* is the mecca of international tennis. A large *Thai temple* is on Wimbledon Hill. Nelson lived in the area from 1801 until leaving for the Battle of Trafalgar (1805). *Wimbledon Common*, covering over 500 ha, has woodlands, open heath, several small lakes and 20km of riding tracks. The *Wimbledon Windmill Museum* (Windmill Rd, Wimbledon Common SW19 ☎ 8947 2825 ⊖ Wimbledon ☛), built in 1817 and restored at the end of the 19thC, has a rich display on the history and development of windmills in Britain.

**NEWHAM** (☎ 8472 1430) changed from an affluent 17thC residential district to an industrial area with the coming of the railway and the expansion of the Port of London. A remarkable building in the borough is the *Abbey Mills Pumping Station*.

Wimbledon Windmill Museum

Lambeth Palace

**REDBRIDGE** (☎ 8478 3020), whose name derives from a red bridge over the river Roding, has a rare breeds farm in the *Hainault Forest Country Park*. Parts still stand of the *Hospital Chapel* of St Mary and St Thomas of Canterbury, founded in the 12thC to house lepers. The monument of Sir Josiah Child (1631–99), chairman of the East India Company, dominates the church of *St Mary's* in Wanstead.

**RICHMOND-UPON-THAMES** (☎ 8891 1411) is blessed with more green spaces and historical sites than any other borough. Richmond (1,000ha) and Bushy (450ha) Parks are the largest of London's royal parks with a unique flavour of medieval England. The royal connection has endowed the borough with a splendid inheritance: the Royal Botanic Gardens at Kew* in the north and Hampton Court Palace* in the south.

*Ham House* (Ham St TW10 ☎ 8940 1950 ⊖ Richmond then Bus ☛) was built by the Thames around 1610, but now stands as it was when home to the Duke and Duchess of Lauderdale during the reign of Charles II. It is a unique monument to Restoration Baroque taste. Of *Orleans House*, (Riverside, Twickenham ☎ 8892 0221 ⊖ Richmond ☞) where Louis-Philippe, Duc d'Orleans, lived whilst exiled-from France 1815–1817, the Gallery

The Richmond Riverside

and its baroque Octagon Room are the only surviving wings. The gallery houses the Borough of Richmond Art Collection of topographical paintings, watercolours and prints. The 18thC *Marble Hill House* (Richmond Rd, Twickenham ☎ 8892 5115 ⊖ Richmond then Bus ☛) is a perfect English Palladian villa with magnificent interiors. Such is the harmonious setting of the borough that even the recent *Richmond Riverside* development echoes the scale and the character of classical language. The *Museum of Richmond* (Old Town Hall, Whittaker Ave TW9 ☎ 8332 1141 ⊖ Richmond ☛) reflects the varied history of Old Richmond while the *Public Record Office* (Ruskin Ave ☎ 8876 3444 ⊖ Kew Gardens, prior application) is the repository of the national archives for England and Wales from the time of the Norman conquest. The 'village' of *Twickenham* underwent a great expansion at the turn of the century with the development of public transport. It is the home of Rugby Football Union and the Museum of Rugby*.

Ham House: Green Closet

**SOUTHWARK** (☎ 7525 5000), the oldest suburb of the metropolis, was the point where two great Roman roads met at the south entrance of the City. By the Thames stands Southwark Cathedral*, the fourth church on the site. The *Globe Theatre* where Shakespeare's plays were performed has been rebuilt. Further south is the Dulwich Picture Gallery*, the oldest public gallery in the country.

For **SUTTON** (☎ 8770 5000), the Palace of Nonsuch, built in the reign of Henry VIII, was the jewel in the crown before being sold for demolition by a mistress of Charles II in 1682. The area underwent a building explosion in the 1920s and 1930s, but some old houses have survived. The timber framed two-storeyed *Whitehall* (1 Malden Rd, Cheam ☎ 8749 1061 ⊖ Morden ☛) dates from approximately1500.

Hawksmoor's magnificent *Christ Church, Spitalfields,* a classic example of English Baroque, is in **TOWER HAMLETS** (☎ 7364 5000), which owes its name to having the Tower of London within its boundaries. Bethnal Green, Poplar and Stepney, areas with a multi-ethnic population which in the past was much involved in shipping activities, merged within it in 1965. A reminder of those times are the markets at Petticoat Lane and Columbia Road in Shoreditch.

The Bethnal Green Museum of Childhood* merits a visit for its celebrated collection of dolls. Canary Wharf* and other areas of Docklands are within this borough.

Queen Elizabeth's Hunting Lodge

**WALTHAM FOREST** (☎ 8527 5544) was a land of forest and agriculture, until the development of public transport brought a dramatic increase in its inhabitants and the building of factories. Epping Forest lies on the eastern side of the borough. *Queen Elizabeth's Hunting Lodge* (Rangers Rd, Chingford ☎ 8529 6681 ⇌ Chingford ☛), was built in Henry VIII's reign as a grandstand from which the monarch could watch in safety the hunting laid on for his amusement in the forest.

The William Morris Gallery* has memorabilia of the 19thC artist. The first British petrol engined car (the Bremer Car) was designed and built locally in 1895. The vehicle can be seen in the *Vestry House Museum* (Vestry Rd E17 ☎ 8509 1917 ⊖ Walthamstow Central ☞).

Vestry House Museum: the Bremer Car

A major feature in **WANDSWORTH** (☎ 8871 6000) is the large Battersea Park with its pleasant walks and the *Buddhist Pagoda*. Putney is one of London's most appealing residential areas. At the *Wandsworth Museum* (The Courthouse, 11 Garratt Lane SW18 ☎ 8871 7074 ⊖ East Putney ☞) paintings, photos and maps show how Battersea, Balham, Putney, Tooting, Earlsfield, Wandsworth and Southfields grew from a scatter of rural riverside villages into a bustling London suburb.

In addition to being the hub of the nation's official and political life the City of **WESTMINSTER** (☎ 7641 6000) contains the highest concentration of landmarks and monuments, museums, places of learning, theatres, art centres and shopping thoroughfares.

In this borough there are 3,768 listed properties: 22.4% of the capital's total. The Romans camped on Thorney Island where Westminster Abbey now stands, but chose to build their capital, Londinium, further down the Thames where the river was deeper. Westminster thus grew as a separate entity from the City of London. King Canute (1016-35) was the first monarch to make Westminster a royal residence by transferring the seat of government from Winchester. The first experiment with gas street lighting was made in Pall Mall in 1807.

❑ **CULTURAL MELTING POT.** For centuries London has acted as a magnet to people from all over the world.

At present around 40% of the 7m inhabitants were born either in other regions of Britain or overseas. Some 275 languages are spoken and over 100 periodicals are printed in a language other than English. The diversity of London is such that synagogues co-exist with mosques, and Buddhist, Hindu and Sikh temples with Church of England, Greek, Russian Orthodox and Roman Catholic churches.

Chinatown: Gerrard Street, Soho

Since the 17thC, expatriates from France have gathered in Spitalfields and later in Soho, Italians in Clerkenwell, Jews in the East End and Greeks in Camden Town. These immigrants, who were preceded by Flemish and German merchants (the Hanseatic League prospered in the City for almost 400 years from the 13thC) and other nationalities brought with them much-needed skills, increasing the stature of London as a premier manufacturing and trading centre.

Before World War II, several thousand Germans were packed in a limited area around Commercial Road, the East End's principal thoroughfare. Southall, in the borough of Ealing, is home to a large community

Notting Hill Carnival, one of the greatest street festivals of Europe

London Central Mosque, Regent's Park. It includes a thriving Islamic Cultural Centre. Completed in 1977, the Mosque's minaret and golden dome can be seen from many places in Regent's Park.

Shop in Southall, Borough of Ealing, where around 42 per cent of the local inhabitants are from the Indian subcontinent.

of Indian immigrants with their temples and colourful shops. Irish workers have been significant in helping to build the metropolis and its transport system as well as making their own distinctive contribution to the armed forces and the national love of horse racing and beer, not to mention their role in music, drama and poetry.

The last twenty years have seen Soho's Gerrard, Newport and Lisle Streets become a focus for Chinese enterprise with scores of restaurants and aroma-filled supermarkets selling oriental produce. A vibrant festival in February celebrates the *Chinese New Year* with traditional lion dances. In summer the *Notting Hill Carnival* is the major show-case of Afro-Caribbean culture. For three days almost a quarter of a million people throng the area around Westbourne Grove, brought alive by colourful floats and cavalcades, loud steel bands and outdoor discos.

The *Ismaili Centre*, South Kensington, housed in a handsome building, is a multi-purpose meeting place established by the Ismaili Muslim Community. The Centre reflects the Community's values and social conscience. The *London Central Mosque* in Regent's Park (Map 1Fc) is one of the largest outside the Islamic world.

As London greets a new millennium the flow of newcomers shows no sign of diminishing. Young people from all over the world make their homes here contributing their own particular talents to the arts, entertainment, sport and other activities.

❑ **THE SUMMER SEASON.** London has something for everyone. Apart from the mainstream tourist attractions, there is always a wide range of events, exhibitions, international conferences and seminars. In recent years the number of visitors attending such occasions has increased substantially.

The Summer Season with all its tradition, pomp, pageantry and strong sporting overtones has long been a feature of the spring and summer months. Its starting point is the Chelsea Flower Show, followed by Trooping the Colour on the Queen's Official Birthday at the beginning of June, the Derby at Epsom (first Wednesday in June) and Royal Ascot soon after. Then Wimbledon for the International Lawn Tennis Championships, Henley-on-Thames for the rowing regatta and horse racing at Goodwood. It ends with the sailing regatta at Cowes, Isle of Wight, in August.

In terms of attendance the *Chelsea Flower Show* comes top of the list. Organised by the Royal Horticultural Society in the grounds of the Royal Hospital, Chelsea, it runs for five days in May attracting over 200,000 visitors. With the Queen as patron, members of the

High Fashion at Royal Ascot

royal family are prominent among the guests. It is the largest display of its kind in the world. The heart is the exhibition of plants in the marquees at the centre of the grounds where the country's greatest gardeners show their best plants and blooms.

The *Summer Exhibition* at the Royal Academy of Arts also in June used to signal the start of the high season. It is unusual in that anyone can submit paintings for consideration by a committee and although many are called, few are chosen for display at Burlington House.

*Royal Ascot*, in the same month, offers one of the highlights of the horse-racing year, giving some of the best flat racing. It is famous for its grey toppers and high fashion (especially ladies' hats) as well as its very fine thoroughbreds.

Highly popular are the international lawn tennis tournaments. The ones at Queen's Club in London for men and at Devonshire Park in Eastbourne for women are also held in June, just before *Wimbledon*, which retains the distinction of being the premier tournament and home of the game played on grass, its original surface.

**Other well-known occasions**

| | |
|---|---|
| January | *New Year Parade*, Westminster.<br>*London International Boat Show*, ExCel, Docklands E16. |
| February | *Chinese New Year celebrations**, Gerrard Street, Soho W1. |
| March | *Chelsea Antiques Fair*, Chelsea Old Town Hall SW3. |
| April | *Easter Parade*, Battersea Park SW11.<br>*The London (International) Marathon*. |
| May | *FA Challenge Cup Final*. |
| June/Aug | *International Cricket Matches*, Lord's NW8/Oval SW9. |
| July | *Hampton Court Palace International Flower Show*. |
| July/Sept | *Promenade Concerts**, Royal Albert Hall SW7. |
| August | *London Riding Horse Parade*, Hyde Park.<br>*Notting Hill Carnival**, Ladbroke Grove W11. |
| September | *Chelsea Antiques Fair*, Chelsea Old Town Hall SW3. |
| Oct/Nov | *State Opening of Parliament**. |
| November | *London to Brighton Veteran Car Run*, Hyde Park W2.<br>*Lord Mayor's Show**, City of London. |
| December | *Norwegian Christmas Tree*, Trafalgar Square WC2. |

The above list offers a glimpse of other main events.
The asterisk (*) marks those described elsewhere.

The Royal Academy: Summer Exhibition

*Glyndebourne* in Sussex, an hour by train from London, is the annual setting for a festival of opera lasting from May well into August, with Mozart's works normally its central feature. It is known for its superb setting, its high musical standards and for the audience's often extravagant picnics held on the lawns during the long interval.

Summer is also a busy period for the antiques trade in books, prints and manuscripts. Dealers and auction houses play an important part but it is the general public that makes the biggest contribution by attending in great numbers the *Summer International Book Fairs* at the Hotel Russell, the *Antiquarian Map Fair* at the Commonwealth Conference Centre and the *ABA Antiquarian Book Fair* at Olympia. As for fine paintings, furniture and objets d'art the *Grosvenor House Art and Antiques Fair* is the most prestigious while the *Fine Art and Antiques Fair* at Olympia attracts more than a quarter of a million visitors in only four days.

Pearly King

In October comes the *Pearly Harvest Festival* at St Martin-in-the-Fields where London's cockney royalty take centre stage. They are known for the profusion of pearl buttons on their clothes and are associated with the East End markets where they originally sold fruit from barrows.

❑ **FAMOUS LONDONERS.** Many of London's buildings have close associations with well-known personalities of the past, both British and foreign. Official blue plaques record such links. In some cases the places where they lived (or worked) have been turned into museums.

**Baden-Powell** Robert (1857–1941), founder of the Scout Movement, is remembered at the ***Baden–Powell House Museum*** (65 Queen's Gate SW7 ☎ 7584 7031 ⊖ South Kensington ☞).

**Bligh** William (1754–1817), commander of the *Bounty*, lived at *100 Lambeth Rd SE1*, and is buried at *St Mary-at-Lambeth Church SE1*.

**Byron** George (Lord) (1788–1824), poet, lived at *8 St James's St SW1*. Statue in *Hyde Park*.

**Canaletto** Antonio (1697–1768), Italian painter, worked and lived for 9 years at *41 Beak St W1*.

**Carlyle** Thomas (1795–1881), essayist and historian, came in 1834 to live at *24 Cheyne Row SW3*. ***Carlyle's House*** (☎ 7352 7087 ⊖ Sloane Square ☛) is open to the public, who may visit the attic studio where most of his principal works were written.

**Chaplin** Charles (1889–1977), actor, lived as a child at *287 Kennington Rd SE11* in a very modest two-room flat. Statue in *Leicester Square WC2*.

**Chaucer** Geoffrey (1340–1400), poet, lived in *Leadenhall St EC3*, and is buried in *Poets' Corner, Westminster Abbey*.

**Churchill** Winston Spencer (1874–1965), statesman and writer lived at *33 Eccleston Sq SW1*, in 1909-13, and died at *28 Hyde Park Gate SW7*. Statue in *Parliament Square SW1*. ***Chartwell*** (☎ (01732) 866 368 ☛), near Westerham, Kent, was Churchill's home for over 40 years. Here he wrote most of his books. Open to the public, it is a museum of memorabilia which includes many of his paintings.

Statue of Churchill in Parliament Square

**Constable** John (1776–1837), painter, lived at *40 Well Walk NW3* and *76 Charlotte St W1*, buried in *St John's Church, Church Row NW3*.

**Cromwell** Oliver (1599–1658), Lord Protector, died at the Palace of Whitehall and was buried in *Westminster Abbey*. Statue in *Old Palace Yard SW1*.

**Darwin** Charles (1809-82), naturalist, lived (1838-42) at *110 Gower Street WC1* and then at ***Down House*** (Luxted Rd, Downe, Orpington ☎ (01689) 859 119 ⇌ Bromley South ☛) from 1842 to his death. The appearance of the Old Study, where nearly all Darwin's scientific work was done, remains as it was during his lifetime.

**Defoe** Daniel (1660–1731), novelist, is buried at *Bunhill Fields EC2*, where are also the tombs of the hymn writer Isaac **Watts** (1674–1748), the poet and painter William **Blake** (1757–1827), John **Bunyan** (1628–1688), author of *The Pilgrim's Progress*, and Susannah **Wesley**, mother of John Wesley.

**Dickens** Charles (1812–70) lived at ***Dickens House*** (48 Doughty St WC1 ☎ 7405 2127 ⊖ Russell Square ☛), now a museum, from 1837–9. It contains the Dickens Library and a vast collection of memorabilia.

**Disraeli** Benjamin (1804–81), statesman, born at *22 Theobalds Road WC1*, lived at *93 Park Lane W1*.

**Doyle** Arthur Conan (1859–1930), creator of Sherlock Holmes, lived at *12 Tennison Rd SE25*. At the ***Sherlock Holmes Museum*** (221 Baker St NW1 ☎ 7935 8866 ⊖ Baker Street ☛) are Holmes' and Watson's possessions. 'Mrs Hudson' the housekeeper is in residence.

**Faraday** Michael (1791–1867), pioneer in the field of electromagnetism, is commemorated at the ***Faraday Museum and Laboratory*** (The Royal Institution, 21 Albemarle St W1 ☎ 7409 2992 ⊖ Green Park ☛).

**Fleming** Alexander (1881–1955) lived and died at *20a Danvers St SW3*. The ***Alexander Fleming Laboratory Museum*** (St Mary's Hospital, Praed St W2 ☎ 7725 6528 ⊖ Paddington ☛) is housed in the small laboratory where he discovered penicillin in 1928.

**Franklin** Benjamin (1706–90), American statesman and scientist, lived at *36 Craven St WC2*, and worked in the Lady Chapel of the Church of *St Bartholomew-the-Great, West Smithfields EC1*, when it was used as a printing press.

**Freud** Sigmund (1856–1939), as a refugee from Nazi–occupied Vienna, lived in 1938–9 in *20 Maresfield Gdns NW3*. The house is now the ***Freud Museum*** (☎ 7435 2002 ⊖ Finchley Road ☛). His extraordinary collection of antiquities and the famous desk and couch are all here, offering a fascinating insight into the sources and nature of his achievements as the founder of psychoanalysis.

Freud Museum: the Study

**Handel** George Frederick (1685-1759), German-born composer, lived at *25 Brook St W1* from 1723 until his death. The building with the adjacent house has become the ***Handel House Museum*** (☎ 7435 2432 ⊖ Bond Street ☛). He is buried in *Westminster Abbey*.

Hogarth's House

**Hogarth** William (1697–1764), painter and engraver, occupied for most of the last 15 years of his life a cottage in Chiswick, transformed into a museum to display drawings, reproductions and other items recording the artist's life: ***Hogarth's House*** (Hogarth Lane W4 ☎ 8994 6757 ⊖ Turnham Green ☞).

**Johnson** Samuel (1709–84), lexicographer and scholar, compiled his *Dictionary of the English Language* and *The Rambler* at *17 Gough Square EC4*, the only surviving house of the many where he lived in London. It is now the ***Dr Johnson's House Museum*** (☎ 7353 3745 ⊖ Chancery Lane ☛). Most of the objects on display are connected with Johnson and his great biographer Boswell.

**Keats** John (1795–1821), poet, lived in *Keats Grove NW3*. The house, set in a pleasant garden where Keats wrote the *Ode to a Nightingale*, has become the ***Keats House*** (☎ 7435 2062 ⊖ Hamsptead ☞) and displays many of his books,and relics.

**Kipling** Rudyard (1865–1936), writer, lived at *43 Villiers St WC2* in 1889-91. He is buried in *Westminster Abbey*.

Karl Marx, Highgate Cemetery

**Lawrence** Thomas Edward (1888–1935), known as 'Lawrence of Arabia', lived at *14 Bruton St SW1*.

**Leighton** Frederic (1830–96), painter and sculptor, lived from 1866 at *12 Holland Park Rd W14* in a building which reflects his own vision of simple exterior and rich interior. ***Leighton House*** (☎ 7602 3316 ⊖ High Street Kensington ☞) contains, in addition to his work and that of other Pre-Raphaelite artists, the Arab Hall, an authentic reconstruction which includes fine oriental tiles.

**Marx** Karl Heinrich (1818–83), German philosopher, lived at *28 Dean St W1* in 1850–56, where he wrote *Das Kapital*. His **grave** in Highgate Cemetery (Swain's Lane N6 ☎ 8340 1834 ⊖ Archway then Bus ☛) is marked by a colossal statue sculpted by L. Bradshaw. The ***Marx Memorial Library*** (37a Clerkenwell Green EC1 ☎ 7253 1485 ⊖ Farringdon ☞) is full of reminders of the 30 years Marx spent in London. In the same house the Russian leader Vladimir Ilyich Ulanovitch **Lenin** (1870–1924) edited the newspaper 'Iskra'.

**Milton** John (1608–74), poet, born in *Bread St EC4*, lived in *Petty France SW1* and *125 Bunhill Rd EC1* from 1662. Bust in *St Giles without Cripplegate EC2* where he is believed to be buried.

**More** Thomas (1478–1535), statesman, scholar and saint, born in *Milk St EC2*. Monument outside *Chelsea Old Church (All Saints), Cheyne Walk SW3*.

**Morris** William (1834–96), architect, painter, poet and designer and social reformer, is remembered by the ***William Morris Gallery*** (Lloyd Park, Forest Rd E17 ☎ 8527 3782 ⊖ Walthamstow Central ☞), set at *Water House*, his boyhood home. It is a monument to all aspects of 19thC art and design with paintings, ceramics, furniture and textiles by the leading contemporary craftsmen and artists.

**Nelson** Horatio (1758–1805), admiral, lived at *103* and *147 New Bond St W1*, buried in *St Paul's Cathedral*. Memorabilia in the National Maritime Museum* and the Lloyd's Nelson Collection*, effigy in the Westminster Abbey Museum*, monument in *Trafalgar Sq WC2*.

**Newton** Isaac (1642–1727), scientist, lodged for 30 years at *87 Jermyn St SW1* before moving to *St Martin's St WC2* and then to *Kensington* where he died. He is buried in *Westminster Abbey*.

**Nightingale** Florence (1820–1910), hospital reformer, is remembered at the ***Florence Nightingale Museum*** (St Thomas' Hospital, 2 Lambeth Palace Rd SE1 ☎ 7620 0374 ⊖ Westminster ☛), located where she established the first school of nursing in 1856, after playing a decisive role in improving the care of wounded soldiers of the Crimean War (1853–6).

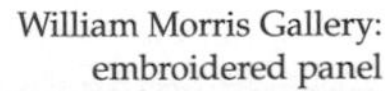

William Morris Gallery: embroidered panel

Nelson, Westminster Abbey Museum

Linley Sambourne House

**Penn** William (1644–1718), Quaker and founder of Pennsylvania, baptised at *All Hallows by the Tower, Byward St EC3*.

**Sambourne** Edward Linley (1844–1910), *Punch* political cartoonist, lived at *18 Stafford Terrace W8* from the early 1870s. The Victorian terraced house has been perfectly preserved in every detail: ***Linley Sambourne House*** (☎ 8742 3438 ⊖ High Street Kensington ☛).

**Wesley** John (1703–91), founder of Methodism, lived and died in *49 City Rd EC1*. Here is ***Wesley's House*** and the ***Museum of Methodism*** (☎ 7253 226 ⊖ Moorgate ☛) with many of his personal belongings. He is buried outside the Chapel, in the forecourt with his bronze statue.

**West** Benjamin (1738–1820), American painter, lived and died at *14 Newman Street W1*.

**Whistler** James Abbot McNeil (1834–1903), American painter, lived at *96 Cheyne Walk SW3*.

**Wilberforce** William (1759–1833), philanthropist who promoted Bill through the House of Commons for abolition of slavery (1807), died at *44 Cadogan Pl SW1*.

**Wilde** Oscar (1856-1900), Anglo-Irish playwright, poet and wit, lived for ten years at *34 Tite St SW3*, from where he left for prison following prosecution for sodomy.

**Woolf** Virginia (1882–1941), novelist and critic, lived (1907-11) at *29 Fitzroy Sq W1*.

**Wren** Christopher (1632–1723), architect, lived at *Gt Scotland Yard SW1* and *Cardinal's Wharf, Bankside SE1*. He is buried in the crypt of *St Paul's Cathedral*.

**Yeats** William Butler (1865–1939), Irish poet, lived at *23 Fitzroy Rd NW1*.

Display in Wesley's House

# CEREMONIES & PAGEANTRY

London's pageantry has evolved through the ages adapting to changing times. Some ceremonies like the Coronation ritual date back over a thousand years while others (Jubilee celebrations, Queen's Birthday Parade, etc) have developed within the last two centuries.

The Changing of the Guard at Buckingham Palace by the Foot Guards and by the Household Cavalry at Whitehall are probably the most popular with Londoners and visitors.

❑ **CHANGING THE GUARD** usually takes place outside Buckingham Palace. When seen marching to and from the ceremony, the *Queen's Guard* is in three main groups. First comes a regimental band, followed by the St James's Palace detachment – who carry the Colour – and then the Buckingham Palace detachment. The order of precedence is governed by the fact that St James's Palace still officially remains the Court and it is there where the Captain of the Queen's Guard establishes his headquarters and the Colour is lodged. At 1130 the New Guard (consisting of officers and men, and the Queen's Colour when the Court is in residence), led by a band, marches into the forecourt of Buckingham Palace. This ceremony takes place every day in summer and every other day in winter, but arrangements can vary.

Life Guards entering Hyde Park

The Queen's Guard is traditionally formed from one of the five regiments of Foot Guards. Each unit, when wearing full dress uniform, is distinguished by the plume on the bearskin, the position of tunic buttons and the epaulettes. Only the *Scots Guards* (established in 1642) have no plume; it is red for the *Coldstream* (1650), *white* for the *Grenadiers* (1656), blue for the *Irish* (1900) and green and white for the *Welsh* (1915). As the Foot Guards have normal service commitments at home and abroad as well as their ceremonial duties, the Queen's Guard is occasionally formed by other regiments.

The **Guards Museum** (Birdcage Walk SW1 ☎ 7930 4466 ⊖ St James's Park ☛) presents a comprehensive display of uniforms, arms and memorabilia covering the history of the five regiments.

*The Queen's Life Guard* at the Horse Guards Building in Whitehall is the oldest and most senior royal guard and is provided by mounted units of the Household Cavalry – the *Life Guards* and the *Blues and Royals*. The Life Guards wear scarlet tunics with white helmet plumes and the Blues and Royals wear blue tunics and red helmet plumes. When the Queen is in London, one mounted officer and 15 other ranks carrying a standard and preceded by a trumpeter (on a grey horse) attend. Changing the Guard at ***Whitehall*** generally takes place at 1100 on weekdays and at 1000 on Sundays. Two mounted troopers of the Household Cavalry are daily posted outside the Horse Guards Building from 1000 to 1600 and relieved every hour.

❑ **TROOPING THE COLOUR** takes place annually on the official birthday of the Sovereign in mid-June. Its origins lie in the early 18thC when the Colour was regularly marched or 'trooped' before the regiment so that every soldier would learn to recognise his own Colour in the smoke of battle. Today the ceremony is a demonstration of loyalty to both the Colour and the Sovereign. On Horse Guards Parade, over a thousand guardsmen and their officers in scarlet tunics await the Queen who, escorted by her Household Cavalry, rides in an open carriage from Buckingham Palace arriving at Horse Guards Parade

Changing the Guard at Buckingham Palace

State Opening of Parliament

at 1100. The Colour is then trooped in her presence after which she returns, with the Sovereign's Escort, to the Palace.

❑ **STATE OPENING OF PARLIAMENT**, perhaps the most splendid of the royal ceremonies, occurs in late October or early November. Essentially this has changed little in the past 400 years. The Queen, wearing the Imperial State Crown, rides in the gilded Irish State Coach from Buckingham Palace to the Palace of Westminster (the official title of the Houses of Parliament), where she is received by the Law Lords of the Realm in their formal black robes and long grey wigs of office and by other Officers of State. In the House of Lords she reads to the assembled Lords and Commons the Speech from the Throne, prepared by the Government, which outlines its programme for the coming session.

❑ **THE LORD MAYOR'S SHOW** takes place on the second Saturday in November. This is a magnificent procession 600 years old which represents pride in the City's history and its strength as a centre of world commerce. The newly elected Lord Mayor rides from Guildhall in the splendid gilded coach (built in 1757), drawn by six horses, past St Paul's Cathedral, down Fleet Street to the Law Courts where he takes his oath of office before the Lord Chief Justice. He/she is attended by senior members of the ancient guilds in their traditional livery, beadles in three-cornered hats wearing the black and gold denoting their civic office in former times and by his/her personal bodyguard of the Company of Pikemen and Musketeers in their scarlet and gold who march alongside the splendid coach.

# BUILDINGS & LANDMARKS

Many of the best-known buildings date from the century between Waterloo (1815) and World War I (1914). Very little remains from the medieval period as a result of the Great Fire of 1666 when 13,000 houses and 89 churches including Old St Paul's were destroyed. There is, however, a great deal to see around the capital. The sheer size of London makes it essential to plan a visit carefully, taking into account traffic congestion. Places, buildings and landmarks are presented in their alphabetical order according to the more familiar names which are not necessarily the official ones (e.g. Houses of Parliament, rather than the Palace of Westminster).

❑ **BUCKINGHAM & ST JAMES'S PALACES** These are the two main residences of the monarch in the capital. BUCKINGHAM PALACE (The Mall SW1 Map 6Hh ⊖ St James's Park) has been the London home of British sovereigns since Queen Victoria acceded to the throne in 1837. When the Sovereign is in residence, the Royal Standard flies above the Palace. Its 300 rooms and grounds occupy the site of Buckingham House, built in 1703 by the Duke of Buckingham and bought by George III in 1762 as a private town dwelling for Queen Charlotte. The present building was started in 1821, and carried out to the design of John Nash. The East Wing, built in 1847, is the part of the palace most

Buckingham Palace from St James's Park

familiar to the general public, being dominated by the Balcony Room with the central window from which the Royal Family steps on to the balcony on special occasions.

At the back of Buckingham Palace is a large garden of about 3.6ha with a fine lake at its centre and a tennis court. The viewing gallery in the restored **Wellington Arch** (☎ 7930 2726 Map 5Gh) at Hyde Park Corner offers an unrivalled vantage point from which to peer at the gardens. These provide the venue for the Royal Garden Parties in summer which were instigated by Queen Victoria and continue to this day.

## Buckingham Palace: State Rooms

(☎ 7839 1377 Aug-Sept ☛)

These have been open to the general public since 1993, during August and September. The tour is confined to major rooms or areas and the visitor is at once absorbed in the grandeur of the palace and the high quality of its contents.

Ten portraits by Sir Thomas Lawrence, Beechey and other distinguished artists dominate the ***Grand Staircase*** while the ***Guard Room*** has 19thC statuary including Queen Victoria herself by John Gibson. The furniture of the ***Green Drawing Room*** includes two exquisite French chests of drawers and a Sèvres porcelain vase in the shape of a boat which belonged to Madame de Pompadour. Seven Regency glass and gilt bronze chandeliers light the ***Throne Room***. Amongst the paintings in the ***Picture Gallery*** are works by Van Dyck, Rubens, Rembrandt, Zuccarelli, Carlevaris and Poussin.

The ***Silk Tapestry Room*** contains a large French clock (1775) and furniture of the same period. Pictures in the ***East Gallery*** and the ***Cross Gallery*** include works by Sir George Hayter, Winterhalter and Benjamin West. Four Gobelin tapestries adorn the ***West Gallery***. The ***State Dining Room***, used for receptions, contains state portraits of the Hanover dynasty and four French gilt bronze candelabra made in 1783 for Versailles.

The ***Blue Drawing Room*** has a portrait of George V by Sir Luke Fildes and the Sèvres porcelain table made for Napoleon. In the ***Music Room*** are the Throne Chairs used by King George V and Queen Mary when Prince and Princess of Wales at the coronation of Edward VII. A concert grand piano by Erard (c1856) is in the ***White Drawing Room***. A mahogany and gilt bronze barograph made in 1765 for George III at a cost of £1,178 (over a million pounds at current prices) and two 18thC Gobelin tapestries adorn the ***Ministers' Staircase*** while the sculpture of *Mars and Venus* by Canova is situated in the ***Marble Hall***. The ***Bow Room***, which concludes the tour, has portraits by Nicaise de Keyser and Winterhalter set into panelling.

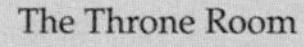

The Throne Room

The Marble Arch, which stood in front of the Palace, was later removed to its present site at the north-east corner of Hyde Park to make room for the **Queen Victoria Memorial** (Map 6Hh), erected in 1911. At the base, facing the Mall, is the seated figure of Queen Victoria carved from a block of white marble.

St James's Palace

The Queen's Gallery and the Royal Mews are in the south wing of the palace, along Buckingham Palace Road. The **Queen's Gallery** (☎ 7839 1377 Map 6Hh ☛), is the venue for temporary exhibitions from the Royal Family collections. In the **Royal Mews** (☎ 7839 1377 Map 6Hj ☛) coaches, landaus, carriage horses and cars used by the Royal Family can be viewed by the public. The carriages include the Gold State Coach built in 1762, and used at the coronation ceremony ever since.

Built for Henry VIII, **ST JAMES'S PALACE** (SW1 Map 5Jh ⊖ Green Park) remains the official court. Foreign ambassadors are always accredited to 'The Court of St James' and Royal Proclamations are first read from the balcony overlooking Friary Court. It was intermittently used by the Royal Family up to 1837. Today it is the London home of the Prince of Wales, the heir to the throne. It also contains the offices of the Lord Chamberlain and is the headquarters of the Queen's Bodyguard: the Yeomen of the Guard (instituted by Henry VII, 1485) and the Gentlemen at Arms (Henry VIII, 1509). The palace was built around four courts of which three still exist: ***Colour Court, Ambassadors' Court*** and ***Friary Court.*** The latter is the scene of a ceremony enacted in connection with Changing the Guard*, when the new Colour is lodged in the palace Guard Room. The proclamation of a new Sovereign also takes place from a balcony overlooking this court.

All the buildings have been much restored, and little remains of the original structure except the ***Clocktower Gatehouse*** on the north front, the ***Guard Chamber***; the ***Presence Chamber*** and most of the ***Chapel Royal***, with a ceiling thought to be in part the work of Holbein.

The beautiful **Queen's Chapel** (Map 5Jh), across Marlborough Road, was designed by Inigo Jones for Henrietta Maria, wife of Charles I. **Clarence House** (Map 5Jh), completed by John Nash in 1828, stands at the south-west wing of St James's Palace and takes its name from the Duke of Clarence, third son of George III who later became William IV. Since 1953 it has been the London residence of Queen Elizabeth, the Queen Mother. The Italianate **Lancaster House** (Map 5Jh) was built in 1825–26 for the then Duke of York and is now used for meetings involving heads of state.

# Kings & Queens

HM Queen Elizabeth II succeded to the throne on 6 February 1952 and HRH Prince Charles, Prince of Wales, is the heir. The Queen is the 43rd Sovereign since Edward the Confessor and her reign is already one of the longest in British history.

**Saxon and Dane**

| | |
|---|---|
| Edward the Confessor | 1042-1066 |
| Harold II | 1066 |

**Norman**

| | |
|---|---|
| William I | 1066-1087 |
| William II | 1087-1100 |
| Henry I | 1100-1135 |
| Stephen | 1135-1154 |

**Plantagenet**

| | |
|---|---|
| Henry II | 1154-1189 |
| Richard I | 1189-1199 |
| John | 1199-1216 |
| Henry III | 1216-1272 |
| Edward I | 1272-1307 |
| Edward II | 1307-1327 |
| Edward III | 1327-1377 |
| Richard II | 1377-1399 |

**Lancaster and York**

| | |
|---|---|
| Henry IV | 1399-1413 |
| Henry V | 1413-1422 |
| Henry VI | 1422-1461 & 1470-1471 |
| Edward IV | 1471-1483 |
| Edward V (Apr-June) | 1483 |
| Richard III | 1483-1485 |

**Tudor**

| | |
|---|---|
| Henry VII | 1485-1509 |
| Henry VIII | 1509-1547 |
| Edward VI | 1547-1553 |
| Mary I | 1553-1558 |
| Elizabeth I | 1558-1603 |

**Stuart**

| | |
|---|---|
| James I | 1603-1625 |
| Charles I | 1625-1649 |
| The Commonwealth | 1649-1660 |
| Charles II | 1660-1685 |
| James II | 1685-1688 |
| William III/Mary | 1688-1702 |
| Anne | 1702-1714 |

**Hanover**

| | |
|---|---|
| George I | 1714-1727 |
| George II | 1727-1760 |
| George III | 1760-1820 |
| George IV | 1820-1830 |
| William IV | 1830-1837 |

**Saxe-Coburg**

| | |
|---|---|
| Victoria | 1837-1901 |
| Edward VII | 1901-1910 |

**Windsor**

| | |
|---|---|
| George V | 1910-1936 |
| Edward VIII | 1936 |
| George VI | 1936-1952 |
| Elizabeth II | 1952- |

Ancient heartland of London: a modern panorama

❑ **THE CITY** (Corporation of London ☎ 7606 3030 Map 2, 3). Founded by the Romans almost 2,000 years ago, the 'Square Mile' (as the City is also known) was the starting point from which London expanded and developed. Throughout the centuries it has influenced each stage of British history. The City is administered by the Corporation of London, which is older than Britain's Parliament. A non-party political body, its structure stems from ancient privileges granted by the Crown and ratified by Charters in 1199 and 1215. It runs its own police force and the nation's Central Criminal Court, commonly known as the **Old Bailey** (EC4 ⊖ St Paul's).

Its merchants were always to the fore in curbing the excesses of religious and political leaders. They organised themselves into powerful **Livery Companies**. There are 104 Livery Companies, many dating back to the Middle Ages. The 12 'Great' in order of precedence are: Mercers, Grocers, Drapers, Fishmongers, Goldsmiths, Skinners, Merchant Taylors, Haberdashers, Salters, Ironmongers, Vintners and Clothworkers. Each company has its own colours, crest and trademarks. The larger ones have their own beautiful halls which may be visited at certain times of the year (details from the Corporation of London). Many are rich in treasures associated with their crafts. The **Clock Museum** (Guildhall Library, Aldermanbury EC2 ☎ 7332 1865 Map 3Pe ⊖ Moorgate ☞) contains all kinds of exquisite and ingenious time-pieces.

Mansion House

The City's headquarters is the **Guildhall** (Aldermanbury EC2 ☎ 7606 3030 Map 3Pe ⊖ Moorgate), erected originally in the 15thC. Severely damaged in World War II, it has been restored and expanded. The **Guildhall Art Gallery** (EC2 ☎ 7332 3700 ☛) displays works from the permanent collection of 4,000 paintings, drawings and sculptures including artists such as Constable, Landseer, Millais and Lord Leighton. The exhibition, arranged thematically, changes periodically to explore different subjects. The gallery is built over

## The Lord Mayor and the City's Coat of Arms

There have been over 600 Lord Mayors since 1192, when Henry FitzAilwin, the first mayor, took office, although the title of "Lord" was not used until the 15thC. Nowadays the office is held for one year. To be elected the candidate must be a Freeman of the City and have served as an Alderman and as a Sheriff. The final selection is made on Michaelmas Day (29 September) and the new Lord Mayor is admitted to office on the second Friday in November at a ceremony in Guildhall called the *Silent Change*.

The Lord Mayor's Procession* takes place the following day. As first citizen of the City he takes precedence over all except the Sovereign and lives for his year of office in Mansion House. On civic or state occasions he wears the 16thC Collar with the Jewel, last replaced in 1799. When he appears in plain morning or evening dress the Jewel is suspended from a ribbon of dark blue silk, worn around the neck.

In the **City's Coat of Arms**, devised in 1381 and modified in 1609, the cross is that of St George, while the sword is the symbol of St Paul, the patron saint of the City. The motto *Domine Dirige Nos* means 'O Lord, guide us'.

The Guildhall

The Royal Exchange

part of a Roman amphitheatre. The nearby **Guildhall Library** (☎ 7332 1839 ☞) has a fine collection of manuscripts, prints and books on all aspects of London.

Opposite the Bank of England* is the **Royal Exchange** (Threadneedle St EC2 Map 3Pf ⊖ Bank), the successor of the original exchange founded by Sir Thomas Gresham in 1566. The present construction dates from 1844. Nearby is **Mansion House** (Map 3Pf), the official residence of the Lord Mayor since 1752, designed by George Dance the Elder. Its interior, behind the majestic portico, is appropriately palatial. Amongst its many treasures is a fine collection of 17thC Dutch and Flemish paintings.

In Queen Victoria Street (EC4), within the courtyard of Bucklersbury House, can be seen the remains of the 1stC AD **Roman Temple of Mithras** (Map 3Pf ⊖ Mansion House). The **Monument** (EC3 ☎ 7606 3030 Map 3Pf ⊖ Monument ☛) stands as a memorial to the Great Fire (1666), which fortunately spared **St Bartholomew-the-Great** (West Smithfield EC1 Map 3Ne ⊖ Barbican). Founded by Rahere in 1123, together with the adjoining hospital, this church is one of London's oldest buildings, and still displays a 13thC Gateway with half-timbered upper storeys and the font (1493) where Hogarth was baptized.

The Monument

St Bartholomew-the-Great

The adjacent **St Bartholomew's Hospital** is London's oldest hospital on its original site. Its medical school, established in 1662, is one of the most illustrious. Two large canvases by Hogarth adorn the walls of the Grand Staircase leading up to the Great Hall. **All Hallows by the Tower** (Byward St EC3 ☎ 7481 2928 Map 3Rg ⊖ Tower Hill ☛) is another church full of historical associations. Although gutted in 1941 (except the 17thC brick tower from which Pepys watched the Great Fire) it has been skilfully restored. It has the largest set of brasses in London dating from 1389–1651. William Penn was baptized and John Quincy Adams married here.

Only 24 of the 50 churches built by Wren survive in the City. As well as St Paul's Cathedral* other masterpieces are **St Lawrence Jewry** (Gresham St EC2 Map 3Pe ⊖ Bank), the Guild Church of the Corporation of the City of London, **St Mary-le-Bow** (Cheapside EC2 Map 3Pf ⊖ Mansion House), and **St Stephen Walbrook** (Walbrook EC4 Map 3Pf ⊖ Bank), with a distinctive dome and for its altar a 10-ton block of marble by the British sculptor Henry Moore. **St Bride's Church** (Fleet St EC4 Map 2Mf ⊖ Blackfriars) has the highest of all Wren's spires (68m). Its ***Museum*** (☎ 7353 1301 ☞), in the Crypt, presents a history of the various churches that have stood on this site since the 6thC.

Fleet Street, once the home of the national newspapers, and the **Inner** and **Middle Temple** (EC4 ⊖ Temple) are also inside the 'Square Mile'. These, the most famous Inns of Court linked to the legal profession since the Middle Ages, occupy a site owned until 1312 by the Knights Templar. In the ***Middle Temple Hall*** the panelling, carved screen, ceiling and heraldic glass date from the 16thC. The Hall contains a serving table made from timbers of Drake's 'Golden Hind'. ***Temple Church*** is one of the few remaining Norman 'round churches' in England.

The Barbican

**Prince Henry's Room** (17 Fleet St EC4 Map 2Mf ⊖ Temple ☞) is a half–timbered house with a fine Jacobean plaster ceiling. In front of this building stands the **Temple Bar Memorial** (Map 2Mf), which marks the western boundary of the City. Here the Lord Mayor meets the Sovereign on royal visits to surrender the City's sword.

**Broadgate** (EC2 Map 3Ne ⊖ Liverpool Street) provides the City with more than one million $m^2$ of office space while the **Barbican** (EC2 ⊖ Barbican, Moorgate), owned, founded and run by the Corporation of London, is the largest residential complex in the 'Square Mile'. As well as 2,110 flats and houses, ornamental lakes, landscaped gardens and the Museum of London* it includes a 2,000 seat concert hall, two theatres, three cinemas and the ***Barbican Art Gallery*** (Silk St EC2 ☎ 7638 4141 Map 3Ne ⊖ Barbican ☛), a major venue for international exhibitions. Of the structures that stood on the site before World War II the historic 16thC church of **St Giles** and a portion of **Roman wall** have been retained.

Many buildings of modern design are scattered throughout the City. The most striking (and controversial) is the headquarters of Lloyd's* by Richard Rogers (1986).

The City has some of the oldest inns in the country and is acquiring a reputation for sophisticated international cuisine. Of the many shops, Marks & Spencer on Finsbury Pavement and Fenchurch Church Street are the biggest. In contrast the refurbished Royal Exchange is a cluster of boutiques selling luxury brands.

Located next to St Paul's Cathedral, the City of London Information Centre provides information on the attractions and events in the 'Square Mile'.

❑ **DOCKLANDS** (☎ 7364 4970). A new London is taking shape along the banks of the Thames, east of London Bridge, in what is one of the most extensive regeneration projects in Europe. Here until the mid 1950s, the Port of London handled some 1,000 ships a week with a workforce in excess of 30,000 dockers.

Then, due to dramatic changes in the management of sea traffic, trade declined, shipping went elsewhere and an area of over 22km$^2$ lay neglected.

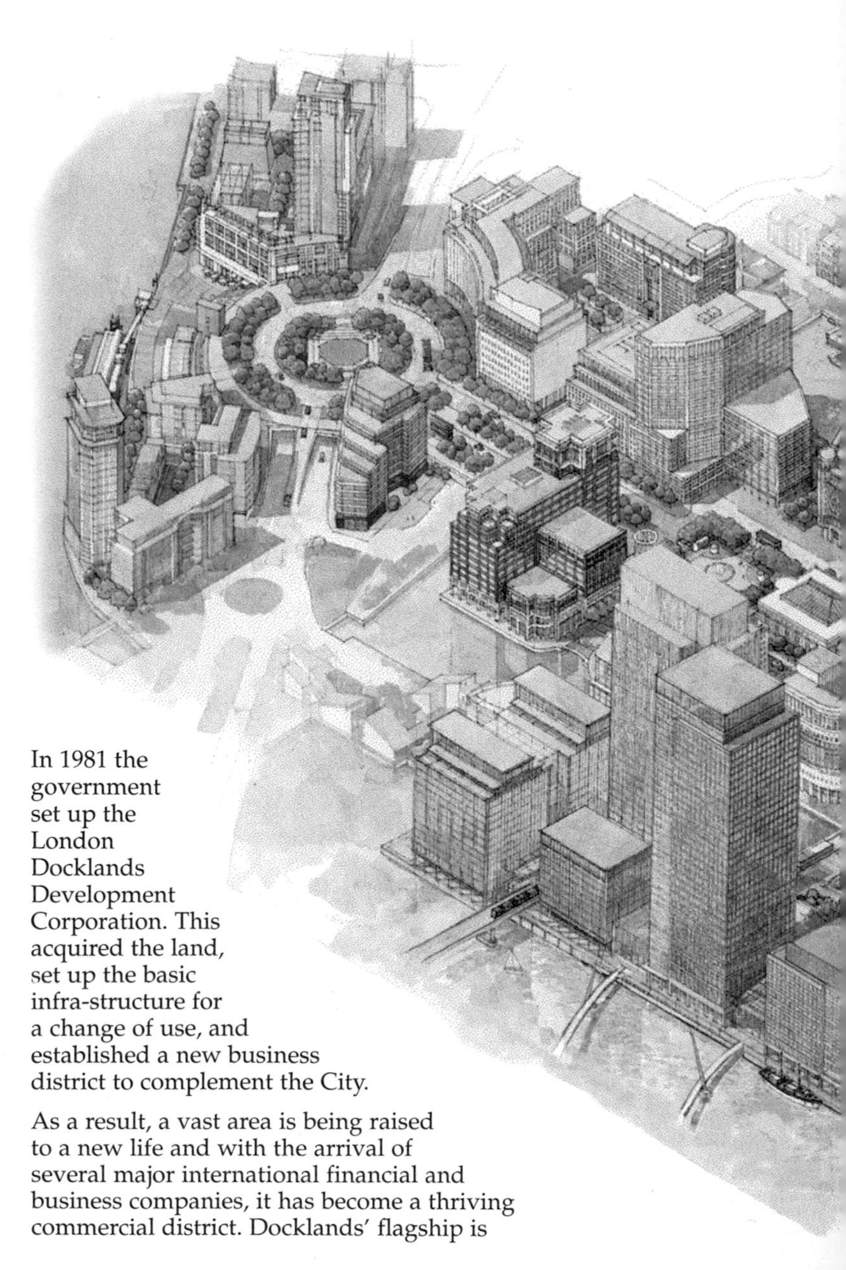

In 1981 the government set up the London Docklands Development Corporation. This acquired the land, set up the basic infra-structure for a change of use, and established a new business district to complement the City.

As a result, a vast area is being raised to a new life and with the arrival of several major international financial and business companies, it has become a thriving commercial district. Docklands' flagship is

**Canary Wharf** (E14 DLR Canary Wharf), so called because, when in use as a dock, many of the goods imported were from the Canary Islands. About 4.2km to the east of the Bank of England, the estate comprises 13 huge office buildings, retail and conference centres and approximately 8ha of landscaped open spaces.

Some of the world's leading architects have been involved in the creation of Canary Wharf. The skyscraper **One Canada Square**, designed by the Argentinian Cesar Pelli, is the tallest building in Britain. Here everything has been conceived on a large scale. Its 50 floors of offices accommodate 7,000 people. It has 3,960 windows, 32 passenger lifts and a 12m high lobby with Italian and Guatemalan marble. The aircraft warning light at the very top of the tower flashes 40 times a minute, 57,600 times a day. Canary Wharf has a daily population of over 35,000 which is due to increase to 90,000 by 2005.

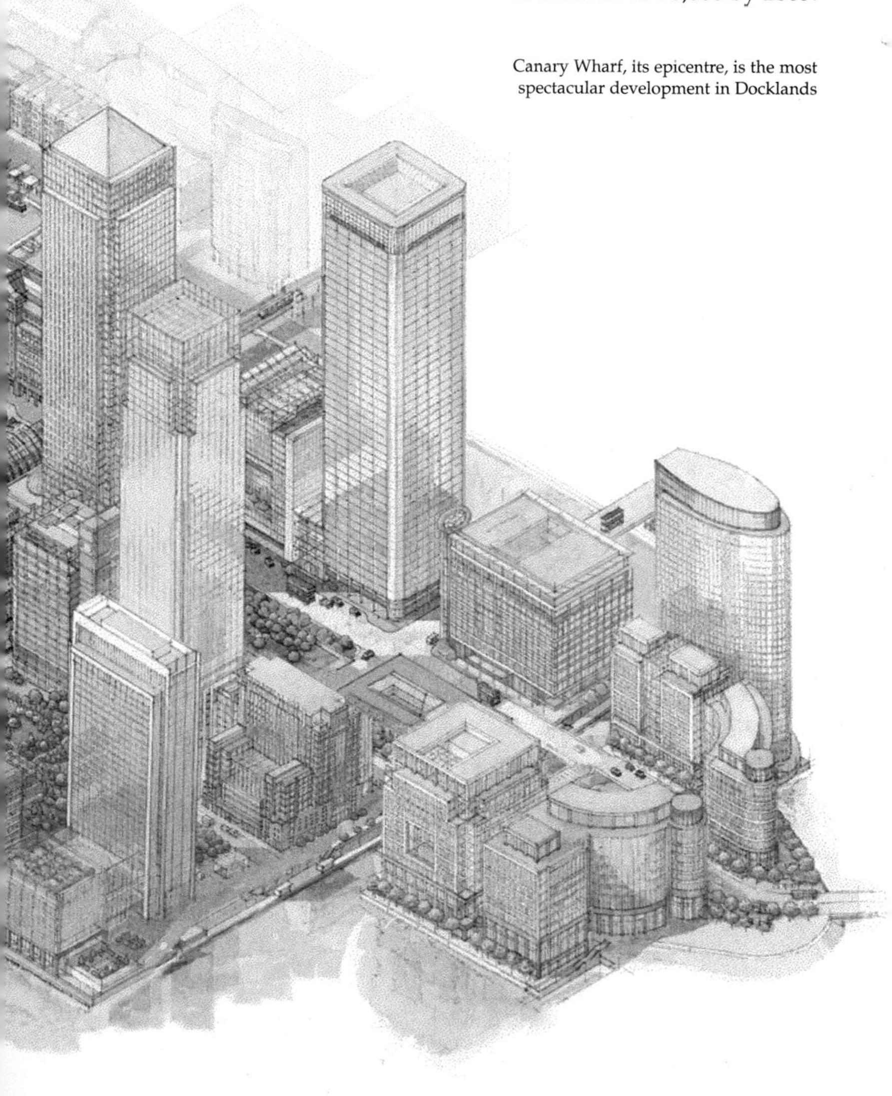

Canary Wharf, its epicentre, is the most spectacular development in Docklands

The Design Museum

Indeed the future of this part of London looks exciting. Two imposing new sky-scrapers have been completed next to One Canada Square and others are planned in adjoining development sites. Major official bodies (e.g.: the Financial Services Authority), several large private firms and many national newspapers have moved their main offices to Docklands.

ExCel, the large state-of-the-art exhibition complex, as well as many restaurants, hotels and shops, opened here at the end of 2000. **Stratford**, north of Canary Wharf, is expected to host the new European rail terminal for the Channel Tunnel and to become the 'capital' of East London with numerous cultural attractions including a centre for the performing arts and the refurbished Victorian Theatre Royal.

Closer to the City of London, just to the south across Tower Bridge, the Butlers Wharf development houses two diverse collections. The **Design Museum** (Butlers Wharf, Shad Thames SE1 ☎ 7403 6933 ⊖ Tower Hill ☛) has a revolving collection of contemporary design exhibits. Also worth a visit is the **Bramah Tea and Coffee Museum** (The Clove Building, 4 Maguire St SE1 ☎ 7378 0222 ⊖ Tower Hill ☛), which shows the effect that coffee and tea have had on Londoners and British society. It not only tells the story of the two great trades which were carried on in the Butlers Wharf area for the last 350 years but also houses a comprehensive collection of over 1,000 coffee makers and teapots.

Bramah Tea and Coffee Museum: ornate teapot

Two other museums farther east are the **North Woolwich Old Station Museum** (Pier Rd E16 ☎ 747 47244 ⊖ East Ham ☞), which tells the story of the Great Eastern Railway, while the **Museum in Docklands** (1 Hertsmere Rd E14 LDR West India Quay ☎ 7515 1162 ☛) shows the history of the London port since Roman times.

With its glorious ticket halls, designed with uncomplicated layout and use of natural light wherever possible, and its ultramodern platforms the *Jubilee Line* connects Docklands to the centre and the northwest of London. The City itself is linked to Canary Wharf by the *Docklands Light Railway* (DLR).

An alternative route by boat during peak hours is offered by the Storm Clipper. This service runs regularly from Blackfriars Bridge, London Bridge City and St Katharine's Dock and the journey takes approximately 8-15 minutes according to the point of departure.

The **London City Airport** (☎ 7646 0088 Bus Shuttle from Liverpool Street Station), 4.8km from Canary Wharf, opened in 1987. It has 13 airlines serving 25 European destinations.

❑ **GREENWICH** (☎ 8854 8888). This London borough, the venue of the official celebrations of the Millennium with the huge Dome being the focus, is situated about 8km to the southeast of the City. It is a place of grand vistas and rare beauty. Birthplace of Henry VIII and Elizabeth I and with nearly 15km of riverside boundaries it has a strong link with the exploration of the sea.

Borough Coat of Arms

The clipper **Cutty Sark** (King William Walk SE10 ☎ 8858 3445 DLR Cutty Sark ☛), in a permanent dry dock by the Thames, commemorates the Golden Age of sail. Launched at Dumbarton (Scotland) in 1869 she won an enduring fame two years later with the fastest voyage from China to England completed in 107 days. Above decks is the complex array of rigging and masts that is characteristic of sail. Below are the exhibits that have been collected from other ships, including the *Long John Silver Collection* of figureheads. Almost alongside the Cutty Sark in a special berth stands the sailing ketch **Gipsy Moth IV** on which Sir Francis Chichester sailed single-handed around the globe in 1966-7 capturing the imagination of the entire world.

Besides its fine architecture, Greenwich is endowed with many open spaces. **Greenwich Park** between Blackheath and the Thames covers 73ha and is the oldest enclosed royal parkland and the only one east of Central London. The London Marathon, one of the major sports events of the year, starts from this park. Amongst Greenwich's glories are the magnificent Royal Naval College, the National Maritime Museum*

Aerial view of historic Greenwich

Royal Naval College: Painted Hall

with the Old Royal Observatory which established Greenwich as the principal meridian of longitude, and thereby Greenwich Mean Time as the global time reference.

The **Royal Naval College** (SE10 ☎ 8858 2154 DLR Cutty Sark ☞) was built during the reign of William and Mary as a home for retired seamen. It has now become part of the campus of the University of Greenwich. Wren was responsible for the general plan of the building but other famous architects, like Hawksmoor and Vanbrugh, were also involved. The ***Painted Hall*** has wall and ceiling paintings by Thornhill. The ***Chapel***, with neo-Grecian interior, was rebuilt by James 'Athenian' Stuart after a fire in 1779.

The 18thC **St Alfege** (Church St SE10 ☎ 8853 2703 DLR Cutty Sark), rebuilt on the foundations of a medieval church where Henry VIII was baptized in 1491, was designed by Nicholas Hawksmoor. General

James Wolfe (1727-1759), hero of Quebec, was buried here and General Gordon of Khartoum baptized in 1833. Restored after its destruction in 1941 during the Blitz, it remains an important landmark.

In the 19th century Greenwich was the forerunner of a communications revolution when a telegraphic cable of over 4,000km, manufactured locally, was laid across the Atlantic. A few years later the largest gas-works in Europe was built on the Peninsula, which was the site of the Millennium Dome.

An extensive background to the borough's long history is provided by the **Greenwich Borough Museum** (233 Plumstead High St SE18 ☎ 8855 3240 ⇌ Plumstead ☞) while the **Woodlands Local History Library** (90 Mycenae Rd SE3 ☎ 8858 4631 ⇌ Westcombe Park ☞), based in an attractive Georgian villa (1774), has a vast array of printed material and manuscripts including a Plumstead deed of 1387. The attached Gallery holds exhibitions of local interest.

St Alfege's Church, Greenwich

The **Fan Museum** (12 Crooms Hill SE10 ☎ 8305 1441 ⇌ Maze Hill ☛) is dedicated to the ancient art and craft of fan making with a fascinating collection of about 3,000 specimens from around the world. The villa **Ranger's House** (Chesterfield Walk, Blackheath SE10 ☎ 8853 0035 ⇌ Maze Hill ☛) provides an ideal setting for the rich Suffolk Collection. This is an astonishing array of 53 full-length portraits with remarkable works by William Larkin (d1619).

Fan Museum:
fan decorated with roses

**Eltham Palace** (Court Rd SE9 ☎ 8294 2548 ⇌ New Eltham ☛) was begun in 1300 by Bishop Bek of Durham. Tradition has it that the Order of the Garter was established here by Edward III in 1347. With the new Great Hall (1480) the old palace reached a new high, but became a ruin during the time of Oliver Cromwell. In 1933 Samuel Courtauld restored the place and added a house for himself marked by the influence of French Art Deco. Lavishly refurbished by English Heritage it deserves a visit. For those keen on military history the museum **Firepower** (Royal Woolwich Arsenal West, Warren Lane SE18 ☎ 8855 7755 ⇌ Woolwich Arsenal ☛) offers an extensive collection tracing the development of the cannon from the Battle of Crécy (1346) onwards.

Ranger's House: the Gallery

❑ **HAMPTON COURT PALACE** (Richmond, Surrey KT8 9AU ☎ 8781 9500 ⇌ Hampton Court, River Launch from Westminster Pier ☛). It occupies a large site beside the Thames, about 15km up river from the centre of the capital. The Palace has been the home of Royalty for several hundred years and its architecture reflects their lives and tastes. It is built around three courtyards: ***Fountain Court***, surrounded by most of the important apartments and State Rooms, ***Clock Court*** next to the Great Hall and ***Base Court*** leading to the main entrance.

Hampton Court Palace

The house was originally a small estate office owned by the Order of St John of Jerusalem. It was leased in 1514 to Henry VIII's Chief Minister, Thomas Wolsey who was responsible for much of the Tudor building including the ***Great Watching Chamber*** and the Chapel situated on the first floor. The ***Chapel*** ceiling is of particular architectural importance being the most splendid Tudor ceiling in the country. Grinling Gibbons later added the great oak reredos behind the altar. Cardinal Wolsey's rooms, south of Base Court, are now home to Renaissance paintings from the collection of the Queen. In 1529 Wolsey had fallen from grace and Henry VIII took over Hampton Court as his own home. Wolsey had entertained on a lavish scale but even his ***kitchens***, situated on the ground floor, could not feed the Tudor Court of over 1,000 people. Henry extended the kitchens, part of which are on view, and built the ***Great Hall***, with its carved hammer beam roof and walls draped with Flemish tapestries. Visitors can also see the indoor ***Tudor tennis court***, still in use. Unlike many other Royal Palaces, Hampton Court escaped demolition under Cromwell's Commonwealth but with the arrival of William and Mary it was subject to sweeping architectural changes under Sir Christopher Wren. Part of the Tudor dwelling was demolished and a new baroque building emerged. The largest of the rooms built by Wren was the ***Cartoon Gallery*** which first housed cartoons by Raphael but is now hung with copies, probably painted by Henry Cooke in the 1690's.

Hampton Court Palace: King's Staircase

Queen Anne did little to enhance the rooms but the ***Queen's Drawing Room*** was decorated by Antonio Verrio with paintings of the British naval victories of her husband, Prince George of Denmark. Verrio also painted the ***King's Staircase***. During the occupation of George I and George II, the last monarchs to make the Palace their home, the Queen's Apartments were completed. James Thornhill painted the portraits of George II, Queen Caroline, the then Prince and Princess of Wales, and their son Frederick on the coving of the painted ceiling of the ***Queen's State Bedchamber***. The ***Cumberland Suite*** of rooms on the first floor was added for the use of the Duke of Cumberland, second son of George II. The ***Wolsey Closet*** gives a glimpse of the colour and richness of the original Wolsey dwelling. The ceiling and wall paintings are all original. During George III's reign, Hampton Court became a Grace-and-Favour home for retired servants of the Crown. This tradition, carried on to this century, was nearly catastrophic in 1986 when fire broke out in one of the flats, destroying part of the King's apartments. These were refurbished and reopened in 1992.

***The Mantegna Gallery***, originally an orangery, holds Andrea Mantegna's Triumph of Caesar, nine of the most valuable paintings in the Queen's collection. The **gardens**, with the famous Maze, are worth a visit. In 1996 the ***Privy Garden*** was restored to the original 18thC layout of the time of William and Mary.

❑ **HOUSES OF PARLIAMENT** (Parliament Sq SW1 ☎ 7219 4272 Map 4Kh ⊖ Westminster. Admission to Strangers' Gallery in either house is by advance application to an MP or a Peer, or by queuing at St Stephen's Entrance ☞). They occupy the site of the former Palace of Westminster which was the principal royal residence in the capital from the middle of the 11thC to 1512. Little now remains of the original buildings, since the palace was burned down in 1834, except for Westminster Hall and the Crypt of St Stephen's Chapel. The present Houses of Parliament are the work of Barry and Pugin – except the Commons Chamber, rebuilt after an air raid in 1941. Barry's design, which incorporated Westminster Hall and the remains of St Stephen's Chapel, covers an area of 3.2ha. The entire complex contains approx 1,200 rooms, 100 staircases and 3.2km of passages.

The furniture and decoration of the interior were designed by Pugin in the intricate style of the Gothic Revival, still preserved in its ornamented glory in the surviving 19thC part of the palace. Painting and sculpture embellish every wall and ceiling, immortalising the great, and monitoring the unfolding of the country's history. They are also a testimony to the craftsmanship of that era, greatly promoted by the Prince Consort, who took a close interest in the rebuilding of the Houses.

The ***Clock Tower*** (A), which rises to almost 100m from the Thames, incorporates the famous bell known to Londoners since 1859 and nicknamed Big Ben after Sir Benjamin Hall, the First Commissioner of Works. The chime is supposed to derive from a phrase in the aria 'I know that my Redeemer liveth' from Handel's Messiah. When the ***Ayrton Light*** shines in the spire above the clock (336 spiralling stairs to the top), it indicates that the Commons are in session. The ***Victoria Tower*** (B) is the repository for over 3 million Parliamentary records. Among them are famous documents, such as the Bill of Rights (1689), second in constitutional importance only to Magna Carta (1215), and the Death Warrant of Charles I (1649). They are all available for consultation in the House of Lords records office.

Houses of Parliament

Houses of Parliament: Central Lobby

***Westminster Hall***, built by William II in 1097-99, was in its time the largest chamber in Europe. In 1394-99 the architect Henry Yevele, whose work can also be seen at Westminster Abbey and Canterbury Cathedral, rebuilt the Hall over the Norman foundations. From the 13thC it was used as the Chief Courts of Law. Sir Thomas More (1535), the Earl of Essex (1601) and Charles I (1649) were all tried here.

Opposite Westminster Hall, on the other side of Parliament Bridge Street, stands **Portcullis House** with a distinctive stone and bronze façade. Designed by Hopkins and opened at the dawn of the new century (and millennium), the new, striking palazzo contains 200 oak-lined and bullet-proof office suites for members of Parliament.

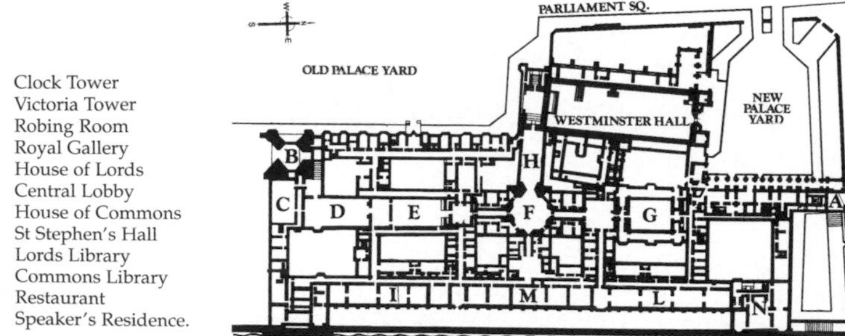

## Houses of Parliament: How they work

### House of Lords

The constitution and function of the Lords is in process of radical change. Before the Throne is the red ottoman known as the *Woolsack* (3) where the Lord Chancellor sits as Speaker of the House of Lords. Two similar but *smaller woolsacks* (4) are used by judges at the Opening of Parliament. The Lords' benches (upholstered in red leather) are arranged with *Government benches* on the right (5) and the *Opposition* on the left (6). The first two benches are reserved for *Bishops* (7). Facing the Woolsack are the *cross benches* (8), for members who do not support either of the main parties.

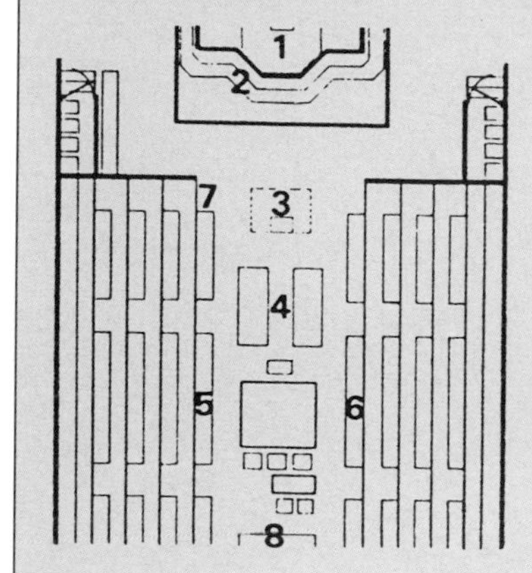


### House of Commons

The name of the 'Commons' does not signify common people, but the local communities in counties and towns of Britain. There are 659 representatives, 529 of whom are elected in England, 72 in Scotland, 40 in Wales and 18 in Northern Ireland. Their Chamber, like that of the House of Lords, is rectangular in shape. Much of the furniture was given by countries of the Commonwealth, when it was rebuilt after World War II. Barry's entrance, rescued from the rubble, was renamed Churchill Arch. In front of the *Speaker's Chair* (1) is the *Table of the House* (2) at which the *Clerk* sits with two assistants (3). The green leather benches for members face each other across a broad gangway known as the 'floor of the House'. The benches to the right of the Speaker are used by the Government supporters and those to the left by the Opposition. The front bench, known as the *Treasury Bench* (4) is reserved for the Prime Minister and other Cabinet members, while the Leader of the Opposition and his senior colleagues occupy seats directly opposite (5). Both debate from the so-called *Dispatch Boxes* (6).

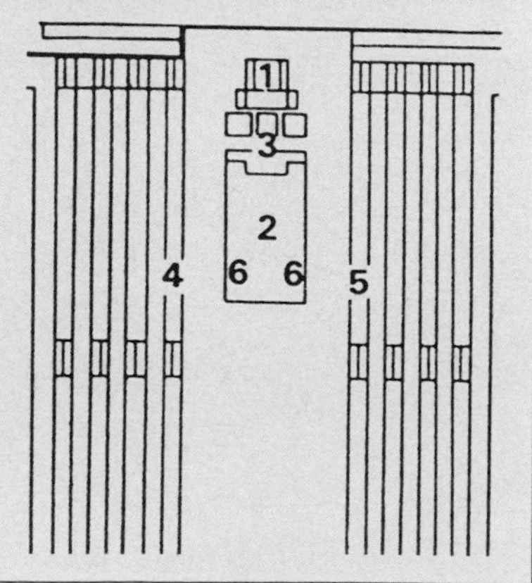


It has become possible for the public to go behind the scenes in the 'Mother of Parliaments', for eight weeks in August-September, when guided tours (in several languages) take place. The 75-minute tour includes a visit to the two Houses and Westminster Hall.

❑ **KENSINGTON & CHELSEA** (☎ 7937 5464 Map 7, 8, 9, 10 ⊖ Kensington High Street, Sloane Square). The Royal Borough of Kensington and Chelsea enjoys the finest residential and shopping facilities and a strong link with the monarchy. Its architecture varies from the rows of pretty cottages of Chelsea to the red brick buildings of 'Albertopolis', the quadrangle south of Kensington Gardens developed under the patronage of Prince Albert, the Consort of Queen Victoria. Here stand the great museums (Natural History, Science and Victoria and Albert), the Royal Albert Hall and several academic and cultural institutions. Before 1965, when the present municipality emerged, the two communities developed separately from each other.

Borough Coat of Arms

The attribute Royal which distinguishes the borough reflects its long connection with royalty. In the case of Chelsea the link began in 1536 following the acquisition of the Manor of Chelsea by Henry VIII. Sir Walter Cope, one of Kensington's earliest inhabitants and a favourite of James I, begun laying the foundation of a great mansion later known as Holland House (demolished after damage during World War II). The large park survives. Called **Holland Park** (W8 Map 10Ah ⊖ High Street Kensington), it is a very pleasant public green space. Venue of concerts and plays in summer, it has the largest area of woodland in Central London and the charming Japanese Koyoto Garden opened in 1991.

The decision by William III in 1680 to live at Nottingham House, reconstructed as Kensington Palace, raised the area's profile. It has been open to the public since 1898 with the exception of those parts retained for royal use. Diana, Princess of Wales, lived here until her tragic death in August 1997.

Kensington Gardens: the broad avenue leading to Kensington Palace

## Kensington Palace: State Apartments

(Kensington Gardens W8 ☎ 7937 9561 Map 9 ⊖ ChQueensway ☛)

Kensington Palace is set in the parkland of Kensington Gardens. The main building was improved by Wren and the interior embellished by William Kent. George II was the last monarch to use the palace. Visitors enter the State Apartments through the garden door on the Queen's side of the palace, so called because it was occupied first by Mary II and later by her sister Queen Anne. The ***Queen's Staircase*** with original panelling by Alexander Fort leads to the spacious ***Queen Mary's Gallery***. Here are gilded mirrors surrounded by an intricate frame carved by Grinling Gibbons in 1691. The portrait of Peter the Great was painted by Kneller during the Czar's visit to London in 1698. The profile portrait of Queen Anne in ***Queen Mary's Closet*** is by Kneller and was used as a model for striking coinage and medals.

The four pictures flanking the fireplace in ***Queen Mary's Drawing Room*** are an *Annunciation* by Carlo Maratti, a *Landscape* after Bassano, an *Infant Christ with St John* by Van Dyck and a *Landscape* by Poelenburgh. The floorboards of ***Queen Mary's Bedchamber*** are the only original ones in the State Apartments. The three Mortlake tapestries in the ***Privy Chamber*** were woven around 1623. G.B. Guelfi created the series of busts in this room and William Kent painted the ceiling with *Mars and Minerva* as central subject. Kent was also responsible for the ceiling of the ***Presence Chamber***; the ceiling and walls of the ***King's Grand Staircase***; the ceiling of both the huge ***King's Gallery*** and the ***King's Drawing Room*** as well as that of the ***Cupola Room***, the principal state room of the palace. Here Queen Victoria was baptized in 1819. The young princess was sleeping in the *Queen Victoria Bedroom* when she was awakened in the early hours of 20 June 1837 with the news of her accession to the throne following the death of her uncle William IV.

The Palace hosts the **Royal Ceremonial Dress Collection** with dresses and uniforms worn at Court dating from the mid-18thC onwards.

The King's Staircase

The fine **Orangery** (1704) was built for Queen Anne's parties and receptions. The **Sunken Garden** (1909), of formal design, has flowers in bloom most of the year.

Another historic landmark of the borough is the Royal Hospital, Chelsea. Originally founded in 1682 by Charles II as a retreat for veterans of the regular army, it still serves that function today providing a home for about 400 Chelsea Pensioners wearing their instantly recognisable scarlet coats and tricorn hats.

## The Royal Hospital, Chelsea

(Royal Hospital Rd SW3 ☎ 7730 0161 Map 7Gl ⊖ Sloane Square ☞)

The main part of the buildings is by Sir Christopher Wren, with later additions by Robert Adam and Sir John Soane. The grounds provide a good setting for the fine architecture. The Chelsea Flower Show* is held here every year in May. On Oak Apple Day (29 May) the statue of Charles II by Grinling Gibbons is wreathed in greenery in memory of the King's escape after the battle of Worcester and a parade is held in his honour.

Royal Hospital, Chelsea: Oak Apple Day

The half dome in the ***Chapel*** was painted by Sebastiano Ricci and his nephew Marco with a fresco of *Christ rising from the Tomb*. The case of the original organ built by Renatus Harris dominates the gallery at the west end. The Great Hall where the pensioners have their meals has a large mural begun by Verrio of Charles II on horseback, and royal portraits by Clostermann, Kneller and Romney of the period.

A small ***Museum***, with objects related to the history of the Hospital, has an interesting collection of former pensioners' medals.

Not far from the Royal Hospital, Chelsea is the National Army Museum*, devoted to the long history of the British Army. The **Chelsea Old Church** (Cheyne Walk SW3 ☎ 7352 5627 ⊖ Sloane Square), one of the best known of the borough, is closely associated with Sir Thomas More (1478-1535), statesman, author and saint, who lived nearby. The general design of the London Oratory, generally but incorrectly known as **Brompton Oratory** (Brompton Rd SW7 ☎ 7808 0900 Map 8Ej ⊖ South Kensington), is baroque. It is one of the capital's largest Roman Catholic churches, once described as 'a museum in a street of museums'. The nave exceeds in width that of St Paul's Cathedral. The Mazzuoli's gigantic 17thC marble statues of the Apostles were originally in the Cathedral in Siena.

Brompton Oratory: Sanctuary

The **Chelsea Physic Garden** (66 Royal Hospital Rd SW3 ☎ 7352 5646 Map 7Fl ⊖ Sloane Square ☛), founded by the Society of Apothecaries in 1673 to train apprentices in identifying medicinal herbs, has been a centre for the study of horticulture ever since. The exhibitions at the **Commonwealth Institute** (Kensington High St W8 ☎ 7603 4535 Map 10Bj ⊖ High Street Kensington ☛) focus on development and achievements of the Commonwealth countries. At the **Royal College of Music** (Prince Consort Rd SW7 Map 8Dj ⊖ South Kensington ☎ 7591 4340) are rich collections of instruments (☛) and portraits (☞).

Leighton House: Arab Hall

The list of Kensington and Chelsea distinguished residents is quite lengthy. Sir Winston Churchill lived in Kensington (Hyde Park Gate) and Margaret Thatcher in Chelsea (Flood Street). Homes of renowned artists of the Victorian era survive. Some of them are open to the public like those associated with Frederic Leighton*, president of the Royal Academy of Arts and foremost exponent of Victorian art.

❑ **PARLIAMENT SQUARE & WHITEHALL.** Within their perimeters is located the 'machine' which for a long time has run Britain's official life. On the east side of PARLIAMENT SQUARE (SW1 Map 4Kh ⊖ Westminster), laid out in the mid-19thC, stand the Houses of Parliament* and on the north the imposing complex of the Treasury.

St Margaret's, Westminster

On the south side of the square is **St Margaret's**, parish church of the House of Commons since 1614 and famous for its Elizabethan and Jacobean monuments. Raleigh, who introduced tobacco into England, is buried before the altar (but his head is interred at West Horsley, Surrey). Pepys, the diarist, and Churchill were both married here.

The nearby **Jewel Tower** (Old Palace Yard SW1 ☎ 7222 2219 Map 4Kj ☛) dates from the 14thC when it held the private fortune of the Sovereign and was used as such until the death of Henry VIII. The spacious green at the centre of the square is ringed by memorials to historical figures. **Churchill's statue** (I. Roberts-Jones, 1973) portrays the statesman in a typically pugnacious pose. On the west side of the square is Middlesex Guildhall, used as a meeting place by exiled governments during World War II. Behind is the modern **Queen Elizabeth II Conference Centre**, opened in 1986, and the huge **Central Hall**, the headquarters of the Methodist Church (the main hall can seat nearly 3,000), where the first session of the United Nations Organization was held in 1946.

Central Hall

Of the government offices in **Parliament Street** (Map 4Kh) the one occupied by the Foreign and Commonwealth Office is by far the most magnificent. Designed in Italianate style by Sir George Scott, it is full of striking neoclassical features including painted domed ceilings, gilt reliefs, patterned walls, murals and marble columns. In front of the building stands the Cenotaph, and at the rear the Cabinet War Rooms.

**The Cenotaph** ('empty tomb' in Greek), sculpted in Portland stone in 1920 and designed by Edwin Lutyens, is the national monument to men and women who died in the services in both World Wars. Many of the most vital decisions of World War II were taken by Churchill at the underground **Cabinet War Rooms** (Clive Steps, King Charles St SW1 ☎ 7930 6961 Map 4Kh ⊖ St James's Park ☛) which also provided protected accommodation for the Prime Minister and key members of his staff.

Parliament Square

**Downing Street** is named after Sir George Downing, nephew of the first Governor of Massachusetts and holder of high office under both Cromwell and Charles II, who in older age turned builder-speculator. ***Number 10*** has been the official residence and office of the head of the national government since 1731 when the house was offered by George I as a personal gift to Sir Robert Walpole who occupied it for 21 years establishing a yet unbroken record. Walpole persuaded the King to allow the house to be used as the London residence of the prime minister for all times. Number 11 is the official residence of the Chancellor of the Exchequer. Since 1985 the street has been closed to the general public for security reasons.

10 Downing Street

WHITEHALL (Map 4Kg ⊖ Charing Cross), the thoroughfare running south from Trafalgar Square, is a street of unique historic memories. It derives its name from the palace built in Cardinal Wolsey's time and appropriated by Henry VIII. It was a focal point of the Court and scene of the execution of Charles I (1649). The Tudor palace was destroyed by fire in 1689 with the exception of a vaulted cellar, which now stands beneath the Ministry of Defence, and the magnificent Banqueting House, designed by Inigo Jones. Almost facing the Banqueting House is the 18thC **Horse Guards Building**, designed by William Kent. In the small courtyard on the Whitehall side the Changing the Guard takes place daily while the large Parade Ground at the rear of the building hosts the annual Trooping the Colour. The **Admiralty** (Map 4Kg), next to the Horse Guards, with a Robert Adam stone screen (1759), was the place where the country's naval affairs were run when the British fleet was regarded as the most powerful in the world.

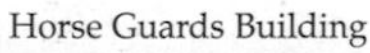

Horse Guards Building

## Banqueting House

(Whitehall SW1 ☎ 7930 4179 Map 4Kh ⊖ Charing Cross ☛)

On the first floor, the ***Banqueting Hall***, has nine large paintings by the Flemish artist Peter Paul Rubens. The works cover the entire ceilings and were commissioned by Charles I to commemorate his father James I. They were put in place in 1635. The best vantage point to admire them is the north entrance doorway of the hall. At the time of the Stuarts, this was the entrance used by visitors seeking audience with the Sovereign.

The central oval, *The Apotheosis of James I*, depicts the King rising to heaven. Flanking it is a procession of cherubs in a kind of Bacchic triumph. The painting *The Benefits of the Government of James I*, placed almost above the throne, shows the Monarch surrounded by Wisdom (attired as Minerva) confronting War (Mars trampling on the King's enemies) while Mercury points to the nether regions as their destination. The King indicates Peace and Plenty while a cherub holds aloft the royal crown. In the oval, to the left, is the figure of Abundance holding the cornucopia bestriding the bound figure of Avarice. In the right oval, Reason holds a bridle above the cramped figure of Intemperate Discord.

The northern pictures describe, in the central square, the *Union of England and Scotland*. Here James I in full regalia is seen commanding the infant Charles to be brought to the throne by personifications of England and Scotland who, with Minerva, hold the two crowns of the kingdom over his head. In the ovals on the sides are, on the left, *Heroic Virtue* in the guise of Hercules crushing Envy, and on the right *Heroic Wisdom* in the form of Minerva striking Ignorance with a spear.

❑ **PICCADILLY** (W1 Map 4Jg). The name, which distinguishes the entire area, derives from Piccadilly Hall, a 17thC mansion built by the tailor Robert Baker who amassed a fortune making and selling 'pickadilles'- high collars with laced or perforated edges.

Once known as the 'hub of the Empire', **Piccadilly Circus** (⊖ Piccadilly Circus) has passed with the Empire into history. Conceived by John Nash, the 19thC architect and planner, it was at first named Regent Circus South. It assumed the current name following the opening of Shaftesbury Avenue (1886). A magnet for generations of Londoners and visitors, it still retains a great appeal as the heart of the capital's entertainment industry.

Prominent is the famous fountain and statue, known officially as the **Shaftesbury Memorial Fountain**, was unveiled in 1893 in memory of Anthony Ashley Cooper, 7th Earl of Shaftesbury (1801-85), politician, philanthropist and social reformer. In 1984 the Memorial was shifted 13m from the original site to stand in a pedestrian piazza. The winged figure 2.4m high, popularly called ***Eros***, was intended by its sculptor (Alfred Gilbert) to represent the 'Angel of Christian Charity'.

The advertisement lights on the Monico building coalesce into a dynamic technicolour scene which in the imagination of millions epitomises London by night. The first electric signs were placed here in 1890 and, except for the years 1939-45, have been alight ever since.

Piccadilly Circus: one of the great meeting places of the capital, where the lights never go out

Other familiar landmarks of the Circus are the London Pavilion and the Trocadero. Behind the floral façade (1885) of the **London Pavilion** a retail and leisure complex has been developed with shops, a restaurant and the **Rock Circus** (☎ 7734 7203 ☛). This depicts in sound, light, animation and hi-tech special effects the birth and development of rock music. The adjoining **Trocadero**, another 19thC building that has undergone several changes since its music-hall times, is a shopping and entertainment centre. It has always been, and remains, a lively corner of the capital.

To the east of the Circus is 'theatreland' with over 30 theatres within a 500m radius. To the west the beautiful **St James** (☎ 7734 4511). The church, designed by Wren, has an 17thC sumptuous interior. Grinling Gibbons contributed the marble font amongst much else.

St James, Piccadilly

Diagonally opposite the church is **Albany**, the most select apartment block in the capital. The 18thC building facing the entrance is by William Chambers and was adapted as apartments for bachelors around 1801. Amongst its residents have been Byron, Gladstone and in more recent times Edward Heath.

**Burlington House**, on the same side to the West, is another important feature of Piccadilly. It is shared by the Royal Academy of Arts* and five learned societies: the Society of Antiquaries, the Royal Astronomical Society, the Royal Society of Chemistry, the Geological Society and the Linnean Society.

Around Piccadilly there are many gentlemen's clubs, a peculiar British institution, which developed in its present form over two centuries ago to replace the early coffee houses. They have often been the centres of political intrigue and membership still retains a certain prestige.

❑ **ROYAL PARKS** (Central London). The capital's huge area of green space is one of its major assets. There is everything, from formal parks to commons, heaths, woods and forests, not to mention the lovingly tended private gardens, the tree-lined streets and garden squares. But the places most enjoyed by the general public are the royal parks. With 3,000ha, 280 buildings, statues, memorials, 29 lakes, over half a million trees, 68km of roads and footpaths, and other amenities they are a source of great delight and relaxation. Many offer sports facilities and the pleasure of listening to open-air concerts during the summer months. In Central London are:

• **St James's Park** (SW1 Map 4Jh ⊖ St James's Park) is the oldest of London's parks. In 1532 Henry VIII acquired the site, a marshy water meadow with the Tyburn stream flowing through it. The name derives from a leper hospital dedicated to St James which was founded in the 13thC. In the days of Elizabeth I, fêtes and tournaments were held here. In the 19thC it was cleverly converted by John Nash to produce a natural landscape effect. The rocky ***Duck Island*** on the lake has a colourful colony of waterfowl, including pelicans, usually fed at 1600 from the Birdkeeper's Cottage. The rose beds on the north side of the lake are a joy to see when in full bloom. There is a fine panorama of the park from the top of the steps where the 38m high **Duke of York's Column** (Map 4Jg), built in 1833, stands.

• **Green Park** (SW1 Map 5Hh ⊖ Green Park) was bought in 1667 by Charles II as an extension to St James's Park and it is called "Green" because there are no flower beds in it. The magnificent 18thC **Spencer House** (27 St James's Pl SW1 ☎ 7514 1964 ⊖ Green Park ☛) with neo-classical interior, fine furniture and pictures, including portraits by Reynolds and Gainsborough, overlooks the park. The house, once owned by Princess Diana's ancestors, is open to the public on most weekends and is used on other days for corporate hospitality.

Hyde Park: young footballers

The Albert Memorial, Kensington Gardens

• **Hyde Park** (W1 Map 5Fg/h ⊖ Hyde Park Corner), opened to the public in 1637, soon became fashionable. The Great Exhibition, a spectacular celebration of art and manufacturing excellence, was held on the south side of this park in 1851 in a specially erected Crystal Palace covering almost 8ha. The large lake is divided by a bridge; the south half is called the ***Serpentine*** (Map 5Fh) and the north half, properly in Kensington Gardens, the ***Long Water*** (Map 5Ff). At ***Speakers' Corner***, near Marble Arch (site of public hangings from 1196 to 1783), the public may exercise their right of free speech. The modern ***Queen Elizabeth Gate***, almost opposite the classical screen (1825) of Apsley Gate by Decimus Burton, marks the south-east entrance to the park. It was erected in honour of the Queen Mother and opened in 1993.

• **Kensington Gardens** (W2 Map 8Dg/h ⊖ Lancaster Gate) cover 111ha and are divided from Hyde Park by the West Carriage Drive running from Alexandra Gate in the south to Victoria Gate in the north. The Gardens date from the 17thC when Kensington Palace* was refurbished and expanded for William III and Mary II to accommodate the court. Other well-known features are the **Albert Memorial**, designed by Gilbert Scott and completed in 1872 as a monument to Queen Victoria's consort, Prince Albert, and facing it on the opposite site of Kensington Gore another memorial to the Prince Consort, the Royal Albert Hall*; the ***Flower Walk***, with its varied and colourful borders; the ***Broad Walk***, the ***Round Pond***, the ***Peter Pan statue*** by Sir George Frampton and the ***Italian Gardens***. These, at the tip of the ***Long Water***, are adorned by a Loggia, which houses a pump for the ponds, four large ornate *fountains* full of water lilies and a memorial bronze statue to *Edward Jenner* (1749-1823), discoverer of vaccination. Also in the area is a classic arched recess known as ***Queen Anne's Alcove*** designed by Christopher Wren. At the **Serpentine Gallery** (Kensington Gardens W2 ☎ 7402 6075 Map 8Eh ⊖ South Kensington ☛) temporary exhibitions of contemporary art are held.

Regent's Park: Queen Mary's Gardens. All the beds are numbered and the roses identified.

Kensington Gardens: the elegantly laid out Italian Gardens

• **Regent's Park** (NW1 Map 1Gc ⊖ Regent's Park). Opened to the public in 1838, it was named after the Prince Regent (later George IV), who appointed Nash to design the layout, its approaches and many of the houses within the park itself. The lake, Queen Mary's Gardens and the London Zoo are landmarks. The lake, covering 9ha, has six mini islands and is the home of the largest waterfowl collection in Britain. ***Queen Mary's Gardens***, named after the consort of George V, date from the early 1930s. They contain the finest assortment of roses in the country with about 30,000 plants representing almost 400 varieties. The Open Air Theatre*, venue of classic performances since 1932 with over a thousand seats, is also located here.

The **London Zoo** (☎ 7722 3333 Map 1Gb ☛) occupies a large area on the north-west of the park. Amongst the biggest in Europe, it was founded by the Zoological Society of London in 1829. The complex includes an Aquarium, Children's Zoo and many architecturally interesting structures such as the Aviary designed by Lord Snowdon (former husband of Princess Margaret), the Elephant House and the open Lion Terraces. Recent additions are the exhibition ***Web of Life***, devoted to biodiversity and its conservation, and a ***Micrarium***, 'the tinest zoo in the world' where visitors can see a world invisible to the human eye.

The minaret and golden dome of the London Central Mosque* (Map 1Fc) can be seen from many places in the park, as can the striking design of the *British Telecom Tower* (177m), erected in 1965 for television and radio transmissions.

**Primrose Hill** (Map 1Fa) was purchased from Eton College in 1841 to extend the parkland available to the poor people of Northern London for open-air recreation.

❑ **ST PAUL'S CATHEDRAL** (EC4 ☎ 7236 4128 Map 3Nf ⊖ St Paul's ☛) The present building was started in 1675 by Wren after the church - the fourth to be erected on the Ludgate Hill site - was destroyed in the Great Fire (1666). St Paul's is a structure of classical and harmonious proportions embellished with baroque detail. It is one of the largest Christian monuments in the world (external measurements are: height 120m and length 170m).

The cathedral is the seat of the Bishop of London. Major national ceremonies have taken place here, among them the funerals of Nelson, the Duke of Wellington and Sir Winston Churchill. Happier events were the Silver Jubilee Service for Elizabeth II (1977) and the wedding of the Prince of Wales (1981).

St Paul's Cathedral: Main Entrance

St Paul's Cathedral: Nave

The interior is dominated by a massive ***Dome*** consisting of an outer wooden frame covered in lead, an inner dome decorated with 19thC mosaics by Salviati and scenes from the life of St Paul by Thornhill, and a brick cone structure wedged between the inner and outer domes to support the weight of the lantern. To the left of the Nave lies the monument to the Duke of Wellington (d1852). The ***Choir*** has the original choir stalls by Grinling Gibbons. The canopy over the High Altar dates from 1958, and, behind it, the American Memorial Chapel contains the names of the 28,000 American servicemen who died in World War II while based in Britain.

St Paul's Cathedral: Dome with scenes from the life of St Paul, by J. Thornhill

The ***Crypt***, running the full length of the building, has many famous tombs including Wren's, with its celebrated Latin epitaph *Lector, si monumentum requiris, circumspice* ('Reader, if you would seek a monument, look around you') and those of Wellington and Nelson. Nelson's remains lie in a Renaissance sarcophagus designed by Benedetto da Rovezzano for Cardinal Wolsey. A monument to Flying Officer Fiske, the first American to lose his life in World War II during the Battle of Britain, also stands there. The crypt also contains the ***Treasury of the Diocese of London***, displaying ecclesiastical plate, regalia and manuscripts covering the whole period of the Church of England from 1500 to the two gold goblets marking the wedding of the Prince and Princess of Wales.

In the upper level of the Cathedral are the ***South Triforium Gallery*** (museum), ***Library*** and ***Trophy Room***. The ***West Gallery*** offers a spectacular view over the nave. Higher still is the ***Whispering Gallery***, the ***Stone Gallery*** with its fine view over London and, above the lantern, the ***Ball***.

Nelson's Tomb: 16thC sarcophagus by Benedetto da Rovezzano

Treasury of the Diocese of London: the Jubilee Cope, 1977

❑ **SOHO & COVENT GARDEN.** These districts which sit next to each other within the City of Westminster are very popular with both Londoners and tourists due to the many attractions offered. The name of **Soho** (Map 2Jf ⊖ Piccadilly Circus) possibly comes from the ancient hunting cry 'So-Ho', used as a password by the forces of the Duke of Monmouth (an early Soho resident) at the Battle of Sedgemoor (1685). Urban encroachment began in the 17thC with the arrival of French Protestant refugees after the Revocation of the Edict of Nantes (1685).

Among the famous who have lived in the area are Canaletto, Constable, Mozart, Rimbaud and Verlaine. ***Old Compton Street*** is the main and most typical street in Soho. The place is regaining its traditional character as London's most cosmopolitan quarter with a multitude of pubs, cafés and restaurants serving and selling food and wines from all over the world. But it is the theatres and nightclubs that give Soho its distinctive appeal.

Statue of Charles Chaplin

On the fringe of Soho are ***Carnaby Street*** (Map 5Jf), famous in the Swinging Sixties for its fashion shops for the younger buyers, the colourful and exotic ***Chinatown*** and ***Leicester Square*** (Map 2Kf). This in late Victorian times was known for its Turkish baths, oyster bars and theatres. Today, fully pedestranised and with gardens at the centre hosting a statue of the famous comedian Charles Chaplin, it is home to some of the capital's premier cinemas, restaurants and discos. The Swiss Centre's modern skyscraper, on the north side of the Square, has become a local landmark.

The fame of **Covent Garden** (Map 2Kf ⊖ Covent Garden) goes back to the 13thC when a thriving garden belonging to the Abbey of Westminster was established on the site. In 1631 an Italianate central

Leicester Square, where the West End's nightlife begins

square, the Piazza, was designed by the architect Inigo Jones on the commission of the Earl of Bedford. An ornate Charter Market was added in 1829 which did a roaring trade in fruit and vegetables for many years before moving to south of the Thames in 1974.

Inigo Jones also conceived for the West of the Piazza the handsome St Paul's Church (1618). It was the first Anglican church to be built in the capital since the Reformation.

Covent Garden: the Piazza

London Transport Museum

Besides shops selling all kinds of wares, there are the Royal Opera House*, several theatres, churches of great historic interest and major museums. The **London Transport Museum** (Covent Garden WC2 ☎ 7379 6344 ⊖ Covent Garden ☛) tells the story of 200 years of the public transport in the capital. Housed in a high Victorian building, it contains a replica of Shillibeer's first London bus of 1829, trams, trolleybuses, and motorbuses including the B-type like the ones which saw service in World War I.

The **Theatre Museum** (Russell St WC2 ☎ 7943 4700 ⊖ Covent Garden ☛) is devoted to all the performing arts. It is amongst the richest collections of its kind in the world. There is a semi-permanent exhibition telling the history of the theatre through the objects in the collections, together with galleries for temporary exhibitions, a painting gallery and a small theatre. The **Library and Museum of Freemasonry** (Freemasons' Hall, 60 Great Queen St WC2 ☎ 7395 9251 Map 2Lf ⊖ Holborn ☞). is concerned with the history and development of Masonic regalia and jewels (as Masonic medals are termed), including fine examples of 18thC hand-painted and embroidered (silks, beadwork and appliqué) aprons and sashes. The large collection of engraved and enamelled drinking glasses and decanters illustrates both the development of English glass and Masonic symbolism.

Theatre Museum

The **Photographers' Gallery** (8 Gt Newport St WC2 ☎ 7831 1772 ⊖ Leicester Square ☛), opened in 1971 as Britain's first independent gallery devoted to photography, hosts temporary exhibitions of international appeal in its three galleries.

❑ **SOUTH BANK & BANKSIDE.** Both these sites, which encompass areas south of the Thames stretching from Westminster Bridge to Tower Bridge, have provided amusement and entertainment for many generations.

Instrumental in the 20thC rise of **SOUTH BANK** (SE1 Map 4Lg ⊖ Waterloo) was the building of County Hall as the administrative headquarters for the London County Council (superseded in 1965 by the Greater London Council which was in turn brought to an end in 1985). The future of the area was strengthened by the decision to hold the Festival of Britain in 1951 in the vicinity. This event was conceived to mark the centenary of the Great Exhibition of 1851 and to celebrate the end of World War II. It proved to be a great success. In addition it offered the opportunity to replace many derelict buildings with examples of modern architecture. Centre pieces were the Royal Festival Hall, the Dome of Discovery and the Skylon, a futuristic form of an obelisk. Of these, only the Royal Festival Hall* survives and still plays a major role in making South Bank the nation's number one art centre.

A stroll along South Bank is rewarding. **County Hall** (Map 4Lh), sold to private developers after the dissolution of the Greater London Council, now contains two major hotels, a restaurant, the **London Aquarium** (☎ 7967 8000 ☛), the biggest of its kind in Britain, and the **Dali Universe** (☎ 7620 2420 ☛), a permanent exhibition of over 500 works of the Spanish Surrealist artist.

The British Airways **London Eye** (☎ 0870 5000 600 ☛), on the river itself, the biggest observation wheel in the world, is a notable addition to the capital's attractions. Standing almost 150m high, it offers spectacular views from its 32 enclosed capsules.

Next to the Royal Festival Hall are two other concert venues (Queen Elizabeth Hall and Purcell Room) and the **Hayward Gallery** (☎ 7928 3144 Map 4Lg ⊖ Waterloo ☛) for major exhibitions. Nearby is the impressive BFI IMAX Cinema*. Continuing the walk and always close to the Thames you pass the National Theatre, and the Oxo Tower with its exclusive high level restaurant.

The London Eye, dominating County Hall

The fame of **Bankside** (SE1 Map 3Ng ⊖ Southwark, London Bridge) goes back to the 16thC when theatrical performances were banned from the City. As a result the Rose opened south of the River in 1586, soon to be followed by the Swan (1594), the Globe (1598) and the Hope, a former bear and bull baiting arena transformed into a playhouse in 1614. The arrival of theatres encouraged the spread of houses of ill repute, pubs and other haunts of pleasure.

After centuries of decline the area, which was heavily bombed during World War II, has been regenerated to a new life. The refurbishment of the huge power station opposite St Paul's to house the Tate Modern* and the opening of a new pedestrian link over the Thames has popularized this part of London.

Near to the Tate Modern is the **Bankside Gallery** (48 Hopton St SE1 ☎ 7928 7521 Map 3Ng ⊖ Southwark ☛), with exhibitions mainly devoted to watercolours and artists' prints. Further east are the reconstructed Globe Theatre* and **Shakespeare's Globe Exhibition** (New Globe Walk, Bankside SE1 ☎ 7902 1500 Map 3Ng ⊖ Southwark ☛), the **Rose Theatre Exhibition** (56 Park St SE1 ☎ 7593 0026 ⊖ Southwark ☛) on the archaeological site of the first playhouse on Bankside and the replica of Drake's **Golden Hinde** (St Mary Overie Dock, Cathedral St SE1 ☎ 7403 0123 Map 3Pg ⊖ Southwark ☛).

Globe Theatre

Not far away is **Vinopolis** (1 Bank End SE1 ☎ 7940 8300 Map 3Pg ⊖ London Bridge ☛), 'the city of wine', where several hundred wines can be tasted and purchased. Also in the area is the **Old Operating Theatre** (9A St Thomas St SE1 ☎ 7955 4791 Map 3Pg ⊖ London Bridge ☛), a surgical theatre for women hidden in the roof of a church, used between 1821 and 1862, and part of the Old St Thomas' Hospital before it moved to Lambeth. The **London Dungeon** (28/34 Tooley St SE1 ☎ 7403 0606 Map 3Pg ⊖ London Bridge ☛) presents an accurate recreation of the harsh realities of life in times past. The effect is one of unredeemed horror. Some exhibits are unsuitable for young children. Southwark Cathedral, next to London Bridge, the location at which Chaucer's *Canterbury Tales* begins, remains one of the capital's most important spiritual centres.

Golden Hinde

## Southwark Cathedral

(SE1 ☎ 7367 6700 Map 3Pg ⊖ London Bridge ☞)

The Cathedral, nicknamed the Cinderella of English cathedrals despite being a rare survivor from the London of Chaucer and Shakespeare and predating Westminster Abbey and St Paul's, stands on the spot which since Roman times has been the traditional southern entrance to the City, across London Bridge. With Lambeth Palace, it is one of the most important medieval buildings in South London.

Its history is rather chequered. Its origin goes back to 606 when a small church was constructed for a sisterhood. In time, this was replaced by a more substantial building, soon destroyed by fire. In its place the present Gothic church arose, which was considerably rebuilt and restored in the 19thC. It became a Cathedral in 1905. Its official name is the Cathedral and Collegiate Church of St Saviour and St Mary Overie (meaning either 'over the river' or 'on the bank').

A £10m Millennium project has funded stonework restoration, reopening of the courtyard looking on to the Thames, a refectory, a library and a visitors' centre with artefacts from the Roman road which runs through the church's grounds. The Cathedral is rich in historic memorabilia, which include the priceless *Bishop Fox's* altar screen (1520), with statues added from 1905 onward; the *effigy of a Knight* (c1275); the medieval canopied *tomb of the poet John Gower;* the magnificent *Nonsuch Chest* (1588) and the *Jacobean Communion table.*

The *Harvard Chapel* (1907) celebrates John Harvard, born in Southwark in 1607 and founder of Harvard University, USA. William Shakespeare is commemorated in the South Transept by a recumbent alabaster figure carved in 1912 by Henry McCarthy. The brother of the great playwright was buried in the church in 1607. The position of his grave is unknown, but an inscribed stone is placed in the Choir.

Within a few hundred metres of the Cathedral are the remains of the 13thC **Winchester Palace**, the former London residence of the Bishop of Winchester, with its own private prison. This has also become a tourist attraction under the name of the **Clink Prison Museum** (1 Clink St SE1 ☎ 7378 1558 ☛) with exhibits showing medieval punishments.

❑ **THE THAMES** London's major river has been celebrated in the paintings of Canaletto, Turner and the French Impressionists. It runs for 338km, cuts the capital in half and was for centuries a main highway. There are some 30 bridges, several tunnels serving pedestrian, road and rail traffic across and under the river and numerous piers for pleasure boats.

Boadicea in her Chariot

The Brunels, father and son, built the first tunnel under the river, which opened as a pedestrian route in 1843. The **Brunel Engine House Museum** (Railway Avenue SE16 ☎ 7231 3840 ⊖ Rotherhithe ☛) occupies the original 19thC boiler house.

Until 1749, London Bridge was the only permanent bridge. The present structure (1972) marks the furthest navigable point up river for large vessels. The new Millennium Bridge (Map 3Ng), linking the area of St Paul's Cathedral with Bankside, is the first pedestrian bridge built across the Thames for 100 years. For a long time heavily polluted, the Thames is nowadays a cleaner river, with over 115 kinds of fish.

The **Victoria Embankment** (Map 4Kg) was built by Sir Joseph Balzagette in 1864–70 by reclaiming 4ha from the river. Apart from improving access to the City, it made the Thames more navigable and run more speedily, which in turn prevented the river from freezing.

A wealth of statues and monuments are set in the gardens from Westminster Bridge to Blackfriars Bridge. Amongst those honoured are *William Tyndale* (1484–1536), the first translator of the New Testament

into English, *General Charles George Gordon* (1833–85) who achieved fame at Khartoum, the Scottish poet *Robert Burns* (1759–1796), the versatile Victorian engineer *Isambard Kingdom Brunel* (1806–59) and *Bazalgette* (1819–91) himself. The ***York Water Gate***, built in 1626, stands by Waterloo Bridge while the ***Boadicea group***, unveiled in 1902 (she was the Queen of the Iceni, who successfully challenged the supremacy of the Roman legions in AD62) is at the approach of Westminster Bridge.

Cleopatra's Needle

The 21m granite obelisk generally known as ***Cleopatra's Needle*** (Map 4Lg), presented to England in 1819, was sculpted 3500 years ago in Aswan, long before the birth of the Egyptian queen, and brought to Heliopolis, near Cairo, by Tuthmosis III. Moved in 23 BC to Alexandria, it eventually fell down and lay in the sand for centuries. When Napoleon was defeated, the Egyptians presented the obelisk to the British in 1819. However the weight and cost of transport prevented the monuments removal to England. Finally, private funds were raised and in 1877 the 'Olga', a stout ocean-going tug, steamed out of Alexandria pulling a barge with the obelisk on board and a small crew to steer it. In the bay of Biscay, a storm upset the barge, the tow-rope snapped and many sailors drowned. Finally, the convoy reached England and the obelisk was erected in 1878. The bronze sphinxes on the base were designed by G. Vulliamy (1917), and modelled by C.H. Mabey. On the south side of the obelisk a plaque commemorates the sailors who died bringing it to London.

Somerset House from the Thames

Gilbert Collection: Table with views of Rome (diameter 83.5cm), mosaic and gilt wood, Rome, 19thC

The main feature of the Embankment is undoubtely **Somerset House** (The Strand WC2 ☎ 7845 4000 Map 2Lf ⊖ Covent Garden) built in the last quarter of the 18thC by Sir William Chambers on the site of the Renaissance palace of the Lord Protector Somerset. Chamber's masterpiece, with almost 1,000 rooms, was originally planned to accommodate government offices (above all the Navy Office) and learned societies such as the Royal Academy of Arts.

Now the building, whose courtyard has been restored to its original 18thC appearance and embellished with new architectural lighting, hosts besides the famous Courtauld Gallery* two other important museums: the Gilbert Collection and the Hermitage Rooms.

The ***Gilbert Collection*** (☎ 7240 5782 ☛) is one of the most important collections of silver, gold and micromosaics. It comprises some 800 objects and was formed over 35 years in California by the real estate developer Arthur Gilbert (born in London 1913) and his wife and given to Britain in 1998. The ***Hermitage Rooms*** (☎ 7845 4630 ☛) display highlights from the State Hermitage Museum in St Petersburg.

Hermitage Rooms

**Tower Bridge** (EC1 Map 3Sg ⊖ Tower Hill) is one of the best-known sights (1894). It incorporates the ***Tower Bridge Experience*** (☎ 7403 3761 ⊖ Tower Hill ☛) showing the interior workings of the only London bridge to open to allow the passage of tall ships. **HMS Belfast** (Morgans Lane, Tooley St SE1 ☎ 7407 6434 Map 3Rg ⊖ London Bridge ☛), moored nearby, is the Navy's last big-gun ship, now a floating museum of World War II at sea.

Tower Bridge

**St Katharine's Dock** (Map 3Sg ⊖ Tower Hill), on the north bank, was started in 1827 and achieved fame for its imports of goods from all over the world. Bomb damage during World War II, the post-war decline of trade in the London docks and the growth in container ships forced its closure, but it has now been brought to life again. It includes a marina, a boat club, a luxury hotel and the World Trade Centre. The *Dickens Inn* stands on one of the quays in a 200-year-old building.

Upstream, not far from Kew Bridge, is **Syon House** (Brentford TW8 ☎ 8560 0881 ⇌ Syon Lane ☛), another historic sight associated with Lord Proctor Somerset who begun to construct a mansion on the land of Syon Abbey suppressed by Henry VIII. Subsequently the Duke of Northumberland got his hands on the estate and it remains in the family's possession today. In 1760 Robert Adam was appointed to remodel the palace. Among the splendid interiors are the *Great Hall* and the *Long Gallery* (41.50m) with 62 pilasters painted by Michelangelo Pergolesi and landscapes by Francesco Zuccarelli.

Syon House: the elegant Dining Room, designed by Robert Adam, the Scottish architect

Regent's Canal at Little Venice

The **Thames Barrier**, downstream at Woolwich, is the world's largest flood barrier and a spectacular sight, spanning the river with 10 moveable steel gates powered by hydraulic machinery within concrete piers. When raised, the main gates each stand 28m high and weigh more than 3,700 tonnes. A *Visitors' Centre* (1 Unity Way, Woolwich SE18 ☎ 8854 1373 ⇌ Charlton Station ☛) hosts an exhibition, shops, a cafeteria and other facilities.

From the north side of Westminster Bridge there are cruises along the river to Greenwich and the Thames Barrier (downstream) and to Windsor, Runnymede and Hampton Court (upstream). Other cruises explore the extensive network of canals which encircle the north of London.

Their history is told by a display at the **London Canal Museum** (12 New Wharf Rd N1 ☎ 7713 0836 ⊖ King's Cross ☛), on a canal side site near King's Cross. The museum presents aspects of the history and working of London's navigable waterways, as well as the traditional art of canal boat people. The building was originally an ice house, used to store ice imported from Norway. The basement contains two large ice wells, each over 10m in diameter, the only ones of industrial scale on view in Britain. The trade in natural ice, and ice cream made from it, have special displays. Working horses are another theme, reflecting their role in ice distribution and transport. The upper floor was used as stables and the horse access ramp and a reconstructed horse stall are featured. There is mooring space to accommodate historic craft which may visit the museum from time to time.

Thames Barrier, at Woolwich

❑ **TOWER OF LONDON** (Tower Hill EC3 ☎ 7709 0765 Map 3Rg ⊖ Tower Hill ☛). Situated on the north bank of the Thames, it has over the centuries been a fortress, a royal palace, a repository for public records, the home of the Royal Mint, a menagerie, an observatory, an arsenal for ordnance and small arms and a State prison. As one of the country's strongest fortresses, the Tower is appropriately the home of the Crown Jewels and of the National Museum of Arms and Armour, better known as the Royal Armouries.

The ***White Tower***, the oldest building, easily distinguished by its four turrets, was begun by William the Conqueror to protect and control the City of London and to dominate the approaches by the river. It is 27.4m high, with walls ranging in thickness from 4.6m at the base to roughly 3.4m at the top. It includes the ***Chapel of St John***, a fine example of early Norman architecture (about 1080). One of the surviving original entrances to the Tower of London is on the south side under the ***Bloody Tower***, believed to have been the scene of the murder of the young Edward V and his brother in 1483.

***Tower Green*** was the site for the execution of those of royal or noble blood while other prisoners were executed on *Tower Hill*. ***Traitors' Gate*** was often used as an entrance to the Tower in days when river transport was more common than today. The ***Chapel Royal of St Peter ad Vincula*** dates from the 13thC but it was rebuilt after a fire in 1512. The dedication to St Peter 'in Chains' is grimly appropriate, for not only was it a place of worship for prisoners but it also housed their remains.

Yeoman Warder, colloquially a Beefeater

## The Crown Jewels

The display, in its super-safe setting, is not, for the most part, quite as old as many believe. After the execution of Charles 1 in 1649 the Parliamentary Party destroyed the royal crowns and sceptres and a new set had to be made for the coronation of Charles II in 1661. For all that, the display is dazzling, and the *St Edward's Crown*, the *Imperial State Crown*, and the *Queen Mother's Crown* with the fabulous Koh-i-Noor or 'Mountain of Light' diamond are an unforgettable sight.

The Constable of the Tower is one of the oldest offices in the country, dating from the 11thC. Day-to-day duties are performed by the Resident Governor, supported by the Yeoman Warders, commonly known as Beefeaters, established as long ago as 1485. One of their functions nowadays is to help visitors.

The *Ceremony of the Keys* takes place nightly when the Chief Yeoman Warder locks the main gates. No one can then enter the Tower until daylight – not even the Queen herself. Ravens form part of the Tower's history, and it is said that the Tower will fall if they disappear.

## The Royal Armouries

Officially entitled the National Museum of Arms and Armour, the Royal Armouries are amongst the finest historic arsenals in the world and constitute Britain's oldest museum. The collection comprises arms and armour, manuscripts and pictures relating to the history of the Armouries and its predecessors in the Tower of London as well as to the Tower itself.

Foot combat armour made for Henry VIII, 1540

❑ **TRAFALGAR SQUARE** (WC2 Map 4Kg ⊖ Charing Cross). The monumental square commemorates the Battle of Trafalgar (21 October 1805) which saw the British fleet under Admiral Nelson's command conquer and destroy the combined forces of France and Spain. Trafalgar Day is still celebrated with a parade up Whitehall to Trafalgar Square. The **statue of Nelson**, who died in the battle, stands at the top of the 51m high Corinthian column designed by William Railton with a bronze capital. The statue, by E. H. Baily, is 5m tall and faces south.

The four bronze lions at the base of the column were sculpted by Edwin Landseer and added in 1867. For many the square is the focal point of Christmas celebrations around the huge tree donated by Norway.

Nelson's Column

Statue of Admiral Nelson by E. H. Baily

The fountains: mermaids and dolphins

St Martin-in-the-Fields

On the north side of the Square is the National Gallery*. Next to it is **St Martin-in-the-Fields** (☎ 7930 1862), the parish church of Buckingham Palace. The present church (1722–26) occupies the site of a medieval chapel, which in turn incorporated Roman remains. It was designed by James Gibbs and built in Portland stone. The plasterwork of the eliptical ceiling is by Artari and Bagutti while the painting of St Martin and the Beggar is by Francesco Solimena and the portrait of Gibbs himself by Jacopo Amigoni. Charles II was christened here. Amongst famous people buried in the church are the miniaturist Nicholas Hilliard, the painters William Hogarth and Joshua Reynolds, the sculptor Roubilliac and Thomas Chippendale, the cabinet maker.

The annual Pearly Harvest Festival Service offers the opportunity to see London's cockney royalty – sellers of food (apples in particular) known for the profusion of pearly buttons on their clothes. It takes place at the church in October.

South of the square is the triangular island of **Charing Cross** on which stands the equestrian ***statue of Charles I*** (Hubert Le Sueur, 1633). This is the oldest freestanding public sculpture and was erected on the spot where the Regicides who signed Charles I death warrant were executed on the return to the throne of Charles II.

Distances to all corners of the British Isles are calculated from a bronze plaque by the statue. Charing Cross derives its name from the last resting place of the funeral procession of Eleanor of Castile (la chère reine, hence Charing), wife of Edward I, as it travelled from Nottinghamshire to Westminster Abbey (1290). The octagonal 'cross' standing in Charing Cross Station Yard is a Victorian reproduction (1863) of the one originally erected nearby. Several main streets radiate from the Square: Whitehall*, where the Banqueting House*, Horse Guards and major ministries are located; the Mall, a broad avenue leading from Admiralty Arch to Buckingham Palace*, and the Strand.

Statue of Charles I, Charing Cross

❑ **WESTMINSTER ABBEY** (Broad Sanctuary SW1 ☎ 7222 5152 Map 4Kj ⊖ Westminster ☛). Westminster Abbey has always been associated with the history of the British Isles both as a centre of worship and a resting place for the noble and the great. Impressive in appearance and size, the Abbey is 156.4m long, 61m broad, across the transepts, and 22.9m broad, across the nave and the aisles. The height of the nave is 31.1m to the vault, while the west towers are 68.6m high. Almost every sovereign, from William the Conqueror in 1066 to Elizabeth II in 1953, has been crowned here, and from about 1270 to 1760 most monarchs were buried here with their consorts.

Westminster Abbey: West Entrance

The Abbey is used for royal weddings, funerals and memorial services of great statesmen and national figures (in addition to the daily services of the Church of England).

It was founded by Edward the Confessor in the 11thC on the site of an earlier church. The present building was begun in about 1245. Most of the eastern end is 13thC. The ***Nave*** was rebuilt by the architect Henry Yevele in the late 14thC and an important later addition was Henry VII's Chapel completed in 1519. In the ***Chapel of St Edward the Confessor*** (22) are tombs of English kings. Close to the entrance of Henry VII's Chapel is the oak *Coronation Chair*. Every monarch since Edward II has been crowned in this chair with the exceptions of Edward V (one of the Princes murdered in 1483) and King Edward VIII who abdicated in 1936 before his coronation.

The magnificent ***Chapel of Henry VII*** (24), one of the glories of English architecture with its fan vaulted roof, consists of a nave, two aisles and five smaller radial chapels. The three oak doors carry bronze ornaments in the colours of the Houses of Lancaster and York, the families of Henry VII and Elizabeth of York, whose marriage ended the Wars of the Roses. Their tomb is the work of Pietro Torrigiano, a Florentine artist of the Renaissance. In the side chapel are tombs of Mary I, Mary Queen of Scots, Elizabeth I and the two princes murdered in the Tower of London in 1483. The ***RAF Chapel*** is dedicated to the airmen of World War II. In the South Transept is ***Poets' Corner*** (29) with tombs and memorials of many major British poets and writers such as the Brontë

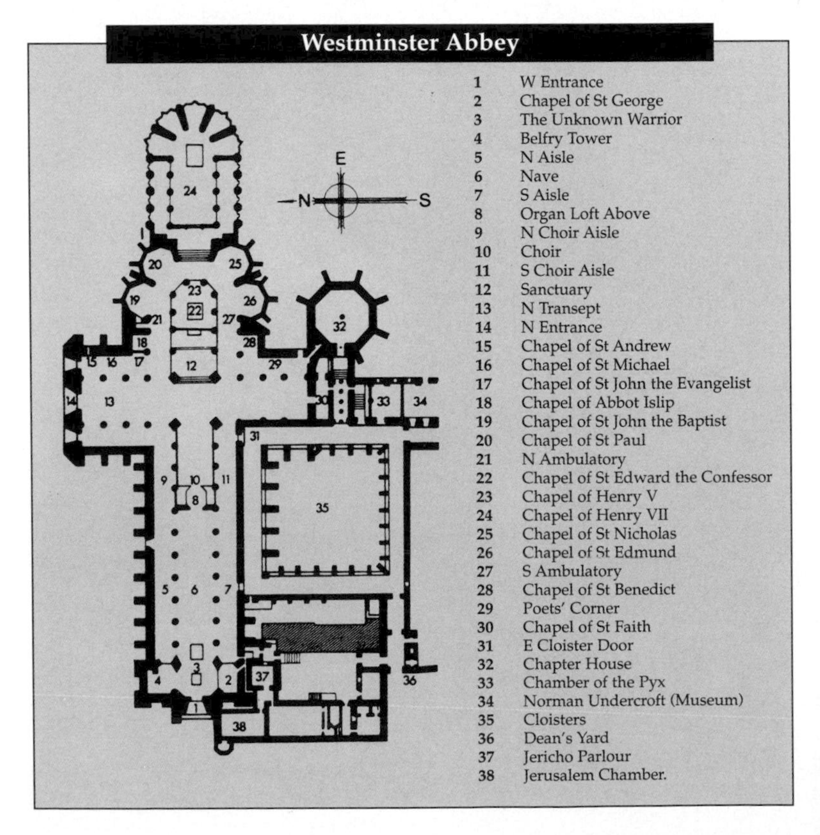

Westminster Abbey: Chapel of Henry VII

sisters, Burns, Byron, Chaucer, Dickens, George Eliot, Thomas Gray, Ben Jonson, Keats, Milton, Shakespeare, Shelley, Spenser, Tennyson, Dylan Thomas and Wordsworth. Scientists buried here include Darwin, Faraday and Isaac Newton. Among musicians are Handel and Purcell. Near the West Door is the ***Grave of the Unknown Warrior*** (3) whose body was brought from France and buried here on 11 November 1920. The grave commemorates those who gave their lives during World War I and whose place of burial is unknown.

Westminster Abbey:
Shrine of Edward the Confessor

Although within the precinct of the Abbey, **Chapter House** (☛) comes under the supervision of English Heritage. Built in 1250 and restored in the 19thC, it contains fine examples of medieval English sculpture. The building (32) is octagonal with a central column and still has its original floor and glazed tiles. It was a meeting place for the Benedictine monks of the Abbey and also for the medieval House of Commons.

## Westminster Abbey Museum

The **Westminster Abbey Museum** (☛) can be reached through the Cloisters. It displays effigies in either wax or wood of royalty and others buried in the Abbey. This collection is situated in the oldest part of Westminster Abbey, the Norman Undercroft of the Monks Dormitory, built between 1066 and 1100.

The earlier effigies are of wood and, of all but two, only the heads survive. Modelled from death–masks, they give an amazingly realistic impression of medieval and Tudor monarchs. The later wax effigies, dating from the 17thC and 18thC, are equally vivid representations, and their clothes and paste jewellery represent in themselves a unique collection of contemporary costume.

As well as the effigies, the museum contains examples of Romanesque carving, a fine relief portrait of Sir Thomas Lovell by Torrigiano, objects connected with the life of the Benedictine Abbey, an architectural model and drawings by Wren and a selection of copes and of silver-gilt plate, mainly of the 17thC.

Effigy of Queen Anne

❑ **WESTMINSTER CATHEDRAL** (Ashley Pl SW1 ☎ 7798 9055 Map 6Jj ⊖ Victoria ☞). The Cathedral, which stands in its own piazza half-way down Victoria Street, is the seat of the Archbishop of Westminster, the senior Roman Catholic prelate in England and Wales.

The main fabric was started in 1895 to the design of J.F. Bentley. It is in neo-Byzantine style, inspired by St Sophia in Istanbul and St Mark's in Venice. Millions of red bricks and a profusion of marbles were used in the building which covers an area of 5,016 $m^2$. The external dimensions are 120m length, 52m width with the bell tower rising almost to 86m.

Westminster Cathedral

Its most important feature is the interior with the nave being the highest and the widest of any cathedral in Britain. It has aisle galleries supported by columns of green marble from the same quarry which provided material for the great St Sophia basilica in Istanbul.

The decorations, though still unfinished, are colourful, especially the mosaics, which depict symbolical and allegorical themes. On the main piers, the bas-reliefs of the ***Stations of the Cross***, made in 1913–18, are by Eric Gill.

Westminster Cathedral: the Lady Chapel

The body of the martyr St John Southworth lies in the ***Chapel of St George and the English Martyrs***, dedicated to those persecuted during the Reformation. The ***Lady Chapel*** is not only the richest with artistic mosaics by Anning Bell and Gilbert Pownall, but it is also at the centre of the cathedral's spiritual life. The first Mass was said here on Lady Day in 1903.

The tomb of the much respected Cardinal Basil Hume, 9th Archbishop of Westminster, who died in June 1999 is in the ***Chapel of St Gregory and St Augustine***.

The ***Millennium Cross***, marking 2,000 years of Christianity, was erected in the piazza outside the Cathedral towards the end of the year 2000. The wooden cross, standing around 17m high, was an initiative of the late Cardinal Hume to strengthen the ecumenical dialogue amongst churches of various denominations.

The Millennium Cross

# MUSEUMS & GALLERIES

There is an enormous variety of museums, galleries and exhibitions in London. Many collections owe their origin to the habit of the British aristocracy and merchant class using their wealth, good taste and shrewdness to acquire works of art from all over the world. This started as a serious pastime in Tudor times and continued through the 18thC in the days of the Grand Tour, reaching its peak in the heyday of the British Empire. Substantial contributions to the growth of the collections were also made by British scientists and adventurers.

A charge is usually made for special exhibitions. Many museums supply floor plans of their displays and portable sound-track commentaries. The majority are open from 1000 to 1800, or later, and closed on Christmas Day and major public holidays.

❑ **APSLEY HOUSE** (Hyde Park Corner W1 ☎ 7499 5676 ⊖ Hyde Park Corner ☛). Built by Robert Adam in the 1770s and known as 'Number One' London, this became the London home of the British hero of the Battle of Waterloo. It houses trophies, uniforms, decorations, fine paintings and sculptures. The Duke of Wellington was an avid collector of pictures: Velázquez, Rubens, Van Dyck, Murillo and Brueghel are all here. Magnificent gifts include the splendid Sèvres Egyptian Service made originally for the Empress Josephine.

British Museum: view of the South Façade

Apsley House: Waterloo Gallery

The huge Canova statue of Napoleon was bought by the British Government in 1816 and given to Wellington. The Duke commissioned Benjamin Dean Wyatt to make alterations to the house, and added the magnificent ***Waterloo Gallery***, where he held his annual dinners with his old comrades-in-arms to commemorate the battle which vanquished Napoleon.

In the ***Dining Room*** on the first floor is the great table with chairs, which the Duke used for his annual dinners, and on the table is the silver centrepiece presented by Portugal in 1816 and described as the 'single great monument of neoclassical silver'. In the Basement is a display of caricatures of Wellington.

❑ **BETHNAL GREEN MUSEUM** (Cambridge Heath Rd E2 ☎ 8980 2415 ⊖ Bethnal Green ☞). A branch of the Victoria and Albert Museum (qv), it has one of the largest collections of toys on display in the world. It is officially known as the National Museum of Childhood. Visitors can explore the process of growing up in the childhood displays showing baby equipment, nursery furniture, children's clothes, and teenage fads and fashions.

❑ **BRITISH LIBRARY** (96 Euston Rd NW1 ☎ 7412 7332 ⊖ Kings Cross ☞). The British Library is the national library of the United Kingdom. Created in 1973 it took over responsibility for the vast assemblage of written and most of the graphic works of the British Museum, and has since acquired other important libraries and archives. It is one of the most extensive collections of books and related materials in the world.

Amongst its treasures is the Old Royal Library donated by George II in 1757, which brought with it the right to a free copy of every work published in the kingdom. The collection, which is open to readers on application, spans almost three millennia and comprises items from all continents of the world. It holds extensive music, map, philatelic and sound collections in addition to books and, digital material.

The new building at St Pancras, designed by Colin St. John Wilson, contains more than 12m books. Dominating the Library's piazza is Paolozzi's bronze statue of Newton, inspired by William Blake's famous image of Isaac Newton seated and bending forward to plot with a pair of dividers the immensity of the universe.

Four exhibition galleries are open to the public:

- ***The John Ritblat Gallery: Treasures of the British Library*** is a permanent exhibition of changing highlights from its rare and unique collection, including the *Lindisfarne Gospels* (c700), the *Diamond Sutra* (868), the *Gutenberg Bible* (c1455), the *Magna Carta* (1215) and Shakespeare's *First Folio* (1623);
- ***Turning the Pages*** is the visitor's chance to turn the pages of electronic copies of some of the Library's most important items;
- ***The Pearson Gallery of Living Words*** contains one special, temporary exhibition per year with thematic displays when there are no special exhibitions;
- ***The Workshop of Words, Sounds and Images*** tells the story of writing, book production and sound recording from the earliest times to the digital revolution.

The King's Library, collected by George III and presented to the nation by his son George IV in 1823, is housed in a six-storey-glass-walled tower at the heart of the building.

British Library: Main Hall

❑ **BRITISH MUSEUM** (Great Russell St WC1 ☎ 7323 8000 ⊖ Holborn, Russell Square, Tottenham Court Road ☞). Founded in 1753, it is one of the world's greatest museums. It is not really a 'British' but a universal institution reflecting the rich variety of human achievement through the millennia. It comprises ten curatorial departments and two scientific departments (Scientific Research and Conservation).

Within the ***Department of Coins and Metals*** is an excellent representation of the world's coinage with a high proportion of significant rarities of various series and the national collection of paper money. The ***HSBC Money Gallery*** traces the growth and development of monetary systems from the 3rd millennium BC to the present.

***Ancient Egypt and Sudan*** illustrates every aspect of ancient Egyptian and Nubian culture from about 4000 BC to the 12thC AD. Among the best known objects are the Predynastic burial from Gebelein c3400 BC, the 196 BC *Rosetta Stone* (the key to the decipherment of hieroglyphic script), the *Shabako Stone* with its creation text 8thC BC and the c530 BC sarcophagus of Nectanebo (last native pharaoh of Egypt).

***The Department of Ethnography*** is concerned with studying and collecting from the cultures of recent and contemporary small-scale indigenous societies (and a number of complex state systems) of Africa, the Americas, Oceania and parts of Europe. It includes the archaeology of the Americas, Oceania and the post-quaternary archaeology of sub-Saharan Africa.

***Greek and Roman Antiquities*** cover the Greek world from the beginning of the Bronze age; Italy and Rome from the Bronze age; and the whole of the Roman Empire except Britain until the Edict of Milan in AD 313. Among the highlights is the *Portland Vase,* the finest piece of Roman glass from 1stC BC/AD.

***Medieval and Modern Europe*** covers European art and archaeology from the Edict of Milan in AD 313 to the present day. It has outstanding collections of Early Christian and Byzantine art, Dark Age European antiquities, Romanesque and Gothic metalwork and ivories, Renaissance and later pottery, porcelain, glass, cameos and jewellery. Amongst the best known items are the *Esquiline treasure* 4thC AD (with the silver casket of Projecta), the *Royal Gold Cup* of the Sovereigns of England and France c1380 AD and the *Sutton Hoo ship burial* cAD 625.

***Oriental Antiquities*** covers the cultures of Asia from the Neolithic period onwards, with the exception of the ancient civilisations of the Near East and the art of Japan. The collections include paintings and prints from all areas as well as antiquities and sculpture. Among the well-known single items are the *Bimaran reliquary* (1st-2ndC AD) and the bronze statue of the goddess *Tara* (8thC). ***Japanese Antiquities*** houses collections of Japanese decorative arts and paintings which are among the finest and most comprehensive in Europe.

***Prehistoric and Early Europe*** has Quaternary material from all over the world and includes many outstanding examples of Upper Palaeolithic art such as the swimming reindeer from Montastruc 10,500 BC. Neolithic and bronze age antiquities derive mainly from sites in Europe, and are extremely comprehensive. The Iron Age collection contains some of the most famous items of Celtic Art, such as the Basse Yutz flagons c400 BC and the Battersea shield 1stC BC found in the Thames. The finds from Roman Britain form one of the best illustrations of provincial culture within the Empire.

1. The Royal Gold Cup, Paris c1380, with scenes from the life of St Agnes; 2. The Rosetta Stone, c196 BC; 3. The Portland Vase, 1stC BC or AD; 4. Horse of Selene from the east pediment of the Parthenon, mid 5thC BC; 5. Human-headed lion from Ashurnasirpal II's palace at Nimrud, c865 BC. British Museum.

British Museum: Queen Elizabeth II Great Court

***Prints and Drawings*** houses one of the most representative collections of Western prints and drawings in existence. The collection of prints covers the development of print making from its beginnings in the 15thC up to modern times and includes many rare and artistically outstanding works. Similarly, the collection of drawings, besides being probably the most diverse extant, includes many works by most of the leading artists of the European schools from 15thC onwards. The collections are not permanently exhibited, but are shown in a programme of temporary exhibitions.

***The Department of the Ancient Near East*** covers the civilisations of this region and adjacent areas (Mesopotamia, Iran, the Arabian Peninsula, Anatolia, the Caucasus, parts of Central Asia, Syria, Palestine and Phoenician settlements in the western Mediterranean) from the prehistoric period until the coming of Islam in the 7thC AD. It is one of the most comprehensive collections of ancient Near Eastern material in the world. Highlights of the collection include the Assyrian sculptures from Nimrud and Nineveh (7th and 8th centuries BC).

To mark its 250th anniversary in 2003 the British Museum is carrying out some major improvements. The most important project has been the transformation of the inner courtyard into Europe's largest covered square: the **Queen Elizabeth II Great Court**. The space round the dome of the Round Reading Room, where Karl Marx wrote Das Kapital and Lenin studied the land question, has been redeveloped. The ***Round Reading Room*** is now home to the *Walter and Leonore Annenberg Centre*, giving access to COMPASS, the museum's multimedia database, and to the Paul Hamlyn Library, a public reference library. The ***Joseph Hotung Great Court Gallery*** is a major new space for temporary exhibitions. There are shops, cafés and a restaurant. Beneath the concourse (south) is the ***Clore Education Centre*** and the ***Ford Young Visitor Centre*** and (north) the ***Sainsbury African Galleries***.

❑ **COURTAULD GALLERY** (Somerset House, Strand WC2 ☎ 7848 2526 ⊖ Covent Garden, Holborn, Temple ☛). The 11 fine art collections in this gallery were privately donated. The two most important donations were made by Samuel Courtauld (1876–1947) (Manet, Degas, Cézanne, Monet, Pissarro, Renoir, Seurat and Toulouse-Lautrec) and by Count Antoine Seilern (1901–1978) (Rubens, Tiepolo and rare early Flemish and Italian paintings).

As well as the Impressionists and Post-Impressionists, highlights of the collection include the Master of Flémalle's *Entombment*, Botticelli's late masterpiece *The Trinity*, Cranach's *Adam and Eve*, the Rubens room (in particular *Landscape by Moonlight* and *Deposition*) and the fine collection of Tiepolo oil sketches.

The gallery also has a world-class collection of 34,000 Old Master drawings and prints. A selection is shown in a special exhibition room on the second floor.

Courtauld Gallery: Manet, *A Bar at the Folies-Bergère*

The Courtauld moved to Somerset House in 1990. This, the masterpiece by Sir William Chambers (1724–1796), architect to George III, is one of the most important 18thC buildings in Europe. The Strand Block, where the gallery is situated, was originally built to house the newly formed Royal Academy of Arts and opened in 1780. The ***Great Room*** on the top floor was the first purpose-built exhibition space in England. In 1837 the Royal Academy* moved to Burlington House, Piccadilly.

❑ **CRAFTS COUNCIL GALLERY** (44 Pentonville Rd N1 ☎ 7278 7700 ⊖ Angel ☞). Periodic displays of work of craftsmen in all media. This is Britain's national collection of contemporary crafts. Its purpose is to lend outstanding works for public display throughout the country. Over 1,200 objects are available for loan. They include ceramics, glass, furniture, textiles, jewellery, metalwork and automata.

❑ **DULWICH PICTURE GALLERY** (Gallery Rd SE21 ☎ 8693 5254 ⇌ West Dulwich ☛). This delightful picture collection in a quiet village setting is England's oldest public art gallery and predates the National Gallery. It is set on the edge of the 38 ha Dulwich Park which remains little changed since it was laid out in 1890 when it was presented to Londoners by Dulwich College.

The building was designed by Sir John Soane and opened in 1814. It contains one of the country's finest collections of Old Master paintings. Here are works by Rembrandt, Van Dyck, Claude and Poussin, an exceptional assembly of other Dutch artists and splendid portraits by Gainsborough and Reynolds.

Dulwich Picture Gallery: West Front, designed by Sir John Soane

Dulwich Picture Gallery: interior.

The oldest part of the gallery's collection dates from the early 17thC when Edward Alleyn, an actor of Shakespeare's time, founded Dulwich College (a well-known school) and bequeathed his 39 paintings to the Foundation.

The most substantial bequest came in the early 19thC from Sir Francis Bourgeois, a landscape painter, who had inherited paintings bought by his

Dulwich Picture Gallery: Rembrandt, *Girl leaning on a Window-sill*

friend Noel Desenfans for the King of Poland. The latter was forced to abdicate in 1795 and his treasures eventually found a permanent home at Dulwich. There are twelve galleries and a mausoleum, the latter an eerie chamber containing the sarcophagi of Bourgeois, Desenfans and Mrs Desenfans.

Major temporary exhibitions are held regularly throughout the year. The gallery reopened in May 2000 after an extensive refurbishment which subtly complements Soane's masterpiece. It provides essential new services: an exhibition space, a lecture theatre and a café. The extension is linked to the gallery by an elegant glass and bronze cloister.

The gallery has received much deserved critical and popular attention. It has a thriving education department. Staff are very friendly and well informed. Private tours can be arranged.

❑ **ESTORICK COLLECTION** (Northampton Lodge, 39A Canonbury Sq N1 ☎ 7704 9522 ⊖ Highbury & Islington ☛). Important collection of Italian Futurist and figurative art in a renovated Georgian building.

Estorick Collection: Luigi Russolo, *La Musica*, 1911

❑ **EUROPEAN ACADEMY FOR THE ARTS** (8 Grosvenor Pl SW1 ☎ 7235 0303 ⊖ Hyde Park Corner ☛). Major temporary presentations relating to the riches of European culture, Italian in particular.

❑ **FENTON HOUSE** (Windmill Hill NW3 ☎ 7435 3471 ⊖ Hampstead ☛). A distinguished building (1693) with formal, very English, walled gardens. The house has fine examples of English 18th furniture, porcelain (Chinese, English and Meissen) and the large and famous Benton-Fletcher collection of keyboard instruments.

❑ **GEFFRYE MUSEUM** (Kingsland Rd E2 ☎ 7739 9893 ⊖ Liverpool Street ☞). Domestic interiors from 1600 to the present day. After entering at the left-hand end, the visitor walks the length of the terrace whose interior is arranged in a chronological series of room settings. These start with an Elizabethan Room, followed by a Stuart Room and so on through the reigns and styles of Queen Anne, the Georgian period, the Regency and Queen Victoria. At the end of the ground floor arrangement are the Aesthetic style room, the Edwardian Room, an Arts and Crafts family parlour of about 1900 and a 1930s suburban lounge. The display culminates with a 1950s Room and the 20thC period galleries. Between the Queen Anne and Early Georgian rooms is the tiny chapel of the 18thC almshouses in which the museum is housed.

Geffrye Museum: the Stuart Room 1660-1685

❑ **HORNIMAN MUSEUM** (100 London Rd SE23 ☎ 8699 1872 ≹ Forest Hill ☞). Impressive ethnographic, musical and natural history exhibits. The exhibition *African World* is the only permanent gallery in London dedicated to African, Afro-Caribbean and Brazilian art and culture.

❑ **ICA GALLERY** (Nash House, The Mall SW1 ☎ 7930 3647 ⊖ Charing Cross ☛). Avant-garde art in multi-media exhibitions at the Institute of Contemporary Arts.

❑ **IMPERIAL WAR MUSEUM** (Lambeth Rd SE1 ☎ 7416 5000 ⊖ Lambeth North ☛). This is a unique institution concerned with the story of war in the 20thC. Founded in 1917, its terms of reference now extend to all conflicts involving British or Commonwealth troops from 1914 to the present day. Military exhibits such as aircraft, tanks, artillery, medals and equipment are central to the museum but there are also extensive collections of works of art, photographs, documents, books, film and sound recordings illustrating land, sea and air warfare and life on the home front.

The spectacular ***Large Exhibits Gallery*** offers dramatic views of more than fifty of the museum's most historically significant large items – the Sopwith 'Camel' veteran of dogfight-days above the Western Front; its successor the 'Spitfire', the P51D 'Mustang', FW190; 'Churchill', 'Sherman', 'Grant' and 'Jagdpanther' tanks; a Biber submarine and Italian human torpedo, V1 and V2 weapons, and 'Thunderbird' and 'Polaris' missiles. Providing more detailed background information are audio-visual displays on general topics like the Battles of Britain and the Atlantic, the North African Campaign, the Eastern Front and missiles and rocket weaponry.

Imperial War Museum: the Large Exhibits Gallery

The Blitz experience recreates what it was like to be caught in the street in an air raid. The ground shakes, smoke fills the air and even the smell is authentic and convincing. Yet another 'experience' awaits the visitor in the form of a 'Tommy' in the trenches of Flanders in World War I.

The 1,400 m$^2$ permanent exhibition on the ***Holocaust*** opened in June 2000. It forms the largest element of the new six storey extension of the museum. The historical display uses original artefacts. While the main focus is the persecution of the Jews in Europe, other groups are included. A 36m long model depicts events of Auschwitz-Birkenau in May-June 1944.

Perhaps unexpectedly, the museum is one of London's most important sources for British 20thC art, with works by Kennington, Paul Nash, Epstein, Sutherland, Piper, Topolski and many more. In all, the ***Department of Art*** holds over 10,000 paintings, drawings, prints and sculptures in what is one of the foremost collections of British art in the world, and some 50,000 posters.

Jewish Museum (Camden Town):
Chanukah lamp, Polish, c1840

❑ **JEWISH MUSEUM**. This institution is split into two. The ***Camden Town*** location (129-131 Albert St NW1 ☎ 7284 1997 ⊖ Camden Town ☛) is devoted to the history and culture of the Jewish people while at ***Finchley*** (80 East End Rd N3 ☎ 8349 1143 ⊖ Finchley Central ☛) there are displays on the Jewish immigration and settlement in London.

❑ **KENWOOD HOUSE** (Kenwood, Hampstead Lane NW3 ☎ 8348 1286 ⊖ Golders Green then Bus ☞). Paintings by Cuyp, Gainsborough, Hals, Rembrandt, Reynolds, Romney, Turner and Vermeer in an 18thC mansion remodelled by Robert Adam in 1767–8 who also designed its interior decoration and furniture. For its public ownership today we must thank Edward Cecil Guinness, 1st Earl of Iveagh, who saved the Kenwood estate from speculators in 1925 and gave it to London.

Kenwood House: Vermeer, *The Guitar Player*

Kenwood House: Main Entrance

❑ **MADAME TUSSAUD'S** (Marylebone Rd NW1 ☎ 7400 3000 ⊖ Baker Street ☛). Life-size wax models and tableaux of events. Its scope is endless, ranging from Beethoven to Michael Jackson, Henry VIII to Elizabeth II. The adjoining ***London Planetarium*** takes visitors on an inter-galactic trek across the Universe.

Madame Tussaud's: Henry VIII and his six wives

❑ **MALL GALLERIES** (The Mall SW1 ☎ 7930 6844 ⊖ Charing Cross ☛). Owned by the Federation of British Artists, it presents changing exhibitions, including those of the Royal Society of Portrait Painters and the Association of Illustrators.

❑ **MUSEUM OF GARDEN HISTORY** (St Mary-at-Lambeth, Lambeth Palace Rd SE1 ☎ 7261 1891 ⊖ Lambeth North ☞). Created in memory of the two Tradescants, father and son, the 17thC gardeners who travelled extensively collecting plants and 'all things strange and rare'. They are buried here, as is Captain William Bligh of the 'Bounty'.

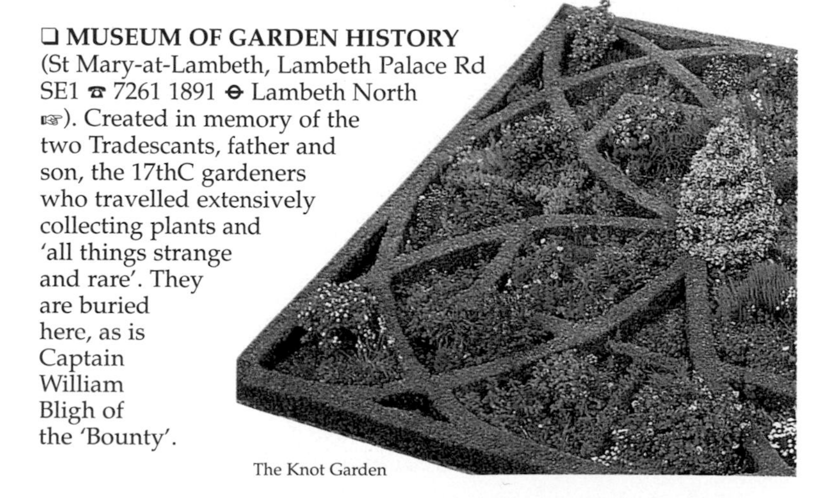

The Knot Garden

❑ **MUSEUM OF LONDON** (150 London Wall EC2 ☎ 7600 3699 ⊖ Barbican, St Paul's ☛). This is Britain's premier social history museum and the repository of the capital's archaeological heritage.

It is a very visual museum, enticing and inviting to the eye. The permanent displays start with pre-historic and Roman London and proceed chronologically through medieval, Tudor and Stuart, Georgian, Victorian and 20thC galleries to tell the story of the evolution of London and its people over the centuries.

The broad themes of London's history are all covered – housing, diet and dress, education and leisure, politics and the Church, trade and industry, religion and culture. But it is also the human story behind London's expansion and change, successes and setbacks, that is conveyed to the visitor. Every object is included because it has something to contribute to the story of the capital, whether it be a medieval leather shoe excavated from a City site or the ceremonial splendour of the Lord Mayor's Coach.

It is this interaction of objects – archaeological with social history and costume, fine and decorative arts with industrial history and ceremonial – that makes this museum particularly colourful, accessible and alive. Certain exhibits clearly fall into the 'top ten' category for all ages, like the collection of Jacobean jewellery known as the *Cheapside Hoard* or the *Great Fire Experience* which recreates through visual and sound effects the Fire of 1666. The costume collections are amongst the finest in the country. The museum has built up an important collection of material relating to the Docklands and London's commercial and industrial activities.

Museum of London: Lord Mayor's State Coach

Museum of London: Cheapside Hoard

The splendid new ***18thC Gallery*** looks at all levels of society and highlights include a recreated façade of Newgate Gaol and stunning Spitalfields silk dresses. The reserve collections and library are important sources of material for scholars of London's history.

❑ **MUSEUM OF THE ORDER OF ST JOHN** (St John's Gate, St John's Lane EC1 ☎ 7253 6644 ⊖ Farringdon ☛). St John's Gate was originally the southern entrance to the Priory of the Knights of St John of Jerusalem in Clerkenwell. The collections relate to the history of the Order of St John from the time of its foundation during the Crusades. They comprise paintings, silver, furniture, ceramics, coins and medals, insignia, books and manuscripts. An important collection of arms and armour of the Knights Hospitaller includes fine Rhodian and Maltese pieces, portrait medals, maps, drawings and a cannon given to the Order by Henry VIII. In the Priory Gallery, adjacent to the Gate, is the ***St John Ambulance Museum***, on the development of the St John Ambulance from its foundation in 1877.

Museum of the Order of St John: St John's Gate

❑ **NATIONAL ARMY MUSEUM** (Royal Hospital Road SW3 ☎ 7730 0717 ⊖ Sloane Square ☞). Housed in a purpose-built building, it is the only museum which records the British Army's activities over the five centuries of its existence. It includes the record of the Indian Army up to Independence in 1947 and of the colonial forces.

National Army Museum: figure of a Private from the 13th Regiment suffering from yellow fever in St Domingo, Caribbean, 1795

In the Basement ***The rise of the Redcoats: The British Soldier 1415-1792*** tells the story of the Army from Agincourt to the American Revolution. The campaigns and battles fought by generals such as Cromwell, Marlborough and Wolfe and their soldiers are covered in detailed displays. Themed displays on recruitment, living conditions, siege warfare, wounds and medicine, personal armour and weapon development give a real insight into the life of the ordinary British soldier. There are recordings too of contemporary soldier's songs. ***Cut, Thrust and Swagger*** is the most detailed display of British military swords in the country featuring nearly 200 swords, supported by contemporary illustrations and a video presentation.

On the First Floor, ***The Road to Waterloo Gallery*** follows the story of the soldier in Wellington's army. The *piece de resistance* is the 37.2m$^2$ model of the Battle of Waterloo with over 70,000 model soldiers. ***The Victorian Soldier*** covers the expansion and defence of the British Empire in the 19thC, while ***The Nation in Arms*** brings us into the 20thC with the reconstruction of a World War I trench and dug out, and views of life in the jungles of Burma and the deserts of North Africa in World War II. The display showing the impact of the machine gun on the Somme (1916) is memorable.

On the Second Floor the exhibition the ***Right to Serve*** highlights the contribution made by women to the Army, from the 'she souldiers' of the 17thC and 18thC who dressed as men in order to follow the Army, to the women serving in uniform today. The ***Art Gallery*** contains a selection of 17thC, 18thC and 19thC paintings. The ***Library*** (prior application) has a comprehensive collection of books and manuscripts covering everyone and everything to do with the Army.

❑ **NATIONAL GALLERY** (Trafalgar Sq WC2 ☎ 7747 2885 ⊖ Charing Cross, Leicester Square ☞). The collection, comprising over 2,300 prime paintings, is remarkably comprehensive. It includes nearly all the major schools of Western European paintings from the 13thC to 19thC. Their quality and variety is a constant source of surprise and delight to the 5 million annual visitors.

National Gallery: Main Entrance

The National Gallery was created in 1824 when the British government acquired 38 paintings from the late Julius Angerstein, a Russian born financier. In 1838 the present building, designed by William Wilkins, was opened by Queen Victoria. Following some generous gifts, the Sainsbury Wing was opened in 1991 and houses the Renaissance collection as well as special exhibition rooms, a lecture theatre, the Micro Gallery computer information room and other facilities. The collection is divided chronologically into four wings: the ***Sainsbury Wing*** with paintings from 1260 to 1510; the ***West Wing*** from 1510 to 1600; the ***North Wing*** from 1600 to 1700; the ***East Wing*** from 1700 to 1900.

Among the Early Italian and 16thC Italian paintings are masterpieces such as Piero della Francesca's *Baptism* (1450s); Uccello's *Battle of San Romano* (probably about 1450–60); Botticelli's *Mystic Nativity* (1500);

National Gallery: Botticelli, *Venus and Mars*

National Gallery: Sainsbury Wing

Leonardo da Vinci's *Virgin of the Rocks* (about 1508), almost the twin of that in the Louvre; Mantegna's *Agony in the Garden* (about 1460); Raphael's *Pope Julius II* (1511–12); Titian's *Bacchus and Ariadne* (1521–23) and Bronzino's *Allegory with Venus and Cupid* (1540–50).

With the Dutch, Flemish and Early Northern masters one can familiarize oneself with the Northern Renaissance. Works such as Van Eyck's *The Arnolfini Marriage* (1434), Dieric Bouts's *Entombment* (probably 1450s), *The Virgin and the Child with Saints and Donors* or the *Donne Triptych* (probably 1478) by Hans Memlinc and Hans Holbein's renowned portrait of *The Ambassadors* (1533). One of Rubens's greatest admirers was *King Charles I*, whose equestrian portrait by Van Dyck (1637–8) hangs in the gallery. There are also two notable acquisitions by Van Dyck, the *Lords John and Bernard Stuart* (about 1638) and the *Balbi Children* (about 1625–7).

Of the 22 Rembrandts in the collection, it is hard for the visitor to single out just one for close study. The two self-portraits – one revealing a confident young man of 34 years (1640), the other a tired and dispirited old figure of 63 (1669) – or his loving portrayal of his mistress *Hendrijke Stoffels*, or the severe and uncompromising features of his old patroness *Margaretha de Geer* (1661), or even the eerie stillness of his deeply shadowed *The Adoration of the Shepherds* (1646); they all evoke an artistic confidence which speaks across the centuries. It is hard also to resist the charm of the other paintings in the Dutch school; Cuyp's placidly grazing cows, Vermeer's steely calm interiors showing a lady at the virginal, and Ruysdael's mighty land, sea and sky scapes.

Among Italian paintings after 1600 will be found Caravaggio's *Supper at Emmaus* (1601) and Luca Giordano's *Perseus turning Phineas and his companions to stone* (early 1680s). Claude and Poussin give way to Chardin and Boucher. Canaletto and Tiepolo lead to Velázquez, Murillo and Goya or Turner, Constable, Reynolds and Gainsborough.

The 19thC rooms present a rich view of European painting in the second half of the 19thC. Impressionist gems – Monet's *Gare St Lazare* (1877), Degas' *Woman Drying Herself* (probably 1888–92), Manet's *Music in the Tuileries Gardens* (1862), Van Gogh's *Chair and Pipe* (1888) and *Sunflowers* (probably 1888), both Seurat's (1884) and Cézanne's *Bathers* (1900–6). Two or three major exhibitions a year are designed to complement the collection. There are lectures, mixed media programmes, quizzes for children, talks for school groups and specialist tours.

National Gallery: Jan van Eyck, *The Arnolfini Marriage*

National Maritime Museum:
Prince Frederick's Barge, 1732

Queen's House: Throne of Estate,
Queen's Presence Chamber

❑ **NATIONAL MARITIME MUSEUM** (Romney Rd SE10 ☎ 8858 4422 ⇌ Greenwich, Maze Hill, DLR Cutty Sark, Boats from Westminster Pier or Tower Pier ☛). Set in the beautiful and ancient Royal Park at Greenwich, the museum includes the 17thC Queen's House and Royal Observatory, Greenwich. Its main galleries, linked by a 19thC colonnade to the Queen's House, have recently undergone major redevelopment (1999). New display themes include *The Future of the Sea, Explorers, Passengers, Trade and Empire, Art and the Sea* and the ever popular *Nelson*. The museum's holdings in most areas relating to British seafaring, especially from the 17thC to late 19thC, are unrivalled and are now increasingly accessible to visitors through an on-site *Search Station*.

The 17thC **Queen's House**, England's first classical building, is one of the few surviving examples of the work of Inigo Jones, who revolutionised English architecture of the period. The Italianate villa was designed in 1616 for Queen Anne of Denmark, wife to James I. It was completed in 1635 for Charles I's consort, Queen Henrietta Maria. Highlights include the magnificent ***Tulip Stairs***, and the ***Great Hall***, a perfect cube with an original black and white marble floor.

The **Royal Observatory, Greenwich**, designed by Christopher Wren in 1675, is the home of Greenwich Mean Time (GMT) and also part of the museum. Visitors can stand in both the eastern and western hemispheres simultaneously by placing their feet either side of the Prime Meridian Line, Longitude $0^{0}$, as well as seeing a camera obscura and many remarkable instruments including John Harrison's famous chronometers. The Observatory unravels the extraordinary phenomena of time, space and astronomy.

National Maritime Museum, looking south towards the Old Royal Observatory on the hill.
On the left, the East Wing; on the right, the West Wing; in the centre, Inigo Jones's Queen's House.

❑ **NATIONAL PORTRAIT GALLERY** (St Martin's Pl WC2 ☎ 7306 0055 ⊖ Charing Cross ☞). It has over 10,000 paintings, drawings, sculptures and photographs of distinguished British men and women. Artistic quality of the exhibits is variable; the great do not always sit to great artists.

National Portrait Gallery: the Victorian and early 20thC rooms

The world's largest portrait gallery occupies four floors covering the 16thC to the 20thC. To see it in chronological order the visitor should start from the top. On the landing between the first and ground floors are John Wonnacott's new portrait of the Royal Family, painted to celebrate the Queen Mother's centenary (2000), Queen Elizabeth II by Pietro Annigoni, Tom Wood's portrait of Prince Charles and Norman Parkinson's photographs of the Royal Family.

The ***Wolfson Gallery*** holds temporary exhibitions, as do the Photography Gallery and the Studio Gallery.

An escalator, London's longest, rises from the new Central Entrance Hall to the second floor Tudor Gallery, while a long ***Balcony Gallery*** provides a setting for portraits embracing figures from every arena of British life from the 1960s to the 1990s including Helmut Newton's portrait of Margaret Thatcher. The *Portrait Explorer*, accessible through 11 touch screens in the ***IT Gallery***, allows visitors to study in depth all the works in the main collection as well as sections of the ***Photographic and Archive Collections*** of over 250,000 portraits.

The Portrait Restaurant and Bar offer views across Trafalgar Square and Whitehall. From time to time actors and musicians give performances based on the lives and works of people in the collections.

❑ **NATURAL HISTORY MUSEUM** (Cromwell Rd SW7 ☎ 7942 5000 ⊖ South Kensington ☛). The museum is made up of two buildings linked at ground floor level by the Waterhouse Way. The building facing Cromwell Road contains the Life Galleries and the one on Exhibition Road, the Earth Galleries.

Natural History Museum: Front Entrance, designed by Alfred Waterhouse

The **Life Galleries** are on three floors. The entrance from the Cromwell Road leads into the Central Hall containing a selection of the ***Wonders*** of the natural world. Outstanding amongst all is the skeleton of a Diplodocus.

***Dinosaurs*** displays a comprehensive view of dino saur life from 230 to 65 million years ago with models, illustrations, animation, interactive video techniques and fossil specimens and, with the addition of the world's most advanced robotic Tyrannosaurus rex, is not to be missed.

***Ecology*** looks at how living things interact with one another and with their environment to form thriving communities and how these, including human beings, cause changes.

The centrepiece of the ***Mammals*** exhibition is the life-size model of a blue whale. ***Human biology*** has sections about the development of body and mind. A slide programme traces the growth of a human embryo. ***Fishes, amphibians and reptiles*** gives a wide display of reptiles, familiar and unusual marine and freshwater species.

The exhibition ***Creepycrawlies*** is devoted to the Arthropod kingdom, the most numerous and diverse on earth, with as many as 80 million specimens, from insects, spiders and crabs to centipedes and millipedes.

***Primates*** takes a look at the group of mammals which currently dominate the planet. Its sister exhibition is ***Our place in evolution*** which sets out the story of our own evolution and our relationship with other primates. ***Origin of Species*** shows how Darwin answered the question 'How do new species evolve?' and the process of natural selection.

One of the most comprehensive collections of minerals in the world is on display in ***Minerals, Rocks and Meteorites***.

Entering the **Earth Galleries** – arranged on three floors – from Exhibition Road, the visitor reaches the Visions of Earth, dominated by a massive globe sculpture of beaten copper, iron and zinc. It symbolizes the Earth's onion-like structure from the atmosphere to the inner core. An escalator carries visitors on a 'journey through the centre of the Earth' to the second floor.

Natural History Museum: Visions of Earth, Earth Galleries

Six giant sculptures in ***Visions of Earth*** exemplify a basic concept of the Earth which is explored in the further exhibitions. *God* (after William Blake) represents Earth's beginnings and stories of the origins of the world and people. *Atlas,* the giant balancing the world on his shoulders and included in the front of one of the earliest maps, is an icon of Earth's shape and place. *Cyclops* represents Earth's past, which we learn from studying and comparing. The ancient Greeks believed that fossil bones were the remains of a race of one-eyed giants, but it is now known that the central eye-like opening in the ancient skulls is actually the location of a trunk. *Medusa,* whose glance was said to be so terrible that it would turn any living thing to stone, embodies the concept of Earth's processes. The figure of a *Scientist* represents the Earth's future and makes us aware of our need to understand how human activity influences the entire Earth's system. The *Astronaut* suggests the Earth's order, introducing us to a future where, according to some scientists, we will mine the Moon to meet our demand for resources.

The ***Power within*** deals with the processes at work inside the Earth. It includes volcanoes and earthquakes and explores the dynamic internal structure of the Earth. ***Restless surface*** explains how external processes have shaped the landscape over millions of years. It shows the power of erosion, whether by scouring glaciers or relentless winds, and its dramatic effect on our surroundings since the Earth formed. ***From the beginning*** deals with Earth's formation and geological time and ***Earth's treasury*** displays specimens of gems and minerals from the museum's famous collections. In the ***Investigate*** on the lower ground floor younger visitors have direct contact with a range of specimens and can carry out experiments and observations with help from museum staff.

Natural History Museum:
the robotic Tyrannosaurus rex

Polish Institute and Sikorski Museum

❑ **POLISH INSTITUTE & SIKORSKI MUSEUM** (20 Princes Gate SW7 ☎ 7589 9249 ⊖ South Kensington ☞). This is by far the most important Polish museum outside Poland with over 10,000 items displayed plus a Library and Archives. A major exhibit in a glass cabinet is General Sikorski's uniform salvaged from the sea after the air disaster in Gibraltar which claimed his life. Another major exhibit is the red and white Polish national flag which was flown over the ruins of the monastery of Monte Cassino in 1944. Separate collections record the history of cavalry, artillery and armoured units with many mementoes of national and sentimental value. Other items are armour from the 17thC, 18thC watercolours, paintings and miniatures and relics from the Napoleonic era.

❑ **POLLOCK'S TOY MUSEUM** (1 Scala St W1 ☎ 7636 3452 ⊖ Goodge Street ☛). Named after Benjamin Pollock (1856-1937), whose shop was well-known for its toy theatres, has toys from all over the world. The items on display are frequently changed.

❑ **RIBA HEINZ GALLERY** (21 Portman Sq W1 ☎ 7580 5533 ⊖ Bond Street). Changing shows from the Royal Institute of British Architects's collection of drawings, plus special exhibitions.

❑ **RIVERSIDE STUDIOS** (Crisp Rd W6 ☎ 8741 2251 ⊖ Hammersmith). 20thC art in all media.

Pollock's Toy Museum

Royal Academy of Arts: The Staircase

❑ **ROYAL ACADEMY OF ARTS** (Burlington House, Piccadilly W1 ☎ 7300 8000 ⊖ Piccadilly Circus ☛) The Royal Academy was founded in 1768 under the patronage of George III to promote the arts in Britain and to provide a free School to train artists. It is one of the world's leading post-graduate art colleges. Since 1868 it has occupied the neo-Palladian Burlington House with a courtyard stretching to Piccadilly. The building, with exquisite paintings by Sebastiano Ricci and other acclaimed artists, reflects the 3rd Earl of Burlington's (1694-1753) refined taste.

The first president, Sir Joshua Reynolds, is commemorated in the courtyard by a statue by Alfred Drury. The courtyard itself, renamed *Annenberg Courtyard*, is at the centre of a major refurbishment involving the addition of fountains and sculpture. A parallel project aims at the renovation and restoration of the *Fine Rooms* for the display of the permanent collection.

Royal Academy of Arts: Michelangelo, *The Taddei Tondo*, c1505

The *Summer Exhibition* of paintings, prints and sculptures which is open to all living artists is held annually. Major international loan exhibitions take place during the rest of the year.

The ***Sackler Galleries*** on the second floor, which were designed by Norman Foster and completed in the early 1990s, accommodate special exhibitions. The *Taddei Tondo*, sculpted by Michelangelo in Florence in about 1505, is one of the Academy's most treasured possessions. In 2001 the Academy took over the building directly behind, previously occupied by the Museum of Mankind. This will create a development which will more than double the Royal Academy's existing space and provide new lecture theatres, workshops, conference facilities and a new large gallery for the showing of art by Academicians, students of the School and other contemporary artists.

❑ **ROYAL ACADEMY OF MUSIC MUSEUM** (Marylebone Rd NW1 ☎ 7873 7373 ⊖ Baker Street ☞). An unparalled collection assembled over many years of musical manuscripts and instruments.

**.R FORCE MUSEUM** (Grahame Park Way NW9 ☎ 8205 .ndale ☛). This complex comprises three quite separate but .entary displays – the Main Aircraft Hall, the Battle of Britain .n and the Bomber Command Hall. The Royal Air Force .um is the only British national museum devoted solely to the his- .y of aviation and to the story of the Royal Air Force, past, present .d future.

The **Main Aircraft Hall** incorporates two hangars dating from World War I. It displays some 40 aircraft ranging from the Bleriot XI of 1909 through the 'Biggles era' of World War I to the supersonic Lightning.

Linking the two hangars is an area which contains the ***Camm Collection*** commemorating the late Sir Sidney Camm who designed such famous aircraft as the Hawker Hart, the immortal Hurricane and the P1127 'jump jet', forerunner of the Harrier.

Royal Air Force Museum: Main Aircraft Hall

The **Battle of Britain Museum** was launched as a national tribute to the men, women and machines involved in the decisive air battle of 1940, and especially to 'The Few', as Winston Churchill named the young pilots of the fighter planes involved.

The Spitfire MkI, which is located in an imaginative replica of a wartime dispersal pen, saw action during the Battle of Britain and participated in the 100th 'kill' of No. 609 Squadron. The German aircraft involved in the struggle are well represented and include a JU88, Heinkel III, Stuka dive bomber and ME 109.

The **Bomber Command Hall** displays and preserves many unique bomber aircraft and artefacts. It also pays tribute to the courage, determination and perseverance of the men and women who built, maintained and flew these aircraft and in particular to the 126,000 aircrew of Bomber Command and the 8th and 9th USAAF who died in the bomber operations during War World II.

The collection includes the only known surviving Wellington (apart from the wreck recovered in 1985 from the depths of Loch Ness) and the dramatically-displayed Halifax which was raised from a lake in Norway. In April 1942 the aircraft flew its first and last operational sortie when it was shot down while attacking the battleship Tirpitz in a Norwegian fjord.

The World War I era is represented by the immaculately-restored DH9A aircraft and tiny Sopwith Tabloid. Post war aircraft include two 'V' Bombers, the Valiant and the Vulcan.

❑ **ROYAL BOTANIC GARDENS** (Kew, Richmond, Surrey TW9 3AB ☎ 8332 5655 ⊖ Kew Gardens ☛). Established under royal patronage more than 250 years ago, the Royal Botanic Gardens at Kew are world-famous. Although around 1.25 million visitors come here each year, few realise that this is primarily a great scientific institution with an outstanding reputation.

The *Sir **Joseph Banks Centre for Economic Botany*** houses global collections of plants, artefacts and implements associated with cultivation. It is only accessible by prior application. In the ***Herbarium*** and ***Library***, open only to researchers, are some 7 million dried plants, over 120,000 books, 140,000 reprints and other items and some 160,000 prints and drawings. There is also the ***Jodrell Laboratory*** where experimental studies take place on the anatomy, cytology and biochemistry of plants.

Royal Botanic Gardens, Kew: Palm House by Decimus Burton

There is much at Kew to interest and delight the ordinary visitor. It is a beautiful and tranquil garden with magnificent trees and impressive vistas. The 50,000 species of plants come from all parts of the world, the more delicate being displayed in the vast ***Temperate House*** and the unique ***Palm House***. The ***Princess of Wales Conservatory***, with 10 climatic zones, is a major greenhouse of modern design. The ***Marianne North Gallery*** contains an astonishing array of botanical subjects painted by this indefatigable Victorian lady in almost every corner of the globe

Royal Botanic Gardens, Kew: Marianne North Gallery

with enormous dedication and considerable talent. The elegant ***Orangery*** has a restaurant and gift shop. The *Victoria Gate Centre* has displays on the work and history at Kew. Guided tours are available.

Within the precinct of the Gardens are **Kew Palace** (built in 1631 when it was known as the Dutch House) and **Queen Charlotte's Cottage**. Both these buildings are full of historic mementoes of King George III, Queen Charlotte and their children.

❑ **SAATCHI GALLERY** (98A Boundary Rd NW8 ☎ 7624 8299 ⊖ St John's Wood ☛). Contemporary art in a converted warehouse in St John's Wood opened in 1985 with the aim of introducing new art, or art largely unseen in Britain, to a wider audience.

❑ **SALVATION ARMY INTERNATIONAL HERITAGE CENTRE** (117/121 Judd St WC1 ☎ 7387 1656 ⊖ King's Cross ☞). It relates the story of the movement, still very much alive in over 100 countries in the name of the Gospel and of social services.

❑ **SCIENCE MUSEUM** (Exhibition Rd SW7 ☎ 0870 870 4868 ⊖ South Kensington ☛). Established with the profits from the Great Exhibition (1851), the museum provides a fascinating insight into the world of Science and Technology. With over 46 galleries and 2000 hands-on exhibits you can see, touch and experience the major scientific advances of the last 300 years, from original working steam engines to the actual Apollo 10 command module and with the latest addition of an IMAX cinema and virtual reality simulator, there is plenty to captivate and inspire everybody.

The Basement is a colourful and vibrant series of inter-active galleries aimed at children and encourages learning and discovery through play. With dozens of puzzles, games and experiments the young can learn about household gizmos and gadgets in the ***The Secret Life of the Home***, test their wits in the hands-on gallery ***Launch Pad*** or splash about in the water area of the ***The Garden***.

With an impressive display of engines, the Ground Floor is also home to the ***Space Gallery*** which explores the past, present and future of space travel. This is the place to design your own rocket, find out about life on Mars and see the *Black Arrow* rocket, Britain's only satellite launcher to date. Also situated on the Ground Floor is ***Making of the Modern World***, which shows off many of the museum's most important artefacts. Telling the story of the development of the modern industrial world, the gallery is an inspirational space with such diverse exhibits as Stephenson's famous *Rocket* locomotive, the first sewing machine and a *Lockheed 10A Electra* plane which hovers over the exhibits from the ceiling.

Science Museum: the Rocket

Science Museum: Space Gallery

Situated on the First Floor is the ***Challenge of Materials*** gallery which explores the complex world of modern materials and is centred around a bridge made entirely of glass and supported by almost-invisible steel wires. Equally impressive is the ***Materials House*** which displays 213 different materials in the form of a massive sculptural structure.

***Computing then and now*** on the Second Floor outlines the development of the computer. A special section, Making the Difference, is devoted to Charles Babbage who designed the forerunner of the modern computer.

Science Museum: Babbage machine

***Flight***, on the Third Floor, is an atmospheric gallery detailing man's desire to fly. Aircraft from the pioneering days of flight are on display as well as a cross-section through a Boeing 747. Also on this floor is ***On Air*** – a radio and sound studio which not only allows visitors to explore the equipment and mechanisms behind broadcasting, but also lets them experiment at compiling their own radio show.

The **Wellcome Wing**, is an impressive theatre of contemporary science. The six new interactive exhibitions explore the latest developments in science and technology and the effect they may have on our lives.

**...N SOANE'S MUSEUM** (13 Lincoln's Inn Fields WC2 ...107 ⊖ Holborn ☞). Filled with the accumulated treasures ... by the architect Sir John Soane (1753–1837) in the house which ...igned for his own occupation. He gathered the best artefacts of ...ptian, Greek, Roman and other civilisations and commissioned ...rks from colleagues and other artists.

Sir John Soane's Museum: sculptures, vases and fragments

The ***Picture Room*** is dominated by Hogarth's *The Rake's Progress* and *The Election*. Also paintings by Turner, Watteau, Piranesi, Henry Howard and a selection of Soane's own works. Amongst the great treasures of the museum is the Sarcophagus of Seti I. Discovered during the exploration of the Necropolis of Thebes in the early 19thC, it was first offered to the British Museum, but rejected because of cost, and then promptly acquired by Soane in 1824. Interpretation of the hieroglyphics was not completed until 1908. Another striking feature is the ***Dome***, which is the oldest part of the museum and can be seen from the basement. The pillars supporting the Dome are covered with sculptures and fragments, vases and other works.

❑ **TATE BRITAIN** (Millbank SW1 ☎ 7887 8008 ⊖ Pimlico ☞). It was started and financed by the sugar magnate Sir Henry Tate, who also donated 67 English pictures, including *Ophelia* by the Pre-Raphaelite John Everett Millais. The gallery, opened in 1897, contains British art from the mid-16thC to the present day, and international art of the 20thC and onwards. The displays are currently hung in a thematic structure but will return to a broadly chronological structure from October 2001.

Tate Britain: Main Entrance

The oldest painting is *A Man in a Black Cap*, dated 1545, by John Bettes, an English follower of Holbein's sharply focused realism. Under Elizabeth I, English painting took an increasingly stylised and decorative character, exemplified by the magnificent portrait of Elizabeth herself from the studio of Nicholas Hilliard, the first great native-born genius of English painting. Moving into the reign of Charles I, there are two other fascinating portraits: *Sir Richard Saltonstall and his Family* by David Des Granges and *Endymion Porter* by William Dobson.

The first important group of works by a single artist is by the 18thC William Hogarth, 'the father of English painting'. His most notable works are the *Self-Portrait* with his pet pug dog, his theatre scene *The Beggar's Opera*, and the anti-French satire *The Roast Beef of England*. Both Stubbs and Gainsborough, perhaps the dominating English artists from about 1760–80, are well represented. In the substantial group of paintings by Reynolds there are three famous and revealing self-portraits. The William Blake collection is the largest anywhere. John Constable is well represented with loans from the Victoria and Albert Museum complementing Tate's own holdings. Constable's work is shown alongside the vast production of J.M.W. Turner in the handsome Clore Gallery.

Tate Britain: British School 17thC, *The Cholmondeley Ladies*, c1600-10

Most notable works of the Pre-Raphaelite collection are Millais's *Ophelia*, Hunt's *Awakening Conscience*, Rossetti's *Beata Beatrix* and Burne-Jones's *King Cophetua and the Beggar Maid*. Their influence extended to the end of the century with artists like J.W. Waterhouse. The American-born James McNeill Whistler marks the beginning of modernism in Britain with his increasingly abstract views of the Thames of the 1870s.

Tate Britain also shares with Tate Modern a huge collection of 20thC British art including greats such as Sickert, Spencer, Moore, Epworth, Bacon, Freud, Hockney, Hamilton, Kapoor, Cragg and Whiteread.

## The Clore Gallery

Over 300 oil paintings and 20,000 works on paper by J.M.W. Turner, a true giant amongst the 19thC landscape artists, have been housed in the Clore Gallery, opened in 1987, thanks to the generosity of the Clore Foundation established by the businessman and philanthropist Charles Clore.

This has fulfilled the dream of the great artist, who left the finished paintings remaining in his studio to the nation, on the understanding that they should be kept and displayed in a home of their own.

J.M.W.Turner, *Self-portrait*

Superb facilities for study and research, including a Study Room where many thousands of drawings and watercolours acquired by the nation at the artist's death can be examined (by appointment), assure the Clore Gallery's future as a focus for Turner studies.

Tate Modern on the night of its official opening (11 May 2000)

❑ **TATE MODERN** (Bankside SE1 ☎ 7887 8008 ⊖ Southwark, Blackfriars ☞). It opened in 2000 in the transformed Bankside Power Station, on the south bank of the Thames. The gallery, the world's largest, is linked to the northern side of the river by the Millennium Bridge. It displays the Tate collection of international 20thC art, featuring major works by the most influential artists, including Bacon, Beuys, Bourgeois, Dali, Duchamp, Giacometti, Matisse, Mondrian, Picasso, Pollock, Rothko and Warhol. It is also a gallery for newly created contemporary art.

International art begins with the early modern movements. Highlights include one of Cézanne's last paintings, *The Gardener*. Italian Futurism is represented by Boccioni's *Unique Forms* of *Continuity in Space* (1913), and there is an important group of works by the British Vorticists led by Wyndham Lewis. Two of the major founders of modern sculpture were the near-contemporaries Edgar Degas and Auguste Rodin.

The early development of pure abstract art is exemplified by *Dynamic Suprematism* (1915) by the Russian pioneer of abstraction Malevich. There is a good group of paintings by Mondrian and very fine examples of the work of Nicholson. Modern sculpture is represented by Brancusi, Epstein, Gabo, Hepworth and Moore.

The development of Expressionism is marked by *The Sick Child* by the Norwegian Munch, and there are works by artists of the German Brücke group (founded 1905). The Tate has one of the best collections of Surrealist art. Among them are the celebrated painting by De Chirico

Tate Modern: Boccioni, *Unique Forms of Continuity in Space*

*The Uncertainty of the Poet* and Dali's most important works of the 1930s. Picasso between the wars is represented by three outstanding paintings: *The Three Dancers, Nude Woman in a Red Armchair* and *Weeping Woman.*

Some highlights of the post-war collection up to the early 1960s are: Matisse's *The Snail;* works by Giacometti and Dubuffet; substantial holdings of American Abstract Expressionism including Newman's *Adam and Eve* and the remarkable group of enormous mural paintings originally intended for the Four Seasons Restaurant in New York but given to the Tate by Rothko in the year of his death (1970); three major paintings by Pollock; substantial holdings of British and American Pop Art including major works by the British Hamilton, Blake and Hockney and by the Americans Oldenburg, Lichtenstein and Warhol, these last two represented respectively by the equally celebrated paintings *Whaam!* and *Marilyn Diptych*. The gallery has substantial holdings of the colourful large-scale abstract sculpture of Caro and his school that flourished in the 1960s.

Tate Modern: Francis Bacon, *Three Figures and Portrait*

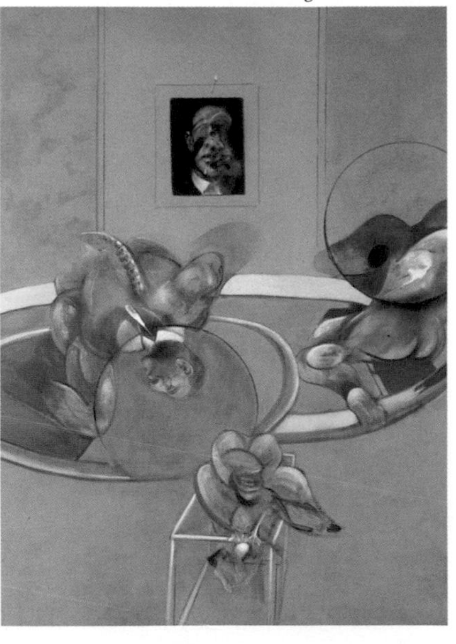

The School of London is portrayed by works of Bacon, Auerbach, Freud and Kossoff. Also represented is international painting and sculpture of the 1980s with works by Americans such as Longo, Salle, Schnabel and Holzer. Of particular interest is the strong collection of recent British sculpture, including works by Cox, Long, Flanagan, Wentworth, Woodrow, Kapoor, Wilding, Houshiary, Deacon and Cragg, shared with Tate Britain.

The Tate Modern building is a remarkable combination of the old and the new. The original Bankside Power Station was designed by Sir

Tate Modern: Picasso, *Nude Woman with Necklace*

Giles Gilbert Scott, architect of the Anglican Liverpool Cathedral and designer of the red telephone box. The building has been converted by the Swiss architects Herzog and de Meuron.

Their design respects the integrity of the building with its soaring central chimney. The ***Swiss Light***, accomplished with generous help from Switzerland's Federal Government, illuminates the top. The most visible change to the building is a glass structure running the length of the roof, which adds two floors to the gallery, provides natural light to the upper galleries, and gives outstanding views across London

The main entrance to Tate Modern is from the west of the building. From here visitors descend down a ramp into the vast former Turbine Hall. Inside the building the display galleries are arranged on three levels with various kinds of spaces. At other levels there are facilities which include an excellent restaurant, cafés, and a large bookshop.

Tate Modern: P. Mondrian, *Church at Zoutelande*

## ...ORIA AND ALBERT MUSEUM

...well Rd SW7 ☎ 7942 2000
...outh Kensington ☛).

V&A: Main Entrance, surmounted by Lanteri's Fame

The Victoria and Albert Museum, or simply the V&A, is a place of superlatives. It owns four million objects in over 8 km of gallery space. The **Henry Cole Wing** alone is a massive store with a million works of art. It houses the ***National Collection of Portrait Miniatures*** which include the celebrated *Young Man among the Roses* by Nicholas Hilliard.

In the main building the galleries have a delightful way of catching the visitor by surprise. On the ground floor the ***Cast Courts*** contain Victorian plaster casts of Europe's great pieces of monumental sculpture and masonry and in many cases they represent a more accurate expression than the original. The Trajan Column in Rome, for instance, is now so

V&A: the plaster cast of Trajan's Column, Cast Courts

badly corroded as to be hardly recognisable while the 1870's plaster cast shows no degradation. In the sumptuous ***Dress Collection*** costume and its creation is seen as a decorative art. Any music lover should not miss the rich ***Historic Musical Instruments Collection***. The ***Raphael Gallery*** displays cartoons executed by the famous Renaissance painter as patterns for tapestries. Regarded as one of the greatest artistic treasures in Britain they form part of the Royal Collection and since 1865 have been on loan to the V&A. The paintings were acquired by Charles, Prince of Wales (later King Charles I), in 1623. In the ***Nehru Gallery of Indian Art*** you will find *Tippoo's Tiger*, an expensive toy made for an Indian sultan in the 18thC. The gigantic *Ardabil carpet* (10.7m by 5.3m) is displayed in the ***Gallery of Islamic Art*** while the ***Chinese Gallery*** has amongst its treasures a jar dating from 2000 BC. The ***European Gallery*** near the main entrance, is dedicated to Continental art of the 19thC. Two other important galleries on the ground floor are the ***Medieval Treasury***, with perhaps the most valuable pieces in the entire collection for their intrinsic value and rarity like the 12thC *Eltenburg Reliquary* and the *Becket Casket*, and the ***Toshiba Gallery***, the biggest Japanese Gallery in Europe.

V&A: Gown, petticoat and stomacher (silk), English, c1760

The ***Ceramic Staircase*** linking the ground floor to the first floor should not be missed. The ***Jewellery Gallery*** displays some of the best Medieval and Renaissance jewellery in the world while the ***Silver Galleries*** have British and Continental items ranging from the 4thC to the present day. Within the ***British Galleries*** are the bust of Henry VII by Torrigiano, Henry VIII's gloves and the four-poster 3.65m wide *Great Bed of Ware*. This appears in Shakespeare and in Dickens and bears the carved signature of hundreds of temporary occupants during its days of hotel service. The ***Glass Gallery*** illustrates the history of 4,000 years of glass-making with over 6,000 objects.

Raphäel Cartoon, *Christ's Charge to St Peter*. The seven Raphäel Cartoons are amongst the greatest artistic treasures in Britain and the most important surviving examples of Renaissance art. They were brought to England in 1623 by Charles, Prince of Wales (later King Charles I). The Cartoons form part of the Royal Collection and since 1865 have been on loan to the V&A.

The whole top floor of the museum is occupied by the ***Ceramic Galleries*** which comprises one of the largest and most comprehensive collections in the world. A futuristic wing on the Exhibition Road side, designed by Daniel Liberskind, will house a multimedia gallery and education facilities on completion.

The ***National Art Library***, part of the V&A, is a vast lexicon of the history of art and a magnificent collection of some of the most beautiful volumes and illustrations ever made.

❑ **WALLACE COLLECTION** (Manchester Sq W1 ☎ 7563 9500 ⊖ Bond Street ☞). This is one of the most outstanding collections ever assembled by one family. It was built up in the 19thC by the third and fourth Marquesses of Hertford and the latter's illegitimate son Sir Richard Wallace, whose wife bequeathed it to the British nation in 1897.

Wallace Collection: Hals, *The Laughing Cavalier*

Wallace Collection: Front State Room

The collection, displayed in 24 galleries on two floors, includes amongst its treasures an array of 18thC French paintings to rival the Louvre, some remarkable pieces of furniture and applied art, Vincennes and Sèvres porcelain and one of the most important assemblies in the world of arms and armour. Amongst its masterpieces is *The Laughing Cavalier* (1624) by Frans Hals.

To celebrate its centenary as a national museum the collection unveiled a vast building development in June 2000, which increased its total space by one third. The ambitious programme involved redesigning the previously neglected basement and transforming the courtyard into the elegant Café Bagatelle with a floating glass roof. As a result four new galleries have been created plus a 150 seat Lecture Theatre, a Seminar Room, an Education Studio and a Visitors' Library.

❑ **WELLCOME TRUST** (183 Euston Rd NW1 ☎ 7611 8888 ⊖ Euston Square ☞). The Trust, the world's largest medical research charity, hosts a series of exhibitions on contemporary medical science and art in its ***Two10 Gallery***. The extensive Library is based on the immense breadth of Sir Henry Wellcome's collections. An Information Service, a Medical Photographic Library and a Medical Film and Video Library are also available to the public.

❑ **WHITECHAPEL ART GALLERY** (Whitechapel High St E1 ☎ 7522 7888 ⊖ Aldgate East ☛). A charitable trust since 1901 for making the best art and design accessible to the people of East London, it has an international reputation for major exhibitions of modern art.

# SHOPPING

A city without shops is like a garden without flowers. This is not the case with London which, along with Paris, Madrid and Milan, is one of the best and most enjoyable European shopping centres. Its main attraction is the very large number of shops offering products from around the globe, not to mention the presence of world-renowned establishments specialising in collecting and auctioning high-quality objets d'art and antiques. Several thousand traders are involved in the antique and art markets, serving a large international clientele.

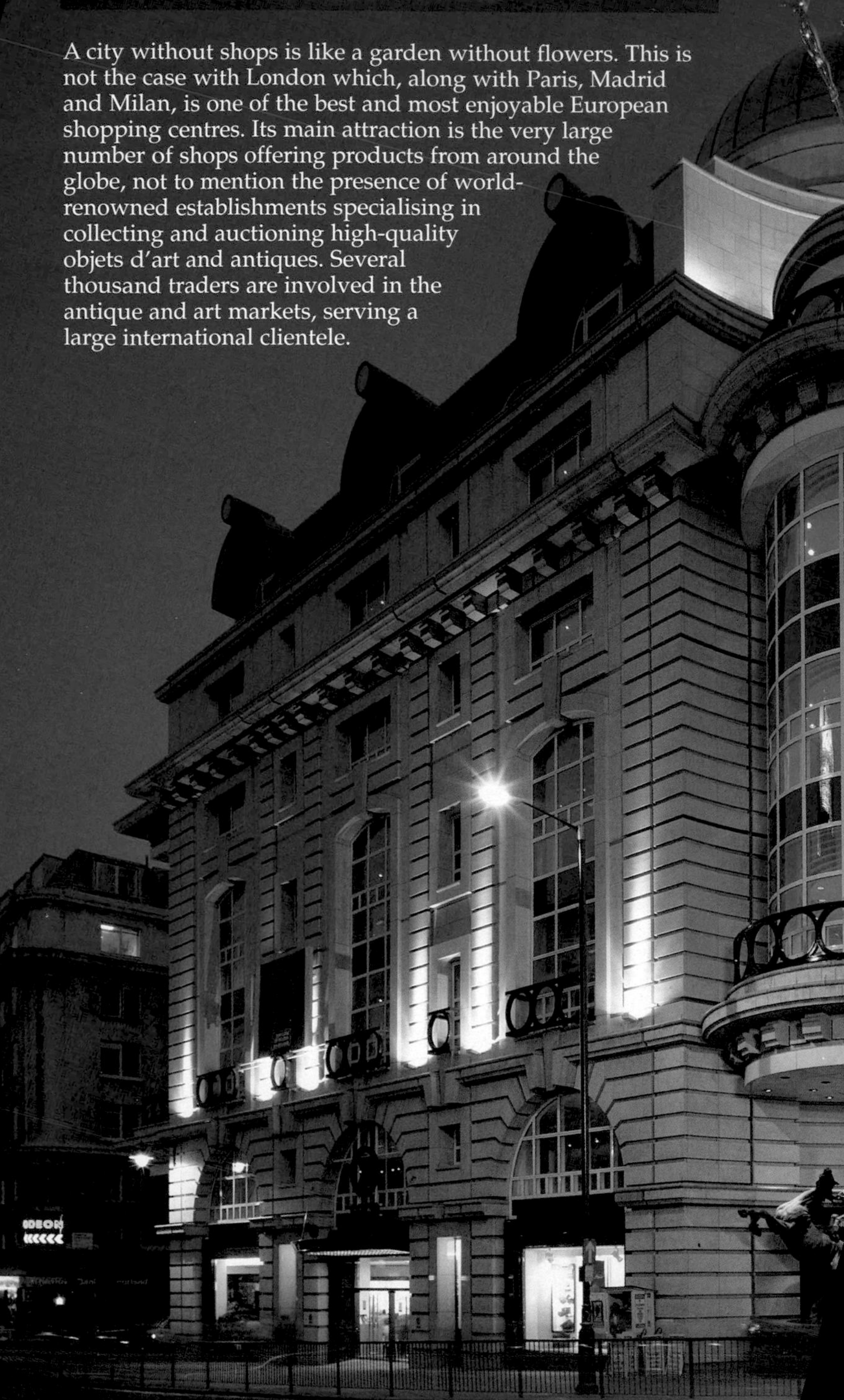

The shopping scene is enhanced by the presence of well-known designers who flock to these shores. The annual *London Fashion Week*, launched in the early 1980s, has given the capital an international reputation for avant-garde clothes.

Londoners and visitors love a bargain and most stores meet their wishes by holding regular seasonal sales. The ***Winter Sales*** usually start in late December and last through January while the ***Summer Sales*** run during July and August. Some shops gild their image by displaying the most prestigious accolade available, the Royal Warrant, which includes the Royal Coat of Arms with the words 'By Appointment'.

*Virgin Megastore*, Piccadilly Circus

## Royal Warrant

The Queen's Royal Warrant

The privilege of the ***Royal Warrant*** has been accorded to certain tradesmen since the reign of George V. Around a thousand shops and companies in Britain hold the Royal Warrant. Even if the applicant is a company, the grantee will always be one of the directors as an individual.To qualify, the establishment must have regularly supplied for three years one of the principal members of the Royal Family or their households. A business may hold warrants for more than one member of the Royal Family.

❑ **STREETS & AREAS**. Shopping is generally geographically compact: shops dealing in the same kind of goods tend to share the same locality. What follows is a selection.

NEW BOND STREET W1

• **Bond Street** W1 (Map 5Hf ⊖ Bond Street). The area retains a whiff of Old England. At the north end you will find New Bond Street, while Old Bond Street runs south into Piccadilly from the bronze statue of the 'Allies' (Churchill and Roosevelt) by Holofcener. At *Burberry* checks in every permutation as well as new ideas. For pick of the top designer clothes, head for *Versace, Yves St Laurent, Giorgio Armani, Donna Karan, Calvin Klein, Salvatore Ferragamo,*

OLD BOND STREET W1

*Donna Karan*, Bond Street

*Chanel* or *Prada*. Equally good, but perhaps a bit easier on the wallet, is *Fenwick*, while opposite *Ralph Lauren* stocks the full range from this popular American designer. Fine shirts can be picked up at *Sulka* and shoes from well-established names like *Church, Fratelli Rossetti* or *Kurt Geiger*. For chocolates *Charbonnel et Walker* is the place, while a range of dazzling gems and jewellery can be inspected at *Cartier, Bulgari, Tiffany, Philip Antrobus, Bentley & Co* and *Asprey and Garrard*.

*Asprey & Garrard*, Bond Street

*Smythson* stocks elegant stationery and *Chappells* high quality pianos. You can buy some timepieces at *Watches of Switzerland.* Discerning travellers visit *Louis Vuitton, Loewe, Hermès* or *Gucci* for their luggage. An Old Master can be sought out at *Agnew's, Colnaghi, Richard Green* or *Sotheby's*. The *Fine Art Society* may also proffer a worthwhile scene or two. *Vivienne Westwood* has been in **Conduit Street** for several years. Children with adults in tow will find a range of clothes at *Please Mum* whilst *Connolly* is just as much appreciated by those in the know for its beautiful interior and its exclusive leather goods.

Expectant mothers stop off at *Formes* (33 Brook St) on their way to nearby **South Molton Street**. This is the place to be seen for London's cool young things with wallets to match their expensive tastes. *Browns* stocks items from all the top designers while *Vidal Sassoon* is a favourite for a quick cut and blow-dry. Tucked in behind Oxford Street, opposite Bond Street station and down Gees Court is **St Christopher's Place.**

A charming pedestrian enclave, it is full of excellent shops such as *Droopy* and *Browns, Hampstead Bazaar, Mulberry Company* (fine leather and accessories), *Woodhouse* (stylish men's wear) and *Nicole Farhi* (similar ladies wear). *Waterstone's* bookshop adds a touch of gravitas and *Under Two Flags* is a haven for model soldier enthusiasts. If you feel peckish, try one of the numerous small restaurants and cafés within the surrounding area especially in Barrett and James's Streets.

*Browns*, South Molton Street

• **Covent Garden** WC2 (Map 2Kf ⊖ Covent Garden) The colonnade, of modern design, at the rear of the Royal Opera House is home to a variety of elegant shops and boutiques. On the other side of the Inigo Jones **Piazza** is the Jubilee Market*. Outside the square in the narrow streets that criss-cross the vicinity there is a whole range of shops catering for everything from high fashion to organic food. Popular fashions can be found up **James Street**, north east of the Piazza, in *Monsoon* and *Gap*, while **Floral Street**, with *Paul Smith*, *Nicole Farhi* and *Jones*, caters for slightly more exclusive tastes. All are very popular with the locally based theatre, television, radio and advertising communities. On **Long Acre**, *Yves St Laurent*, *Timberland* and *Stanford's* (maps) are just three of the places worth a visit. Another delight, slightly hidden away to the north of the square up Neal Street, is **Neal's Yard** (off Shorts Gardens). With its various shops selling newly crushed peanut butter, pulses, grains, honeys, mustards and fine authentic English cheeses, it is a must for all food-lovers.

COVENT GARDEN WC2
CITY OF WESTMINSTER

Leaving the Piazza to the north west by King Street, and before you hit theatreland, you will see the *Irish Shop* which stocks Waterford crystal, Belleek china, Irish hand-knitted sweaters, tweeds and linen. There is also a good selection of cafés and bistros where you can take a break if the strain is getting too much. For those interested in old prints, and theatre memorabilia, it is worth crossing St Martin's Lane into **Cecil Court**. If you tread a more terpsichorean line, then leave the Piazza to the east via Russell Street, past the Royal Opera House, to 187 **Drury Lane** where you can step out in dancers' shoes of all sorts from *Dancia International*. Remember, above all, that Covent Garden is to London what Les Halles is to Paris – always changing, always lively, a place to get lost in for the afternoon.

CECIL COURT WC2
CITY OF WESTMINSTER

Covent Garden: shopping colonnade behind the Royal Opera House

• **King's Road** SW3 (Map 7Fk ⊖ Sloane Square), in the middle of Chelsea, is the main shopping venue for the fashionable young that live in and around the area.

*Peter Jones*, Sloane Square

Starting in **Sloane Square**, your first port of call should be the department store *Peter Jones*. Founded as a department shop in 1887, it has been the holder of Royal Warrants of Appointment as draper and furnisher since the time of King George VI in 1938. As you walk further down the King's Road, the shops become more adventurous, evoking the times when punk ruled supreme in the 1970s. *Antiquarius* for small antiques and curios, and *Designers Guild* and *Habitat* for furnishings are also popular.

*Designers Guild*, King's Road

Borough of Chelsea
SLOANE SQUARE
S.W.1

**'Brompton Cross'** (⊖ South Kensington) is a fashionable shopping area round the junction of the Fulham Road, Draycott Avenue and Sloane Avenue. The *Conran Shop*, part of the burgeoning empire of Sir Terence Conran, is a beguiling mixture of things in the beautifully restored and revamped Michelin Building. Originally opened in 1973 a few hundred metres from its present location, the shop mixes together a wide variety of original items: from furniture to fabrics, lighting, glass, vases of all shapes and colours, luggage, etc. This is also the place to indulge your gastronomic passion, especially for seafood. Just along the road is *Agnes B*, whose Paris rue du Jour empire has long been a must in many a fashion editor's diary.

*Conran Shop*, 'Brompton Cross'

• **Knightsbridge** SW1, SW7 (Map 5Fh, 5Gh ⊖ Knightsbridge) is home to a host of luxury hotels and fine shops on the south side of Hyde Park. The pick of the shops are *Harrods*, *Harvey Nichols* and The *Scotch House* which has almost every known tartan, as well as Shetlands and scarves galore.

KNIGHTSBRIDGE SW1

Further down **Brompton Road** past Harrods, is *Emporio Armani*, the diffusion label of the famous Italian designer. The clothes are neatly laid out over two floors and retain the same classical lines and attention to detail of Armani's more expensive creations. The store includes a stylish café on the first floor.

In glossy **Beauchamp Place** pick up some jewellery at *Annabel Jones* or an evening dress at *Caroline Charles* or even indulge in a snack at a suitably elegant Pizza Express.

**Sloane Street** (Map 5Fh ⊖ Sloane Square, Knightsbridge) is another place synonymous with elegant shopping. Besides such quintessentially English establishments as *The General Trading Company* (favourite place for wedding lists), which is in nearby Symons Street, there is an invasion of foreign chic. Top names like *Christian Dior*, *Joseph*, *Kenzo*, *Chanel*, *Gucci* and *Valentino* all offer expensive alternatives to home-based designers. Classy shoes with a Gallic touch are at *Stephane Kélian*.

*Christian Dior*, Sloane Street

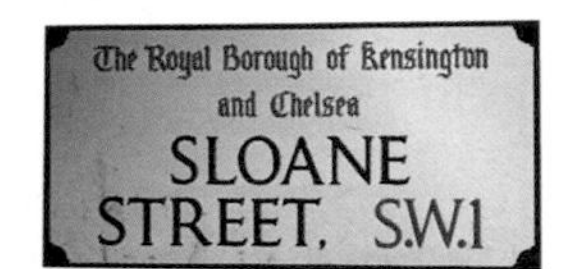


*The Scotch House*, Knightsbridge

A typical day in busy Oxford Street

• **Oxford Street** W1 (Map 5Gf ⊖ Bond Street, Marble Arch, Oxford Circus) remains London's and probably even Europe's, main shopping street. Throughout the year, but especially during the Sales, crowds flock to pick up reasonably-priced goods from one of the many household names. Starting at Marble Arch, you will come across the largest, most adventurous branch of *Marks & Spencer*. Nearby is Selfridges* which rivals Harrods for the range of products on offer. Towards Oxford Circus past *Debenhams, D.H. Evans, John Lewis* and *BHS*, where Londoners go for value and reliability, *World of Football, Olympus, JD Sports* and *Niketown*, all cater for sporting enthusiasts.

# PICCADILLY W1

*Waterstone's*, Piccadilly

• **Piccadilly** W1 (Map 4Jg ⊖ Piccadilly Circus, Green Park) runs all the way to Hyde Park Corner. Almost opposite Burlington House is Fortnum & Mason*. The nearby *Waterford Wedgwood* stocks classic porcelain. Take a passing glance at *Kent & Curwen*, purveyors of clothes with an authentic English sporting flavour, while *Hatchards*, which first opened for business in 1797, and *Waterstone's*, the largest bookshop in Europe, are unbeatable for books in print and out of print. Under the Ritz Hotel arcade is the *London Store*, a good place to stop for hand-knitted British knitwear. Turn back to the **Burlington Arcade** ( ⊖ Green Park). This charming Regency covered arcade runs parallel to Old Bond Street, lodging the sort of shops that Anglophiles dream about such as *Peal & Co* for cashmeres and *Richard Ogden* for antique jewellery.

Cashmeres at *Peal & Co*, Burlington Arcade

Down **St James's Street** a piece of traditional England can be sampled: hats from *Herbert Johnson* or from *Locks*, shoes by *John Lobb*, countryware from *William Evans* gun and rifle maker, luggage and umbrellas from *Swaine Adeney Brigg*, and cigars from *Davidoff* or *James J.Fox*. At the south of the street you will see the sentries outside St James's Palace. Return to Piccadilly via *Justerini & Brooks* (est. 1749) or *Berry Bros & Rudd* to pick up a bottle of wine or maybe call in at Balls Bros wine cellars in Ryder Street for a civilised and reasonably priced glass and a snack. Otherwise, sample some real ale at the Red Lion in Crown Passage, the oldest village inn in London. The area bordered by Pall Mall, St James's Street and Piccadilly, contains the premises of many art dealers and sellers of expensive antiques or objets d'art. Both *Christies* and *Spinks* salerooms are located in **King Street**. Walk up **Bury Street** past *Longmire*, cufflink jeweller, into **Jermyn Street** where the man-about-town buys what some call the finest shirts in the world at *Turnbull & Asser*, his monogrammed velvet slippers and more shirts from *Harvie & Hudson*, his cheese from *Paxton & Whitfield* and his soaps and toiletries from *Floris*, and tobacco (and much more) from *Dunhill*, established in 1893. He might also dine at Wiltons' fish restaurant or turn into Duke of York Street for oysters from Wheelers or Greens.

*Paxton & Whitfield*, Jermyn Street

*Laura Ashley*, Regent Street

• **Regent Street** W1, SW1 (Map 4Jg ⊖ Oxford Circus, Piccadilly Circus) is an elegant, slightly curved road lined with shops. At the north end is a large and comprehensive branch of *Laura Ashley*, the popular interior furnisher and fashion shop. *Godiva* and *Thorntons* cater for chocoholics. *Dickins & Jones* is a progressive department store of long standing. Opposite is *London House* which has a good choice of reasonably priced cashmeres, Shetlands and lambswool. Further down is Liberty*. Next-door, there is *Jaeger* for traditional ladies' and mens' wear, *Hamleys* and *Disney Store* for toys, *Mappin & Webb* for fine jewellery and *Waterford Wedgwood* for glassware and china. *Zara* and *Mango* have the most up-to-date fashion for the young. *Aquascutum* has a reputation for beautiful clothes for men and women and especially for raincoats. As far back as the Great Exhibition of 1851 its waterproof coat was the hallmark of a well-dressed gentleman.

In **Piccadilly Circus** itself, *Virgin Megastore* and *Tower Records* are the one-stop stores for all music. *Lillywhites* is London's biggest department store for sporting goods and sportswear. Back on Regent Street, you will find *Austin Reed* for traditional English outfits, and *Talbots* for ladies' American clothes. London's premier showcase for Scottish merchandise is to be found at the *Scotch House*, famous for its fine woollens.

SAVILE
ROW W1

**Savile Row** has had an international reputation for the excellence of its gentlemen's bespoke tailors for a very long time. Happily the old profession still persists in this little lane behind Regent Street. Some of the establishments have been there for centuries, but not many tailors look like shops and fewer would deign to advertise. To have a suit made by any of them now costs more than a pretty penny. The long-established *Gieves & Hawkes* provides uniforms to the Royals, as well as suits for town and country and an excellent range of accessories. Among their early customers were two of Britain's military and naval heroes: the Duke of Wellington and Lord Nelson. Just to the east of Regent Street, behind Liberty, is **Carnaby Street**, famous in the 'Swinging Sixties'. Here various outlets offer trendy merchandise, much sought-after by the younger generation. By contrast, *Whittards* appeals to more traditional tastes with its wide range of teas and coffees.

*Gieves & Hawkes*, Savile Row

❑ **DEPARTMENT STORES**. These are generally massive shops arranged over several floors with thousands of items on sale. They differ from chain stores like Marks and Spencer in that they tend to trade mainly at a single location. Also, many are worth a visit simply for the painstaking window displays they arrange for each season. The more popular are:

## Harrods

**Harrods** (Brompton Rd, Knightsbridge SW1 ☎ 7730 1234 ⊖ Knightsbridge), founded in 1849 in much smaller premises, occupies an impressive building (1901-5), with windows topped with canopies. It has 6,000m² of selling space and nearly 300 departments over seven floors. The store is known for being able to provide anything from a pin to an elephant – quite literally. The amazing range of goods is probably the widest in Europe. For example, the renowned *Food Hall* on the ground floor offers, among other things, more than 150 whiskies. There are also restaurants, hairdressers, drycleaners, banking, insurance, tourist information, theatre tickets, renting and sale of houses and flats, and many other services.

## FORTNUM & MASON

**Fortnum & Mason** (181 Piccadilly W1 ☎ 7734 8040 ⊖ Piccadilly Circus) opened in 1707 and is famous around the world for the food hall on the ground floor. It has been a royal purveyor of food for centuries and royalty from all over the world are amongst their faithful clients. The store is renowned for its hampers, preserves, sauces, mustard, tea and spices, all of which make for coveted gifts. Clothing, accessories and antique furniture are also important. Particularly exclusive is the china, glass and silverware department, on the lower ground floor, with all the best British and foreign makes. Stop off in the *Fountain Restaurant* for coffee, tea and cake, or if you fancy something with more sparkle head for the Salmon and Champagne Bar.

## HARVEY NICHOLS

**Harvey Nichols** (109 Knightsbridge SW1 ☎ 7235 5000 ⊖ Knightsbridge) has a reputation for being the most elegant department store in London with a location to match amongst the top fashion houses at this end of Sloane Street. Its window displays have often been voted the best in town. The store is mainly devoted to fashion and accessories, selling the best designer clothes for both women and men. There is also a highly selective choice of china, linen and gifts. Everything is in impeccable taste.

## LIBERTY

**Liberty** (210-220 Regent St W1 ☎ 7734 1234 ⊖ Oxford Circus) has had strong links with the artistic world since its foundation in 1875 and this connection continues to this day. It is particularly popular for its range of exclusive printed fabrics (cotton, wool and silks), pewter, ceramics and modern and antique furniture (some originally made for Liberty by well-known artists and craftsmen). An entire department is devoted to oriental goods. The carpet section is worth mentioning and has acquired a reputation amongst connoisseurs. Designer fashion for ladies and children, menswear and accessories, jewellery and gifts are also available.

## Selfridges

**Selfridges** (400 Oxford St W1 ☎ 7629 1234 ⊖ Bond Street) is the second major department store in London after Harrods. Its massive façade is graced by a clock with the gigantic figure of the 'Queen of Time'. It has recently undergone a vast refurbishment that has dramatically modernised its interior. It has one of the largest cosmetics and perfumery departments in Europe and its food hall is a by-word for variety and quality. The fashion departments cover a huge range of excellent British and international names. There is a great choice of china, glass, leather goods, furniture, wine and tobacco. Customers can find several useful services readily available: a hairdressing salon, a theatre ticket agency, restaurants, etc.

## Useful Addresses

| | | ☎ |
|---|---|---|
| ABA | Sackville Ho, Piccadilly W1 | 7439 3118 |
| Abbott & Holder | 30 Museum St WC1 | 7637 3981 |
| Adams, Norman | 8 Hans Rd SW3 | 7589 5266 |
| Agnew's | 43 Old Bond St W1 | 7629 6176 |
| Alfie's | 13 Church St NW8 | 7723 6066 |
| Annely Juda | 23 Dering St W1 | 7629 7578 |
| Anthony d'Offay | 9 Dering St W1 | 7499 4100 |
| Antiquarius Antiques Market | 131 King's Rd SW3 | 7351 5353 |
| BADA | 20 Rutland Gate SW7 | 7589 4128 |
| Bernard J. Shapero | 72 St George St W1 | 7493 8076 |
| Biblion | 1-7 Davies Mews W1 | 7629 1374 |
| Bond Street Antiques Centre | 124 New Bond St W1 | 7351 5353 |
| Bonhams, W. & F.C. | Montpelier St SW7 | 7393 3900 |
| Christie's | 8 King St W1 | 7839 9060 |
| Colnaghi | 15 Old Bond St W1 | 7491 7408 |
| David J. Wilkins | 27 Princess Rd NW1 | 7722 7608 |
| Eskenazi (Oriental Art) | 10 Clifford St W1 | 7493 5464 |
| Fine Art Society | 148 New Bond St W1 | 7629 5116 |
| Gray's | 58 Davies St W1 | 7629 7034 |
| Haughton, Brian | 31 Old Burlington St W1 | 7734 5491 |
| Henry Sotheran | 2 Sackville St W1 | 7439 6151 |
| Koopman Rare Art | 53-64 Chancery Lane W2 | 7242 7624 |
| Lefevre Gallery | 30 Bruton St W1 | 7493 2107 |
| London Silver Vaults | 53-64 Chancery Lane WC2 | 7242 3844 |
| Maas Gallery | 15a Clifford St W1 | 7734 2302 |
| Maggs Bros | 50 Berkeley Sq W1 | 7493 7160 |
| Mallett | 141 New Bond St W1 | 7499 7411 |
| Mansour Gallery | 46 Davies St W1 | 7499 0510 |
| Mark Gallery | 9 Porchester Pl W2 | 7262 4906 |
| Marlborough Fine Art | 6 Albemarle St W1 | 7629 5161 |
| Moss, Sidney | 51 Brook St W1 | 7629 4670 |
| Oriental Carpets Co. | 105 Eade Rd N4 | 8802 1010 |
| O' Shea Gallery | 120a Mount St W1 | 7629 1122 |
| Partridge | 144 New Bond St W1 | 7629 0834 |
| Phillips Son & Neale | 101 New Bond St W1 | 7629 6602 |
| Phillips, S.J. | 139 New Bond St W1 | 7629 6261 |
| Potter, Jonathan | 125 New Bond St W1 | 7491 3520 |
| Quaritch, Bernard | 5-8 Lower John St W1 | 7734 2983 |
| Redfern Gallery | 20 Cork St W1 | 7734 1732 |
| Richard Green | 39 Dover St W1 | 7499 4738 |
| Robin Symes | 3 Ormond Yard SW1 | 7930 9856 |
| Simon Finch | 53 Maddox St W1 | 7499 0974 |
| Society of London Art Dealers | 91a Jermyn St SW1 | 7930 6137 |
| Sotheby's | 34 New Bond St W1 | 7493 8080 |
| Spink & Son | 5-7 King St SW1 | 7930 7888 |
| Symes, Robin | 3 Ormond Yard SW1 | 7930 9856 |
| Thomas Gibson | 44 Old Bond St W1 | 7499 8572 |
| Waddington | 11 Cork St W1 | 7437 8611 |
| Wildenstein & Co | 46 St James's Place SW1 | 7629 0602 |

❑ **ART & COLLECTABLES**. A visit to an auction house, in which field *Bonham's, Christie's, Phillips* and *Sotheby's* lead the way, is one of the great, free pleasures of London. Usually sales are held in the morning of silver or furniture, for example. If the items are not of international appeal, the crowds can be thin - perhaps only twenty or thirty people, spread around the room, the majority of them dealers. At other times, the rooms can be packed, the interest trans-national, the pace hectic. Most of the lots in the catalogues show an estimate of the likely prices of the objects up for auction. The 'low' estimate is usually the reserve price, below which the vendor is unwilling to let a sale take place.

*Sotheby's*, New Bond Street

To an extent, the salesrooms have been too successful in pushing up the price of antiques and works of art, especially in the field of Impressionist paintings, a chief sector in international trading. Here London is the entrepôt rather than the leading player. Even so, the premises of *Wildenstein* always carry some choice Impressionists, as will *Marlborough Fine Art* and the *Lefèvre Gallery*. And then there is *Thomas Gibson* where 'museum quality' pictures are often available, although the stock can be more limited.

Another major art dealer in Impressionists and modern art is *Richard Green* who has four galleries, two in Dover Street and two around the corner in New Bond Street. Green is probably the busiest fine art dealer in London and is unusual in that he deals across the field, from 20thC art to Old Masters. The *Fine Art Society*, which for a century has occupied grand, arty premises in Bond Street, has made a particular success in marketing indigenous artists like Dorothea Sharp and Sir George Clausen to a wider, international market.

Bibliophily at *Maggs*

When it comes to Contemporary Art, like the Impressionists, London can hold its own with any other city. Conveniently, many of the leading dealers – *Waddington and Redfern* - are concentrated in Cork Street and its environs. This is where to come if you are after examples of those British artists who have broken through to the world stage - Bacon, Moore, Hockney, etc - as well as American and modern continental masters. Around the corner in Dering Street is another cluster of dealers built around *Annely Juda* and *Anthony d'Offay*.

Aesthetics and social pleasures combine at *Sotheby's*

One sector where London predominates is Old Masters. Dealers who began by advising 18thC English aristocratic collectors on their purchases, notably *Agnew's* and *Colnaghi*, still face each other in Old Bond Street. Agnew's has diversified into modern art and Colnaghi now specialises in Italian drawings and prints but their vaults still contain some of the finest Old Masters in London.

Pictures aside, London's eminence is based on the breadth of its treasures. It is particularly strong in exotic foreign wares, an expertise acquired in Imperial times. Chinese works of art abound. *Eskenazi* has a penchant towards the earlier periods, Chinese archaic bronzes and the like, rather than the more fanciful Ching wares now so popular. Other well-established dealers in oriental items are *Sidney Moss* and *Spink*. Look out for silver, pictures, coins, medals and objets.

For antiquities there is *Robin Symes* and the *Mansour Gallery*; for silver *Koopman Rare Art*, and *S.J.Phillips* (the latter also for jewels), not forgetting the *London Silver Vaults* for a large number of dealers in silver, plate and other objets d'art. For 18thC ceramics there is *Brian Haughton* and for icons the *Mark Gallery*. Dealers in fine furniture are spread along Mount Street. Satellite stars are *Norman Adams* near Harrods and *Mallett* and *Partridge* in Bond Street.

Valuable books and manuscripts can be found at *Bernard Quaritch*, established in 1847. You can also try *Simon Finch*, *Maggs Bros* (founded in 1853), *Bernard J. Shapero* and *Henry Sotheran*, the world's oldest antiquarian bookshop, almost a book fair in itself. At *Biblion*, a hundred of Britain's bookdealers present the widest range of old books to be found in London. The *O'Shea Gallery* has a vast range of fine old maps and engravings, as has *Jonathan Potter*.

*London Silver Vaults*

The best spot for oriental carpets is the appropriately named *Oriental Carpets Company* where the dealers serve the trade as well as private collectors.

*O'Shea Gallery*

***Antiques arcades,*** notably *Alfies's, Antiquarius,* the *Bond Street Antiques Centre* and *Gray's,* are home to scores of traders. They sell the small change of the antique world - jewels, coins, costumes, prints, with the odd masterpiece thrown in for good measure. The most prestigious ***antiques fair*** is the *Grosvenor House Art & Antiques Fair* held every June in the Grosvenor House in Park Lane. In turn the periodical antiques fairs at Alexandra Palace, Earl's Court and Olympia cater for all tastes and and budgets. The *Chelsea Antiques Fairs* are held twice a year, in Spring and Autumn, at the Old Town Hall, Chelsea. The exhibitors are dealers from London and from all over Britain so that visitors have the advantage of viewing a wide selection of pieces all under one roof. London also plays host to specialist fairs of silver, netsuke, books, manuscripts, stamps, watercolours and ephemera.

The *British Antique Dealers' Association* (BADA), the *Society of London Art Dealers* and the *Antiquarian Booksellers Association* (ABA) are representative bodies that oversee the dealers. Not only do they safeguard the integrity of the trade, but can also help in locating particular items.

*Christie's*: the sale in 1987 of Van Gogh's *Sunflowers* for £24.7m, the world record at the time

❑ **MARKETS & SHOPPING CENTRES**. In almost every part of London indoor and street **markets**, originated as places supplying local inhabitants with fruit and vegetables, are to be found. However in recent years some have attracted traders selling minor collectables. Hours of trading can vary, but as a rule, it is best to get there early. Amongst the better known are:

• **Camden Lock** (Chalk Farm Rd NW1 ☎ 7485 7963 ⊖ Camden Town). Daily from 1000 –1800 – a focal point for many Londoners and visitors, it gets very busy at the weekend. Situated on the canal-side, the stalls offer a mix of old and new including local and international arts and crafts, small pieces of furniture, bric-à-brac, army uniforms, and clothing.

• **Camden Passage** (Islington High St N1 ☎ 7359 9969 ⊖ Angel). In fashionable Islington, a mixture of outdoor stalls, usually laden with small antique objects, jewellery, clothing, linen, books, postcards, silver and nearby shops sell everything from very fine furniture to clocks. Most shops open Tuesday, Thursday, Friday 1000 –1700, with the full market operating on Wednesdays from 0800 to 1600 and Saturdays from 0900 to 1700.

• **Jubilee Market** (Covent Garden WC2 ☎ 7836 2139 ⊖ Covent Garden). Tucked in behind Covent Garden, the general market is open Tuesdays – Fridays from 0900 to 1800. English crafts are available on Saturdays and Sundays from 0900 to 1800. A variety of small antiques are on offer from 0500 – 1700 on Mondays.

• **New Caledonian** (SE1 ⊖ Bermondsey). Also known as **Bermondsey Market** being just off Bermondsey Street, it is open (usually) from 0600 to 1200 Fridays. The earlier you get there the better - take your torch in winter. Try the main dealers' market for antiques of all sorts - furniture, china, glass, silver, jewellery, and bric-à-brac.

• **Petticoat Lane** (E1 ⊖ Liverpool Street). Open Monday to Friday 0800 to 1600 and Sunday 0900 to 1400. Visit Petticoat Lane, Wentworth Street and Middlesex Street for nearly new clothes, handbags, leatherwear, kitchen equipment and toys; Strype Street for food and New Goulston Street for antiques which lately has expanded to the nearby area of ***Spitalfields Market***, previously the largest horticultural wholesale market north of the Thames.

Petticoat Lane

• **Portobello Road** (W11 ⊖ Notting Hill Gate). On Saturdays from 0800 to 1700 this market served by 1,500 dealers is by far the most popular, with an international appeal. Bill Clinton visited the place himself in December 2000, when the American President bought a necklace for his wife and a ring for his daughter Chelsea.

A stall in *Portobello Road*

Taking their lead from North America, **shopping centres** have grown in popularity often helping to regenerate local economies by bringing under one roof a range of high street names, cafés, restaurants and even cinemas. Some of the largest are ***Brent Cross*** (NW4 ⊖ Hendon Central), a pioneer in the field, in the borough of Brent and the ***Ealing Broadway Centre*** (W5 ⊖ Ealing Broadway).

*Ealing Broadway Centre*

***The Plaza*** (W1 ⊖ Oxford Circus), in Oxford Street, ***Whiteleys*** (W2 ⊖ Queensway), and ***Victoria Place*** (SW1 ⊖ Victoria) are more central. ***$O_2$*** (NW3 ⊖ Finchley Road), within walking distance from Swiss Cottage, is the most recent one. ***West One*** (W1) is directly above Bond Street Underground Station. The ***Trocadero*** and the ***London Pavilion*** (W1 ⊖ Piccadilly Circus) also offer several different types of entertainment alongside the usual shopping experience. The ***Hay's Galleria*** (SE ⊖ London Bridge), off Tooley Street and next to London Bridge, is one of the most striking with its barrel vaulted roof of glass and steel covering shops, wine bars, restaurants and an interesting dolphin-cum-ship-shaped kinetic water sculpture.

The $O_2$ Centre, Finchley Road

# HOTELS & RESTAURANTS

The range of accommodation in the capital extends from the huge *Forum Hotel* in South Kensington, which boasts over 900 rooms in a modern skyscraper, to smaller ones like the cosy *Durley House*, conceived in a grand English mansion style. Alternatively visitors can opt for fully serviced apartments or for a B&B which besides providing a bed for the night serves a large breakfast to start the day off well.

In the past, it might have been said that when it came to dining out, London lagged behind comparable world cities. That has all changed. In the year 2000, 27 out of 300 restaurants reviewed by Michelin were described either as 'exceptional' (two), 'excellent' (five) or 'very good' (twenty). But the rise in standards have affected prices which in recent times have escalated considerably.

A prominent hotel in Piccadilly

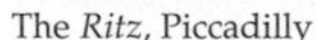

The *Ritz*, Piccadilly

*47 Park Street*, Mayfair

❑ **HOTELS, B&B & SERVICE APARTMENTS**. Hotels can be divided into premier; de luxe; hotels with character; medium-sized and moderately priced. Most offer lower tariffs at weekends.

*Claridge's* is a perennial favourite for lovers of ***premier*** hotels. It is the top choice for visiting aristocrats and heads of state. Its keenest rivals are the *Mayfair* and the *Connaught*, both in Mayfair; the *Savoy*, in the Strand; the *Dorchester* and *Grosvenor House*, in Park Lane; the *Ritz* in Piccadilly and the *Berkeley* and the *Mandarin Oriental Hyde Park*, renowned for its Edwardian ambience, in Knightsbridge.

A number of smaller hotels with long histories have recently undergone extensive modernization without losing any of their character. A good example is *Brown's Hotel*, founded in 1837 by J. Brown, Lord Byron's valet, and still providing open fireplaces, antiques and afternoon tea. You might also want to consider either *Duke's Hotel* or the *Athenaeum*. Both are in, or very close to, Piccadilly.

The ***de luxe*** include most of the best-known international chains. The large *Inter-Continental* and the *Lanesborough*, on different sides of Hyde Park Corner, are ideal for executive business visitors. Just around the corner in Park Lane is the *London Hilton*, favoured by American travellers who prefer a taste of home. Next door is the *Four Seasons*. Other similar establishments include the *Churchill* and the *Portman*, both in Portman Square; the *Britannia* and the *London Marriott*, in Grosvenor Square; *Le Meridien* near Piccadilly Circus; the *Landmark*, which boasts a stunning six storey atrium, next to Marylebone Station; the *Sheraton Park Tower* and the *Berkeley* in Knightsbridge; and the

The *Hempel* in Bayswater

*Hyatt Carlton Tower*, halfway between Knightsbridge and Sloane Square.

The *Dorchester*: Front Hall

The *Thistle Tower*, in the shadow of Tower Bridge, is handy for the City and is popular with business visitors. Other Thistle establishments can be found in Marble Arch, Charing Cross and Victoria. Also in this category are the *Kensington Hilton*, at the Shepherds Bush end of Holland Park Avenue, the *Langham Hilton*, the *St James's Court* and the *Royal Lancaster* overlooking Kensington Gardens. The *Conrad* in ultra-chic Chelsea Harbour overlooks the Marina, a stone's throw from the King's Road. The *Great Eastern* with 267 bedrooms and suites in a pleasing mix of modern and classic design is the only hotel of substance within the City's boundaries. The very smart *Sanderson* and the *St Martin's Lane* are the creation of the interior designer Philippe Starck.

For those who find traditional hotels too formal, and de luxe modern hotels too large, ***hotels with character*** may be the answer. One of the most popular is *Blake's*, which mixes the traditional with the modern. It occupies three unassuming 19thC terraced houses in South Kensington. The establishment's glamorous interiors, international menu and attentive staff attract a cosmopolitan and smart clientele. Anouska Hempel, who also created the *Hempel* in Bayswater, which is equally chic and stylish, designed the hotel.

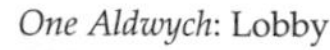
*One Aldwych*: Lobby

*Beaufort Hotel*, Knightsbridge

The elegant *One Aldwych* is housed in a turn of the century Parisian-style building. In ultra-fashionable Notting Hill Gate you will find the *Portobello* which leans more towards Victoriana. For the nearby *Westbourne* a group of Britain's most successful artists have provided works for its 20 rooms which also have DVD players and queen-size beds. The *Basil Street Hotel*, in Knightsbridge, is like an exclusive club while *Halkin* has more technical features than a moon launch. The *Metropolitan* is a triumph of minimalism. *Eleven Cadogan Gardens*, an elegant townhouse, was once the home of the mistress of King Edward VII, Lillie Langtry. 47 *Park Street*, with 52 individual appointed suites in the heart of Mayfair, is one of London's best kept secrets.

The *Beaufort* may be a stone's-throw from Harrods but remains nonetheless a peaceful establishment in a quiet and charming cul-de-sac minutes away from many of the best shops in town. *Number Sixteen*, also in South Kensington, has a secluded flower garden with a fountain. The *Durrants*, first opened in 1790 and owned and managed by the Miller family since 1921, offers quality and individual style in the heart of the West End.

There are some 300 ***medium-sized modern*** hotels, each with a variety of levels of comfort and price. Amongst the most recent additions are the *Hampshire*, the *Mountbatten*, the *Grafton*, the *Kenilworth* and the *Marlborough*. ***Moderately priced*** hotels are often family-run establishments. The *Lincoln House Hotel* is commended by the London Tourist Board. ***B&B*** are mainly to be found in residential areas, but a few are next to Euston, Paddington and Victoria Stations. Many belong to a sort of loose consortium like Bed & Breakfast UK.

*Lincoln House Hotel*

For visitors planning a longer stay, a good solution can be renting a ***service apartment*** from one of the specialist estate agents that deal in this field. Some can rival the best hotels for luxury and comfort. Among the better known are *51 Buckingham Gate* with luxury suites set in an Edwardian courtyard and *13 Half Moon Street* where the apartments all feature different décor, from High Regency to Luis XV.

❑ **WHEN, WHERE & WHAT TO EAT**. Restaurants normally open for lunch and dinner from Monday to Friday and many on Saturdays and Sundays as well, although some only serve either lunch or supper at weekends. It is advisable to reserve a table in good time especially for the more fashionable and expensive ones. Almost all take major international credit cards, but once again it is best to check in advance.

• **Breakfast**. From 0730 onwards, most of the larger hotels serve what the British novelist Somerset Maugham defined as the best meal of the day. A full English (or American) breakfast is available at several department stores (Harrods and Fortnum & Mason included) as well as in a number of restaurants. At *Bank* you can even indulge in having caviar from 0700 Monday to Friday and at *Pizza on the Park* breakfast is served all day, from 0815 Monday to Saturday.

• **Afternoon Tea**. Tea at the *Ritz* is an English classic. Amid ornate décor, you eat wafer-thin cucumber sandwiches while at the *Connaught Hotel* tea includes wild strawberry mille feuilles. At *Brown's Hotel* the setting resembles a country house drawing room as you eat toasted scones on chintzy sofas and chairs. At the *Churchill Hotel* your finger sandwiches, brandy snaps, scones, cream and jam come accompanied by a pianist. Real devotees can try their luck at the *Mandarin Oriental Hyde Park* where you can take your pick from seven different teas while enjoying a leafy view of the park. The *Waldorf Hotel* in Aldwych is also highly recommended.

Tea at the *Waldorf Hotel*, Aldwych

• **Lunch & Dinner**. The *Gordon Ramsay* is the only restaurant in the capital to mark the new century (and millennium) with a top score of three stars. Others which are pick of the the bunch with a clutch of two Michelin stars to match, are the restaurant at the Capital Hotel, *John Burton-Race* at the Landmark Hotel, *Le Gavroche, La Tante Claire* and *The Square*. Five of the twenty-five one-star restaurants are part of well-known West End hotels like the Connaught and Halkin. Eating at the Ritz remains a great experience. The *Terrace* at the Dorchester Hotel and the *Axis* at One Aldwych are also very pleasant.

For traditional English fare, head for *Simpson's-in-the-Strand*. Within its vast panelled dining rooms, the speciality is huge joints of meat wheeled up and carved at your table; the same can be enjoyed at *Rules* and *Shepherd's*. At *Launceston Place*, the dining area is divided up into a series of interconnected rooms and offers a blend of old and new cuisine. The clubby *Boisdale* takes its inspiration from North of the border with haggis and Highland venison both on offer. Irish food and traditional beers are served at *Ard Ri Dining Room*, *Minogues* and *The Toucan*.

The *Café Royal*, once the haunt of Oscar Wilde, Max Beerbohm, Beardsley, Whistler and their generation, is now the flagship of the Granada corporate empire. Equally glamorous is *Langan's*, the brasserie part-owned by international film star Michael Caine; look out for straight-forward English/French food like Toulouse sausages, salmon hollandaise and champagne. Terence Conran's *Quaglino* is a massive place serving hundreds of diners at a time. It also has a good bar. *Odins* serves rich, luxurious food - red mullet pâté, melting chocolate pudding - while the *Langan's Bistro*, hung with open umbrellas and paintings by David Hockney (a regular for years) serves lighter food. *Zafferano* is one of the West End's smartest Italian places. Nico Landenis's *Incognico*, Marcus Wareing's *Petrus*, *Le Caprice* and *Mirabelle* cater for similarly expensive tastes.

SOHO has become the media centre of town and there are plenty of cool places to keep them entertained. *Leith's* and *Alastair Little* are worth

*Axis Restaurant* at One Aldwych

trying for their fine cooking. The *Gay Hussar* has become an institution for its Hungarian specialities while *L'Escargot*, with lithographs by Chagall and Miro, remains a favourite. At *Soho Soho* the menus contain Provençal dishes which can be hard to find elsewhere in London and *Café Lazeez* serves an innovative light Indian cuisine. *Mezzo*, with space for 700 customers, is another big eaterie from the ubiquitous Sir Terence Conran. It has live music from Wednesday to Saturday.

One of the latest arrivals in the area is the *Titanic*, another project from Marco Pierre White, who has also revamped the *Criterion*, in Piccadilly Circus.

Onwards towards COVENT GARDEN, the *Ivy* is one of the best – if you can get a table! The *Neal Street Restaurant* has a varied menu, with wild mushrooms a speciality, which are in many cases collected by the proprietor himself, Antonio Carluccio author and television presenter on Mediterranean food. Somewhat cheaper is *Mon Plaisir* with its bustling atmosphere and typical French café menu. *Luigi's* also presents good Italian cooking in elegant Georgian surroundings.

In the CITY wine lovers can enjoy *Corney & Barrow* where the list is twenty pages long. *Tatsuso* excels in Japanese cooking as does *Moshi Moshi*. Chinese cuisine has reached the vaults under the Royal Exchange in *Imperial City* where the TV chef Ken Hom has concocted an original menu. Light French food is served at *Whittington's*, named after the medieval lord mayor of London and located in a cellar of his old house. At the *Rupee Room* batata puri and grilled meats from the tandoori and chicken daalwala make a pleasant change from the more restricted Indian fare. The brasserie at *One Lombard Street*, which occupies a former banking hall, and *Prism*, a monumental, posh gastrodrome, are popular as well. If you are looking for classic Italian with excellent service and impressive surroundings, try *Caravaggio*. Also worth a visit are *Aurora* and *Terminus* at the Great Eastern Hotel, *Searcy's* at the Barbican, *Gradwins* (lunch only), *City Rhodes*, *Coq d'Argent*, *Brasserie Rocque* and the French *Le Omai*. For meat-eaters only, *Chez Gerard* has numerous branches throughout the City. Bring your own binoculars in visiting *Twenty Four* located in the City's tallest building. The view is stunning and, if height doesn't bother you, you can climb right to the top for a drink at the 42nd floor *Vertigo*.

*Vertigo*, City of London

Looking west to CHELSEA, the *Canteen* of Marco Pierre White has an interesting décor of playing cards. The *Bluebird* in King's Road, favoured by the local fashion set, is another Conran establishment, with its own fruit and vegetable market outside and modern decor within. *Dan's* is set in a typical Chelsea house where the food is mainly French. One can eat 'al fresco' in the large garden during the warm, summer months.

In KNIGHTSBRIDGE, *St Quentin's*, all dark wood and chandeliers, gives a Left Bank ambience. *Bibendum*, yet another Conran enterprise housed in the splendidly restored Michelin building, offers French and English dishes, with a long and wide-ranging wine list. *San Lorenzo*, a favourite with royalty and footballers alike, has a roof that opens on warm days. The *Montpeliano* offers Italian specialities in a fine setting, while *Piccola Venezia* is handy for visiting the great museums in the South Kensington area.

In KENSINGTON *Clarke's* no-choice evening menu is popular with the locals; original cooking based on Californian food and wines; good English cheeses. *Kensington Place* has a bustling atmosphere to complement good British fare. Further over towards PADDINGTON is *Concordia Notte*, which has provided excellent Sicilian food, live music and dancing for years and there are plenty of other good eating places in nearby Westbourne Grove and Edgware Road. The latter has the greatest concentration of restaurants and cafés with a Middle Eastern flavour and atmosphere.

In HAMMERSMITH the *River Café* has become a mecca for lovers of Italian food. *Novelli*, in CLERKENWELL, puts its own distinctive spin on the art of cooking. *Casa Giovanni*, in SWISS COTTAGE, has fine 'pappardelle' and grilled 'gamberoni'. Captivating Italian food is proposed by the chefs Maurizio Morelli and Francesco Apreda at the *Green Olive* in LITTLE VENICE. At the Genoese V*egia Zena* in PRIMROSE HILL lunch and dinner can be taken al fresco in summertime. For a great view up and down the THAMES the *Oxo Tower* is the place to visit. The food is excellent although on the pricey side.

Some department stores and museums have stylish eating places. *Harvey Nichols* in Knightsbridge is one of the places to be seen. *Emporio Armani* has a gallery room where modern Italian food is served. The restaurant at the *British Museum* is within the stunning conversion of the Great Court and those of the *National Gallery* and the *National Portrait Gallery* offer views over Trafalgar Square and Whitehall. Even more stunning are the views from the restaurant at the top of *Tate Modern*. At *Tate Britain* you can lunch in a Whistler-muralled room. The fare is also good at the *Bagatelle* in the glass-covered courtyard of the Wallace Collection. Many other galleries have their own cafés worth using even if art is not on your menu.

*Oxo Tower Restaurant*

• **All through the Night**. If you know where to go, it is possible to eat at almost any hour. Over two dozen restaurants are open until well after midnight all the week round. Very popular are the *New Diamond* in Soho, which serves Chinese food every day up to 0300, and *Kitchen* in Covent Garden. In the latter, located on the ground floor of the New Connaught Rooms, the space is designed to impress and the fare is high class-rotisserie.

*Tamarind Restaurant*, Mayfair

• **Ethnic Cuisine.** The rise of the Beatles, of Pop music and of the King's Road 'dolce vita' coincided with a gastronomic explosion of exotic cuisine. This has not only withstood the test of time but has spread throughout London. Places serving genuine Chinese, Malaysian, Pakistani, Greek, Nepalese, Polynesian, Arabic, Japanese, French, Portuguese, Spanish and Italian cuisine have become common. The choice, however, does not stop here. Chinese food, for example, varies from Cantonese to Szechuan and Indian/Pakistani meals include vegetarian dishes, fish recipes or tandoori-cooked meat.

Chinese delicacies

*Suntory* is one of the most famous ***Japanese*** restaurants, marked out by its classic dishes, formally served. The cooking at *Nobu*, part-owned by Robert De Niro, at the Metropolitan Hotel, shows South American influence. Also good are *Asuka* and the chain *Benihana*. The Michelin star given to both *Tamarind* and *Zaika* confirms London's status as leading centre of ***Indian*** cooking in Europe. The *Bombay Brasserie* is smart: huge, with banana trees, vast conservatory and sophisticated menu. *Café Spice* has an eclectic selection of delicacies (Parsee, Goa, North India, Hyderabad and Kashmir). The *Red Fort* and *Bengal Clipper* are elegant and enticing, although their repertoire is limited. *Pied a Terre* has some real surprises while *Khan's* is an archetypal establishment. *Veeraswamy* and *Chutney Mary* tend to offer more traditional recipes in an authentic ambience. The *Salloos* specializes in ***Pakistani*** dishes.

*Ken Lo's Memories* is regarded as being the best for ***Chinese*** food, and dim sum and noodle bar are excellent at *China House*. *Poons* has made a name for itself thanks to its selection of wind-dried meat. *Lee Ho Fook* is one of the Chinese community's own favourites while at the pretty *Mao Tai*, Szechuan dishes can be sampled.

***Thai*** food has become all the rage in recent years. Amongst the better known are the *Blue Elephant* and the *Churchill Arms*. A new kid on the block is ***Korean*** cookery, a blend of Chinese and its own native spicy Bulgogi style of barbecue. The *Arirang* is amongst the more popular as is *Kaya*. The ***Vietnamese*** recipes at *Viet-Hoa* are original, light and aromatic. The compact *Mandalay*, probably the only ***Burmese*** restaurant in England, is more than a curiosity: the cooking is good as well as unusual.

Several places concentrate on ***Middle Eastern*** cooking with recipes lost in the mists of time. Amongst the leaders are *Noura* and *Al Hamra*. Handy for Harley Street and enthusiastically patronised by locals and visitors alike, *Topkapi* offers authentic ***Turkish*** cuisine in Central London such as Adana doner kebabs, hot boreks and Anatolian wines. Turkish accent also at *Ozer*. *Lemonia* excels in ***Greek*** food and wine, like the *Real Greek*. If in a wilder mood, you can smash plates and dance at *Apollonia*. Still wild? The *Borshtch 'N' Tears* is crowded and youthful with ***Russian*** music and flying bread rolls. *Firebird* is also noted for its Russian cooking, although the general flair is classically French. If you want to indulge in vodka while nibbling on cured herring, smoked eel, salmon and cold roast stuffed pork *Potemkin* is the place to visit. *Bloom's* is the best-known ***Jewish*** restaurant in London; it is strictly Kosher and closed Friday evenings and Saturdays.

*Cambio de Tercio* has a good choice of ***Spanish*** food. *Rebato's* provides excellent zarzuelas, paellas and much more. Iberian cooking can be found at *Don Pepe* as well. ***Mexican*** specialities are well represented at the classy *Chiquito*. The menu at *Fina Estampa* is traditional ***Peruvian*** and the emphasis is on seafood. The *Mandola* describes itself as being 'urban ***Sudanese***' while *Lalibela* is most certainly ***Ethiopian***, where well-prepared dishes are complemented by delicious (and expensive) coffee served in typical manner.

• **Fish Restaurants.** Londoners have always had a passion for fish. Until a few decades ago, the streets of London had stalls selling prawns, cockles, mussels and eels as well as shops which turned out fried cod day and night with chips dressed with malt vinegar: the famous 'fish and chips'. Most of the stalls and many of the shops have disappeared, but the number of good fish restaurants is on the increase.

*One-O-One*, at the Sheraton Park Tower, Knightsbridge, is amongst the best. At *Fish* you can choose from a list of 20 fish and decide to have your choice grilled or steamed and which of the five sauces should accompany it. *Lou Pescadou* gets its fresh fish from Brittany. The intimate *Poissonerie de l'Avenue* has a loyal following amongst fish connoisseurs; fine puddings, too. Club-like *Wiltons* is a refuge for 'nouvelle cuisine' haters. *Manzi's* has a check tableclothed café-type atmosphere downstairs and a varied menu upstairs. *Flounders* employ a bistro approach, serving scampi provençale, cod and haddock pie. *Wheeler's* has a reliable selection of classic dishes, as does *Sheekey's*, a traditional favourite for theatregoers. Some of the best oyster bars are *Scotts*, *Delfina* and *Bentley's*.

*Lou Pescadou*, Old Brompton Road

• **Fast Food**. Tourists have made a big contribution towards making London the fast-food capital of Europe. Hamburger is the most popular, followed by pizza and fried chicken. The *Hard Rock Café* is still a mecca for diners prepared to queue for hours. *Planet Hollywood* serves burgers amidst movie memorabilia. *Maxwell's*, behind the Royal Opera House in Covent Garden, has more of the same and a large bar. The *Pizza Express* is perhaps the most elegant of the many pizza chains in the capital. *Pizza Metro* has made a name for itself by selling Neapolitan pizza by the metre.

❑ **OLD ENGLISH PUBS**. Pubs are the bedrock of social life to many Londoners. Children under 18 are not allowed to buy alcoholic drinks but may sit with an adult, at the publican's discretion. *Free Houses* are mainly one-man businesses with a wide selection of beers. Pubs have always cashed in on their association with distinguished people. What follows is only a sample of the better-known and traditional pubs.

• **The Anchor** (1 Bankside SE1 ☎ 7407 1577). Historic riverside inn by the site of Shakespeare's Globe Theatre. Rebuilt 1750. Displays of Elizabethan objects found during renovation. Restaurant.

• **Bull and Bush** (North End Way NW3 ☎ 8455 3685). Of music-hall song fame. 'Victorian interior'. Mementoes of Florrie Ford.

• **George Inn** (77 Borough High St SE1 ☎ 7407 2056). Only surviving galleried pub in London. Restaurant.

*George Inn*, Southwark

• **Hoop and Grapes** (47 Aldgate High St EC3 ☎ 7480 5739). It claims to be London's oldest pub, dating back to the early 13thC.

• **London Apprentice** (62 Church St, Old Isleworth, Middx ☎ 8560 3538). Named after the City Livery Companies apprentices who used to row up to Isleworth. 15thC and Georgian architecture. Riverside restaurant.

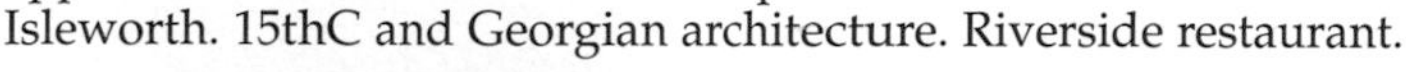

*Prospect of Whitby*

• **Prospect of Whitby** (57 Wapping Wall E1 ☎ 7481 1095). This pub dates from about 1520 and is considered to be London's oldest riverside tavern. A favourite resort of the diarist Samuel Pepys in the 17thC, it was given the present name in 1777 after a ship called the 'Prospect', moored off the pub, had become a local landmark. Restaurant upstairs with a fine view of the Thames.

• **Sherlock Holmes** (10 Northumberland St WC2 ☎ 7930 2644). Reconstruction of the Baker Street apartment of the detective created by A. Conan Doyle. Restaurant.

• **Ye Olde Cheshire Cheese** (Wine Office Court EC4 ☎ 7353 6170). Very famous with history going back to the 16thC. Puddings are a speciality.

• **Ye Olde Watling** (29 Watling St EC4 ☎ 7248 6235). It was built about 1668 and used as Wren's office and a hostel for builders during the construction of St Paul's Cathedral.

# ENTERTAINMENT & NIGHTLIFE

If the day is for work, evenings and nights are for pleasure. Whatever your tastes or interests are, it is not hard to find somewhere in London the type of entertainment which will suit you. The choice is wide, whether it be a visit to the theatre, opera, ballet, concert or cinema, or in pursuit of more mundane pleasures in nightclubs or discos.

The City of Westminster is the centre of mainstream theatre. Apart from six evening performances every week, the majority have matinees. Guided tours of some theatres, including a backstage visit, are arranged by the establishments themselves or by specialised agencies.

The *Lyric*, Hammersmith

❑ **THEATRES.** A number of theatres still bear traces of their historic past. The *Drury Lane, Theatre Royal* was patronised by Charles II; 'God Save the King' was first sung here in 1741 and 'Rule Britannia' in 1750. Most theatres date from the second half of the 19thC, many standing on the sites of old playhouses. The *Savoy*, the first theatre to have electric light in London, was built in 1881 for Richard D'Oyly Carte, as a venue for the operettas of Gilbert and Sullivan. It stands beside the Savoy Hotel; the theatre has been lovingly restored. Several theatres were also built in the 1930s, including the *Adelphi* and the *Cambridge*. Others, like the *Lyric Hammersmith*, are more recent.

The *Royal Court*, Sloane Square

The Royal Shakespeare Company (RSC) stages a continuous repertory, not only of Shakespeare, including the productions transferred from Stratford-upon-Avon, but also modern plays and classics. It is resident in the *Barbican Centre* (Silk St EC2) where in addition to a 1,180-seat theatre there is a smaller stage, The Pit. The advanced computerised ticket reservation and printing system enables anyone in any part of the world to book a seat and be allocated a ticket immediately. Performances of Shakespeare's plays are also to be enjoyed during the summer months in the delightful woodland setting of the *Open Air Theatre* (Regent's Park NW1), or, from mid-May to September, in the newly built spiritual home of the Bard, *The Globe* (Bankside SE1). This is a replica of an original Elizabethan round theatre and the audience may stand in the open or sit on benches under cover.

## Theatres & Concert Halls

☎ ADELPHI 7344 0055 • ALBANY 7369 1730 • ALDWYCH 7416 6003 ALMEIDA 7359 4404 • APOLLO 7494 5070 • APOLLO VICTORIA 7416 6070 ARTS CLUB 7836 2132 • BARBICAN 7638 8891 • CAMBRIDGE 7494 5080 COCHRANE 7242 7040 • COLISEUM 7836 8300 • COMEDY 7369 1731 CRITERION 7369 1747 • DONMAR WAREHOUSE 7389 1732 • DOMINION 7656 1888 • DRURY LANE 7494 5000/1 • DUCHESS 7494 5075 • DUKE OF YORK'S 7565 5000 • FORTUNE 7836 2238 • GARRICK 7494 5085 GIELGUD 7494 5065 • GLOBE 7401 9919 • HAYMARKET 7930 8800 • HER MAJESTY'S 7494 5400 • ICA 7930 3647 • KING'S HEAD 7226 1916 • LYCEUM 7420 8100 • LYRIC 7494 5045 • LYRIC HAMMERSMITH 7741 2311 • NEW END 7794 0022 • NEW LONDON 7405 0072 • OLD VIC 7928 7616 • OPEN AIR 7935 5756 • PALACE 7434 0909 • PALLADIUM 7494 5020 • PEACOCK 7314 8800 • PHOENIX 7369 1733 • PICCADILLY 7369 1734 • PLAYERS 7839 1134 • PLAYHOUSE 7839 4401 • PRINCE EDWARD 7447 5400 • PRINCE OF WALES 7839 5987 • QUEEN'S 7494 5040 • RAYMOND REVUEBAR (Nude Show) 7734 1593 • RIVERSIDE STUDIOS 8237 1111 • ROYAL ALBERT HALL 7589 8212 • ROYAL COURT 7565 5000 • ROYAL FESTIVAL HALL 7960 4242 • ROYAL NATIONAL THEATRE (OLIVIER, COTTESLOE, LYTTLETON) 8452 3000 • ROYAL OPERA HOUSE 7304 4000 • SADLER'S WELLS 7863 8000 • ST JOHN'S SMITH SQUARE 7222 1061 • ST MARTIN'S 7836 1443 • SAVOY 7240 1166/836 8888 • SHAFTESBURY 7379 5399 • SOHO 7478 0100 • STRAND 7930 8800 • TRICYCLE 7328 1000 • VAUDEVILLE 7836 9987 • VICTORIA PALACE 7834 1317 • WESTMINSTER 7828 9361 WHITEHALL 7369 1735 • WIGMORE HALL 7935 2141 • WILTON'S 7702 9555 • WYNDHAM'S 7369 1736

Tickets Direct ☎ 0870 606 3441 serve most of the London theatres.

The Globe, Bankside: *Henry V*

The imposing *Royal National Theatre* (South Bank SE1) is a large complex consisting of three auditoriums (Olivier, Lyttleton and Cottesloe) where performances of the classics, new plays and experimental works take place throughout the year. There are also exhibitions, workshops, bookstalls, bars, buffet counters and a restaurant, open before and after performances. A short distance away, down Waterloo Road (SE1), stands the *Old Vic*. Designed in 1818 by Rudolph Cabanel, the strong square building has a classical foyer. In the 1930s it was the first theatre to stage Shakespearian plays as well as spectacular dramas and experimental works. Following an extensive refurbishment audiences at the *Royal Court* no longer need fear the creaky seats which so angered G.B.Shaw in 1906 and Harold Pinter ninety years later. Every part of the building has been cleverly renovated including the dressing room Lawrence Olivier complained about.

Fringe theatre has now established a firm and flourishing reputation. Productions are not luxurious and seating capacity is usually small, but the acting is first-class. Amongst the better-known are the theatres attached to the *Institute of Contemporary Arts* (ICA, The Mall SW1), the *Almeida* (1a Almeida St N1), the *King's Head Theatre Club* (115 Upper St N1), *New End Theatre* (27 New End NW3), the *Tricycle* (269 Kilburn High Rd NW6) and the *Riverside Studios* (Crisp Rd, Hammersmith W6).

## The 'Big Hit' Scene

Outstanding productions are always on offer at West End theatres, some of which run for years and show no sign of ever coming to an end. The musical *The Phantom of the Opera* (Her Majesty's), a phenomenal success from the pen of Andrew Lloyd Webber, is yet again breaking box office records, as is *Les Misérables* (Palace). *The Mousetrap* (St Martin's), the thriller by Agatha Christie, has been running for 50 years.

The latter, formerly film and television studios, offers a mixed programme of theatre, music, dance, films, children's activities, exhibitions and mounts its own productions of the classics, as well as encouraging visiting groups and artists.

❑ **OPERA & BALLET**. Lovers of opera and ballet can choose from many theatres. Chief among these is the newly restored, and beautifully appointed, *Royal Opera House* (Covent Garden WC2) where operas given by the *Royal Opera* in the original language, with singers and conductors of international repute, take their turn in the repertoire with performances by the world-famous Royal Ballet. The English National Ballet also has regular annual seasons at the Royal Festival Hall and elsewhere.

*Romeo and Juliet*, Royal Ballet

At the *Coliseum* (St Martin's Lane WC2), the home of the English National Opera (ENO), there is a large repertoire of classical and modern operas, all sung in English. *Sadler's Wells Theatre* (Rosebery Ave EC1), rebuilt in 1998, acts as host to visiting opera and dance companies. It is named after Thomas Sadler who in 1683 opened a music house on the site which was known for its medical wells since Roman times. The famous clown Joseph Grimaldi performed here from 1802 up to his death in 1837. From time to time at *Wilton's Music Hall* (Grace's Alley, Wellclose Sq E1) you can catch a first class production of an opera directed by a renowned name like Jonathan Miller. There is also a season of opera in the open air in *Holland Park* (June – August).

❑ **CONCERT VENUES**. London has a thriving musical life and concerts of all sorts can be heard every night of the year, ranging from orchestral, choral and chamber music to jazz and rock. Five professional orchestras of international repute are based in the capital the London Philharmonic, the London Symphony Orchestra (LSO), the Royal Philharmonic, the New Philharmonia and the BBC Symphony Orchestra. There are also specialised string and chamber orchestras such as the English Chamber Orchestra, the Academy of St Martin-in-the-Fields and the London Sinfonietta. It is also worthwhile checking London and City churches for lunch time concert programmes eg. St Martin-in-the-Fields.

The main concert halls include the *Royal Festival Hall*, the *Queen Elizabeth Hall*, and the small *Purcell Room* (recitals only), all in South Bank. The *Royal Albert Hall* (Kensington Gore SW7) is the largest, with a seating capacity of 10,000, and the oldest. It opened in March 1871, in memory of Prince Albert, the consort of Queen Victoria. Here the annual season of Henry Wood Promenade Concerts takes place from July to September. *The Barbican Hall* (Silk St EC2) seats 2,000 and is the home of the LSO for three months in the spring.

## The Royal Opera House, Covent Garden

The Royal Opera House is one of the principal world centres of both opera and ballet and is the permanent home of the Royal Opera and the Royal Ballet. Its splendour and sumptuousness make it a place of great enchantment. There has been a theatre on its site for almost 250 years, the land having once been a convent garden. The first and second theatres were burned down. The present building, designed by E.M. Barry and opened in 1858, has been restored and refurbished. Most opera productions are staged in the original language.

Covent Garden has produced its own singers of international repute – among them, Joan Sutherland, Jon Vickers, Kiri Te Kanawa and Thomas Allen. Its list of distinguished Music Directors includes Kubelik, Solti, Colin Davis and Bernard Haitink. Ninette de Valois, founder and first director of the Royal Ballet, played a decisive role in creating what has become one of the world's foremost ballet companies. The repertoire has always featured the great 19thC classics, alongside modern masterpieces.

Other principal concert venues are the elegant *Wigmore Hall* (36 Wigmore St W1), best-known for solo recitals, and the beautiful *St John's Smith Square* (SW1), an 18thC church destroyed in World War II and restored and converted into a concert hall in 1969.

In the summer months open air concerts are given all around the capital. The most popular are those in the setting of Kenwood House (Hampstead Heath) and Holland Park as well as the performances by military and police bands in Royal Parks.

*Royal Albert Hall*: the Proms

❑ **CABARET & JAZZ**. Most jazz fans have heard of the famous *Ronnie Scott's Club* (Frith St ☎ 7439 0747), *Pizza Express Jazz Club* (Dean St W1 ☎ 7439 8722), *100 Club* (Oxford St W1 ☎ 7636 0933), near St Giles Circus, but may not have visited *Larry's Room, Pizza on the Park* (11 Knightsbridge SW1 ☎ 7235 5273). This reasonably priced, delightfully atmospheric cabaret room, plays host to a rich variety of jazz and cabaret talent and is the ideal rendezvous for all ages to enjoy listening to good music whilst dining. Old Time Music Hall, this very British institution of the Victorian and Edwardian era, is kept alive at the *Players Theatre Club* in the shopping arcade off Villiers Street (WC2). The bill changes every two weeks, there is a master of ceremonies and customers are expected to join in the choruses. Visitors may become members for the night.

❑ **CINEMAS.** The largest and most comfortable in the West End showing the latest releases are those clustered in an area spreading out from Leicester Square. The British Film Institute, founded in 1933 to promote greater understanding and access to film in the United Kingdom, runs the *National Film Theatre* (South Bank SE1 ☎ 7928 3232 ). In 1999 it brought a new feature to London's entertainment scene: the *BFI IMAX Cinema* in a building at the roundabout outside Waterloo Station, with the largest screen in the country. Its sophisticated 360-degree projection system provides exceptional visual and audio quality, making viewers feels as if they were literally 'in the picture'.

*BFI IMAX Cinema*

❑ **NIGHTCLUBS & DISCOS**. Going clubbing has become an egalitarian pursuit. The distinction between 'disco' and 'nightclub' is a fine one. In general, while at the former you are bound to find taped music, in the latter the 'menu' may include extras such as live shows. Table dancing is offered by many establishments in Central London as well as in other areas of the metropolis. Visitors can always enter membership clubs as the guest of a member, or by telephoning in advance.

*Stringfellows*

The **nightclub** scene has been dominated for many years by the elegant and exclusive *Annabel's* (44 Berkeley Square W1 ☎ 7629 2350) where access may prove difficult owing to the management's established policy of screening their clientele. But there are many places with a more free-and-easy approach. The *Café de Paris* (3 Coventry St W1 ☎ 7734 7700) has acquired some popularity after reopening in 1996 following an extensive refurbishment. Built on the site of a Tudor bear pit and originally known as the Elysée Restaurant, it was an instant hit when it first opened in 1920. Here the Queen, when Princess Elizabeth, held her 23rd birthday party and Marlene Dietrich made her London debut.

Everybody is also welcome at the *Hippodrome* (1 Cranbourn St WC2 ☎ 7437 4311). The *Limelight* (136 Shaftesbury Ave W1 ☎ 7434 0572) is unusual in that it occupies a large former Welsh Presbyterian Chapel, dating back to 1754. At *Iceni* (11 White Horse St W1 ☎ 7495 5333) money talks as loudly as the music while at *Raffles* (287 King's Rd SW3 ☎ 7352 1091) landed gentry rub shoulders with young yuppies. *Stringfellows* (16 Upper St Martin's Lane WC2 ☎ 7240 5534) is popular with out-of-town and overseas businessmen. Since opening in 2001 *Attica* (24 Kingly St W1 ☎ 7287 5882) has attracted an international party crowd from the world of music, film and fashion. The *Walbrook* (37a Walbrook EC4 ☎ 7623 6100), just behind Mansion House, is fashionable with people working in the City.

**Discos** with pounding music, darkness and large bars in general appeal to the younger clientele. Amongst the most popular is the *Equinox Discotheque* (Leicester Sq WC2 ☎ 7437 1446) which claims to be one of the largest in Europe. It is on two floors and can hold 2,180. Also on the large size is the nearby *Home* (1 Leicester Sq W1 ☎ 7909 0000) with its seven floors of minimalist design. The *Ministry of Sound* (Newington Causeway SE1 ☎ 7378 6528) is another well-known spot. Many boat operators on the Thames have vessels with disco facilities.

*Ministry of Sound*

# EDUCATION & SPORT

The University of London: Senate House

For a long time, London has attracted a large, and increasing, number of students from all parts of the world. Several factors account for the wide popularity of the British educational system: the general use of English as a lingua franca, the high standards of tuition offered, the low student-to-staff ratio (11 to 1 at universities, which is one of the most favourable in the world), and the possibility of obtaining professional qualifications recognised internationally.

Throughout the year sporting events take place in and around London. Some of these are open to spectators on the day but most require booking in advance. Visitors are advised to plan ahead if they wish to attend any of the major and international fixtures.

❑ **UNIVERSITIES & COLLEGES**. Annual study fees depend on the type of course taken. Candidates from EU countries benefit from considerable reductions and other foreign students can receive financial assistance through a variety of official and charitable schemes. Several thousand enjoy grants provided within the framework of the aid programme for developing countries. Outside this programme, the Overseas Research Students Awards Scheme can assist researchers of known ability.

The **University of London** is by far the major academic body in the capital: it is also the largest and most diverse university in Britain. It has its origins with the foundation of University College in Bloomsbury (1828), the first in England to admit students irrespective of their religion, race or sex, and with ***King's College*** in the Strand established by Royal Charter in 1829. Nowadays the University is a federation of 40 schools, colleges and institutes with 900 independent courses, some 400 graduate degree courses and the widest range of advanced research in the British Isles.

Within its framework are ***St Bartholomew's Medical Hospital,*** one of the oldest schools of medicine in Europe, the ***Imperial College of Science and Technology,*** whose alumni have included several Nobel Prize winners, and the ***London School of Economics and Political Science,*** renowned for its teaching and research.

University College: aerial view

## Useful Addresses

| | ☎ |
|---|---|
| ARELS, 56 Buckingham Gate SW1 | 7802 9200 |
| British Council, 10 Spring Gdns SW1 | 7930 8466 |
| City University, Northampton Sq EC1 | 7477 8000 |
| Universities Central Council on Admissions (UCCA), PO Box 28, Cheltenham, Gloucestershire GL50 3SA | |
| University of London, Senate House, Malet St WC1 | 7636 8000 |

Remarkable collections are linked directly or indirectly to the University of London. Amongst these are the ***Percival David Foundation of Chinese Art*** (53 Gordon Sq WC1 ☎ 7387 3909 ⊖ Euston Square ☞) with very fine Chinese ceramics from the 10thC onwards, the Courtauld Institute of Art and the very fine Courtauld Gallery*. The ***College Art Collections*** (University College, Gower St WC1 ☎ 7387 7050 ⊖ Euston Square ☞), with over 800 drawings by John Flaxman (1755-1820), Old Master prints and paintings and drawings from the Slade School of Fine Art, and the ***Petrie Museum of Egyptian Archaeology*** (Malet Pl WC1 ☎ 7679 2884 ⊖ Euston Square ☞), known worldwide for its antiquities, are connected with University College. The ***Brunei Gallery*** (Thornhaugh St WC1 ☎ 7898 4915 ⊖ Russell Square ☞), with its unique exhibitions, is part of the School of Oriental and African Studies (SOAS). This is Europe's largest institution for the study of all aspects of Asia and Africa.

The **City University** emerged officially in 1966, when it received a charter, completing the transition from a much older and respected institution, the Northampton Polytechnic. In spite of being a relative newcomer, the University has managed to establish itself at the forefront of the cultural and educational life of the Square Mile. Among the newer additions to the university scene are **Brunel** and other former polytechnics like the **South Bank** which have been raised in status.

London Business School

Governments and private industry have been active in promoting management and administrative courses. In this field, the **London Business School** is a front-runner. It occupies a fine building facing Regent's Park. Scores of other organisations, private and public, provide specialist training in accountancy, banking, law, tourism and other subjects.

London hosts many schools of English. Some are supported by public funds and belong to the *British Association of State Colleges in English Language Teaching* (BASCELT). Private enterprises, if conforming to standards laid down by the *Association of Recognised English Language Services* (ARELS), can be approved by the British Council which is Britain's principal agent for cultural relations abroad. Although supported by the Government, the Council operates independently in providing a network of contacts between universities and professional and business organisations in Britain and overseas. It is represented in 90 countries where it maintains libraries and organises the teaching of English amongst its many other activities.

❑ **SPECTATOR SPORTS**. Followers of **athletics** can watch the Amateur Athletics Association championships held during the summer at Crystal Palace as well as many other indoor and outdoor meetings at other tracks throughout the year. The All England **Badminton** tournament in which teams from the several thousand clubs in Britain take part annually is held in March, normally at the Wembley Arena. There are numerous venues in and around the capital for **basketball**, **bowls** and **boxing** matches.

Cricket at Old Richmond Park

In the summer months many village greens are used for playing **cricket**, the quintessential English game. At professional level the two major venues are Lord's and the Oval. Lord's is the headquarters of cricket both domestic and international and home of the Middlesex county team. Here the visitor can tour the ground and visit the ***MCC Museum*** (Lord's Ground, St John's Wood Rd NW8 ☎ 7289 1611 ⊖ St John's Wood ☛) with its unique collection of pictures, trophies, bats and other memorabilia including the "Ashes", contested by England and Australia since 1883. The Oval, where the Surrey County Cricket Club is based, has a magnificent pavilion.

**Football** dominates the winter calendar (August to June) and tickets for matches can be bought at the grounds up to the day of the match, usually played on a Saturday and midweek. But tickets for big matches in domestic and European competitions are hard to come by and may be very expensive. London's leading teams Arsenal, Tottenham, Hotspur and Chelsea are regularly sold out. The legendary Wembley Stadium is being redeveloped to meet the demands of today's fans for comfort and accessibility. The ***Arsenal Museum*** (Arsenal Football Club, Arsenal Stadium, Highbury N5 ☎ 7704 4100 ⊖ Arsenal ☛) has the largest, most extensive archive of one club's football history and memorabilia in Britain. It reflects its success over many decades.

## Useful Telephone Numbers

| | ☎ |
|---|---|
| *Ascot Racecourse* Berks | (01990) 22211 |
| *Brands Hatch* Kent | (01474) 872331 |
| *Crystal Palace National Sports Centre* SE19 | 8778 0131 |
| *Epsom Racecourse* Surrey | (01372) 726311 |
| *Henley Royal Regatta* Oxfordshire | (01491) 22626 |
| *Lord's* St John's Wood NW8 | 7289 1611 |
| *Oval* Kennington SE11 | 7582 6660 |
| *Queen's Club* Palliser Rd W14 | 7385 3421 |
| *Twickenham Stadium* Twickenham | 8892 8161 |
| *Wembley Stadium* NW9 | 8902 1234 |
| *Wimbledon Lawn Tennis Championships* SW19 | 8946 2244 |
| *Windsor Guards Polo Club* Berks | (01784) 434212 |

In the London region and its vicinity there are many racecourses for **horse racing** enthusiasts. The chief events are the Derby Stakes run at Epsom on the last Wednesday in May or the first in June, the Oaks, run at Epsom the following week, and in mid-June the Four Day Royal Meeting at Ascot. Inaugurated by Queen Anne in 1711 and, since that time, attended by the Sovereign and members of the Royal Family driving in state carriages from Windsor Castle, the Ascot meeting is almost as famous for hats and high fashion as for its racing and gold cup. **Motor racing** (car and motorcycle) can best be seen at the famous Brands Hatch circuit in Kent. **Polo** is mainly played at Windsor Great Park.

Riding in Rotten Row, Hyde Park

The Thames provides the setting for the spectacular **rowing** races and regattas of the spring and summer. The Boat Race between Oxford and Cambridge Universities is rowed from Putney to Mortlake on a Saturday in late March or early April and attracts huge crowds of spectators who line the banks. The most celebrated of the regattas is held at Henley-on-Thames during the first week of July. Crews from overseas and Britain compete in the various events.

Twickenham is the home of the Rugby Union and the England XV. Although **rugby** is now a professional sport it is only the spring international matches between the four home countries (England, Ireland, Scotland and Wales), France and newcomers Italy and occasional visits by the All Blacks (NZ), Wallabies (Aus) and Springboks (SA) which gain wide public attention. Memorabilia of the game can be seen at the ***Museum of Rugby*** (Rugby Rd, Twickenham ☎ 8892 2000 ⊖ Richmond ☛). During the winter and spring, international matches are played at Twickenham and, in December, the long standing Oxford-Cambridge "Varsity" match.

Anyone for tennis?

The most famous international lawn **tennis** championship is held by the All England Tennis and Croquet Club at Wimbledon for two weeks at the end of June. Bookings should be made well in advance because there is enormous demand for tickets, particularly for the Centre Court. During the week before Wimbledon the Stella Artois tournament takes place at Queen's Club where many of the men's world champions perfect their form on grass courts. At The **Wimbledon Lawn Tennis Museum** (All England Lawn Tennis and Croquet Club SW19 ☎ 8946 6131 ⊖ Southfields ☛) the visitor can savour those special moments from past Championships.

# BUSINESS & FINANCE

The reputation of the City as a leading financial centre is long-established. Logic, co-incidence and accident contributed to such a pre-eminence. In the 17thC, for instance, when the first modern institutions were developing, Britain's capital was already the nexus of the international trade forged by wool traders and other merchants.

By this time the use of bills of exchange was common, as was the circulation of notes issued by goldsmiths against the deposit of bullion held by them, in trust.

As companies with limited liabilities became popular, their shares provided scope for the development of the London Stock Exchange. The spread of business was helped by the government-of-the-day's policy of interfering as little as possible with the free working of the City.

Baltic Exchange: the Boardroom

Set within the European time zone the City is the natural apex of the global financial triangle of New York-Tokyo-London. Companies from all over the globe benefit by joining the élite community of London-listed businesses. More than 65% of the Fortune Global 500 Companies are represented in London and more than 550 international banks and 170 global securities houses have offices here. The headquarters of the *European Bank for Reconstruction and Development*, established here in the 1990s, is probably the most prestigious of all.

London remains the hub of insurance business and has a powerful concentration of legal firms, accountants and management consultants. Canary Wharf in Docklands* is challenging the City's supremacy as the main address for financial services. The trend is bound to strengthen because of lack of space within the boundaries of old Londinium.

❑ **FINANCIAL INSTITUTIONS.** While the leading position is held by the Bank of England, the UK central bank, other institutions are also of considerable importance.

• **Bank of England.** Established in 1694 as a private company, the Bank remained independent until 1946 when it was nationalised. It acts as banker to the Government, implements monetary policy, provides facilities for the banking system, and issues banknotes for which it holds a monopoly in England and Wales. Scottish and Northern Irish banks have a limited right to issue their own notes. Since 1997, the Bank has been responsible for setting short-term interest rates. The Bank occupies a massive building in Threadneedle Street. Sir John Soane was responsible for the external curtain wall, which is relieved somewhat by mock Corinthian columns.

Bank of England Museum: the Bank Stock Office (1792), restored.

The ***Bank of England Museum*** (entrance on Bartholomew Lane EC3 ☎ 7601 5545 ⊖ Bank ☞) illustrates the long history of the Bank. It is set around the original Bank Stock Office. Its neoclassical interior, also designed by Soane, is regarded as one of the finest in Europe.

*Bank of England* Threadneedle St EC2 ☎ 7601 4444

• **Retail Banks.** With the growth of financial services and the relaxation of restrictions from 1971 onwards, the role of retail banks in Britain has increased. Barclays Bank, HSBC and Lloyds TSB all have their headquarters in the 'Square Mile'. The number of retail banks has increased as several large building societies have joined in. Some banks open their archives to researchers.

*British Bankers Association* 105-108 Old Broad St EC2 ☎ 7216 8800

• **Building Societies.** Another variety of retail banking institution, building societies are owned by their members and specialise in providing mortgages and other personal financial services.

*Building Societies Association* 3 Savile Row W1 ☎ 7437 0655

Gate-Keepers
Bank of England

Merrill Lynch headquarters for Europe, Middle East and Africa, accommodating 4,000 employees and two high-tech trading floors, each capable of supporting up to 1,000 professionals.

• **Investment Banks**. They occupy a pre-eminent position in international finance and have moved far beyond their original function of guaranteeing commercial bills and overseeing capital issues. They provide financial backing and advice on all forms of corporate finance, including the issue of equity and debt, and mergers and acquisitions. It is not unusual for continental European company shares to be traded on a larger scale between dealers in London investment houses than on the floor of their own home exchange. The London Investment Banking Association (LIBA) is the sector's main corporate body. Established in 1989, it represents the interests of firms active in the investment and securities industry on all aspects of their business and promotes their views to the authorities in the UK, the EU and elsewhere.

*LIBA* 6 Frederick's Pl EC2 ☎ 7796 3606

• **Foreign & Overseas Banks**. Over 500 foreign institutions have offices, branches, subsidiaries or representative offices in the City. As well as providing additional employment, these banks contribute additional expertise and resources to the financial community. Around 170 banks belong to the Foreign Banks & Securities Houses Association (FBSA). Foreign banks began to open branches in London in the 1860s. First were the French, followed by the Swiss, German, Italian, Russian and American.

*FBSA* 5 Laurence Pountney Lane EC4 ☎ 7621 9557

• **Insurance Companies**. The London Insurance market is the world's leading market for internationally traded insurance and reinsurance. Its business comprises mainly large and high-exposure non-life business from overseas, and also from the UK. The market is centred on the City of London, although an increasing number of participants from across London participate in it electronically. As well as an unrivalled concentration of insurance expertise within a small geographical area, the City provides the required international, financial, banking, legal and other support services. The market provides employment for around 50,000 people in the UK through 100 companies, over 100 Lloyd's syndicates and 39 marine protection and indemnity clubs, as well as the suppliers of ancillary services such as accountants, actuaries and loss adjusters.

Over 400 companies which between them represent 95% of the UK insurance business belong to the Association of British Insurers (ABI) and several have offices at the modern London Underwriting Centre (LUC). The ***Chartered Insurance Institute Museum*** (20 Aldermanbury EC2 ☎ 7417 4412 ⊖ Moorgate, prior application) contains artefacts relating to the early history of insurance companies and is run by the Chartered Insurance Institute. The display includes original fire-marks (plates).

London Underwriting Centre

*ABI* 51 Gresham St EC4 ☎ 7600 3333

*LUC* 3 Minster Court St EC3 ☎ 7617 5000

• **Pension Funds**. Many occupational and personal pension schemes are invested through money managers based in the City of London. The assets invested in pension funds have mushroomed from £2 billion in 1957 to over £600 billion in 1999. In fact approximately 30% of the securities listed on the London Stock Exchange* are held by UK pension funds. Many are members of the National Association of Pension Funds (NAPS).

*NAPS* 4 Victoria St SW1 ☎ 7808 1300

❑ **FINANCIAL MARKETS**. Most of the City's financial markets are the oldest of their kind in the western world and are the largest in terms of volumes traded. Some markets operate from purpose-built premises. Others are electronic in nature and are connected to a world wide network.

• **Baltic Exchange**. An international market whose members arrange the bulk of the world's movements in raw materials - namely oil, grain, iron ore, coal and chemicals. It traces its origins back to the Virginia and Baltick coffee house established in 1744.

*Baltic Exchange* St Mary Axe EC3 ☎ 7623 5501

Baltic Exchange Coat of Arms

• **Euromarkets**. These electronic markets form a prominent part of the international capital markets. Participants include governments and multinational companies. Originally the markets centred on currencies lent or invested outside their national boundaries. Today, debt instruments such as euro commercial paper and eurobonds form the backbone. Transactions on the euromarkets exceed £6,000 billion annually. London's virtual capture of the Eurodollar market in the 1960s also ensured that the techniques relating to such new international lending were centred here.

• **Foreign Exchange Market**. Over 30% of the world trade in currencies is conducted in the City of London. Daily turnover is nearly $650 billion. Foreign exchange trading is another market that is linked electronically.

• **International Petroleum Exchange**. The IPE is Europe's leading energy futures and options exchange and the second largest in the world. The IPE provides a highly regulated marketplace where industry participants can manage their exposure to highly volatile energy prices. Incorporated in 1980, the IPE lists five main energy contracts: Brent Crude futures and options, Gas Oil futures and options and Natural Gas futures.

*IPE* 1 St Katharine's Way E1 ☎ 7481 0643

• **Lloyd's of London**. Almost anything can be insured at Lloyd's. Business is carried out on behalf of individual underwriting members or 'names'. Lloyd's includes individual members with unlimited liability and corporate members with limited liability as well. Members operate through about 108 syndicates and business is placed through authorised brokers. In 2000 the market had a capacity of about £11 billion. Reinsurance contributes a large part of Lloyd's business. The famous Lutine Bell used to be rung for both good (two strokes) and bad (one stroke) news. It came from the French frigate 'La Lutine' which surrendered to the British in 1793.

The ***Lloyd's Nelson Collection*** (Lloyd's of London, Lime Street EC3 ☎ 7623 7100 ⊖ Liverpool Street, prior application) bears witness to Lloyd's connection with Lord Nelson, which dates back to 1798. In addition to silver and swords, there are many letters from the Admiral, most in his well-known left hand script. Lloyd's and the Nelson Collection are not open to the general public.

*Lloyd's of London* 1 Lime St EC3 ☎ 7327 1000

Lloyd's of London: The Lutine Bell

• **London Bullion Market**. This is the hub of global OTC (Over-The-Counter) precious metal trading. Its representative body, the London Bullion Market Association (LBMA), has members from all market sectors, including banks, fabricators, refiners, shippers and brokers. The responsibility for fixing the gold price (twice daily, Mon-Fri) rests with a group of five long-standing gold dealers; the silver price is fixed once a day.

Bullion Vaults

*LBMA* 6 Frederick's Pl EC2 ☎ 7796 3067

• **London International Financial Futures Exchange**. LIFFE is the world's leading electronic exchange, offering the widest range of products with contracts denominated in five major currencies across the following asset classes: bond, money, swap, equity, equity index and commodity. It trades futures and options on its electronic trading system Connect. Every day € 656 billion of business is entrusted to it. The system is available in 23 countries and 380 trading rooms worldwide. At the beginning of 2001 the exchange had more than 200 members made up of banks and brokers. Connect was linked to 223 dealing rooms overseas and 180 in Britain.

*LIFFE* Cannon Bridge House, 1 Cousin Lane EC4 ☎ 7623 0444

• **London Metal Exchange**.The LME is the world's leading non-ferrous metals futures and traded options exchange. It had an annual turnover of $2,500 billion in 2001. The prices agreed for futures settlement dates for aluminium, aluminium alloy, copper, tin, lead, nickel and zinc are used by physical metal dealers to determine raw material prices. The exchange contracts allow buyers and sellers of metal to lock in future prices, thus avoiding the risk of future price movements. This ensures that prices for consumers are stabilised.

London Metal Exchange

*LME* 56 Leadenhall St EC3
☎ 7264 5555

• **London Stock Exchange**. It is the world's most international stock exchange, and the largest in Europe by a wide margin. It provides companies in the United Kingdom and around the world with the means to raise capital by issuing shares, bonds and securities, as well as a transparent and well-regulated marketplace for these securities to be bought and sold. The attraction of London as a venue for the listing and trading of shares in companies of all types has established it as the fourth largest equities exchange in the world by market capitalisation, and the third largest by value of trading. While London's historic origins make it the world's oldest marketplace for the buying and selling of shares, its advanced trading systems mean it is also one of the most modern. The LSE runs different markets suited to the needs of different

Clara Furse

kinds of companies. The main market is where most UK and international shares are listed, while the Alternative Investment Market (AIM) is a first step into the public market for growing and fledgling companies. TechMARK, within the main market, is the exchange's market for innovative technology companies. After 228 years of being run almost exclusively by men LSE chose a woman, Clara Furse, as its Chief Executive at the beginning of 2001. There are plans to move the LSE headquarters to a new building near St Paul's Cathedral.

*LSE* Old Broad St EC2 ☎ 7797 1000

• **virt-x**. Launched in June 2001, it is the operator of a pan-European blue chip equities exchange. The market emerged following a joint undertaking between Tradepoint Financial Networks, the Swiss Exchange and the Tradepoint Consortium which is made up of leading international brokers and financial services firms.

*virt-x* 1 Canada Sq E14 ☎ 7864 4300

• **Wholesale Markets**. These cover a wide spectrum of dealings. The parallel markets are dominated by banks involved in channelling short-term public sector and corporate securities from lenders to borrowers. Based on negotiations conducted primarily by telephone, these markets handle a great volume of business.

❑ **EXHIBITION & CONFERENCE CENTRES**. As far back as the 19thC, when Britain led the world in manufacturing, London was a traditional venue for major exhibitions. The pioneering Great Exhibition of 1851 covered an extensive area, part of which subsequently developed into the famous museums around South Kensington.

Nowadays the main location for large **exhibitions** is the *ExCel* in Docklands. When completed it will be Britain's largest single centre for events. It already offers 65,000 m$^2$. Other important venues are *Earl's Court* (59,000m$^2$), *Olympia* (41,000m$^2$), *Wembley Centre* (34,000m$^2$), *Alexandra Palace* (10,000m$^2$ indoor and 809,400m$^2$ outdoor), the *London Arena* (8,820m$^2$), the *Barbican Centre* (8,000m$^2$) and the *Business Design Centre* (3,745m$^2$).

## Useful Addresses

| | ☎ |
|---|---|
| *Alexandra Palace* Wood Green N22 | 8365 2121 |
| *Barbican Centre* Silk St, Barbican EC2 | 7638 4141 |
| *Business Design Centre* 52 Upper St N1 | 7359 3535 |
| *Earl's Court* Warwick Rd SW5 | 7385 1200 |
| *ExCel* Royal Docks E16 | 7476 0101 |
| *London Arena* Limeharbour, Isle of Dogs E14 | 7538 8880 |
| *London Chamber of Commerce* 69 Cannon St EC4 | 7248 4444 |
| *London First* 1 Hobstone Ct, Suffolk St SW1 | 7665 1500 |
| *London Tourist Board & Convention Bureau* Glen Ho, Stag Pl SW1 | 7932 2000 |
| *Olympia* Hammersmith Rd W14 | 7603 3344 |
| *Queen Elizabeth II Conference Centre* Broad Sanctuary SW1 | 7222 5000 |
| *Wembley Conference Centre* NW9 | 8902 8833 |

ExCel, in Docklands

For **conferences** in Central London one of the most modern and extensive is the *Queen Elizabeth II Conference Centre* adjoining Parliament Square and facing Westminster Abbey. Planned and designed for meetings ranging from international gatherings up to 2,000 delegates to rooms suitable for just a handful of people, the Centre spreads over 10 floors. In addition to studios, 12 channels of simultaneous interpretation and a closed circuit television which can broadcast to 150 monitor screens installed throughout the building, it has good and varied catering facilities. The 18thC Spencer House* facing Green Park is one of the most exclusive venues for small assemblies. *Logan Hall* (University of London), equipped with advance audiovisual aids and almost 1,000 fixed and raked seats, is an ideal place to hire for medium-size conferences and lectures.

All major hotels have business centres for the benefit of their guests and provide secretarial assistance, e-mail and other similar services. The Hilton London Metropole in Edgware Road (W2) can accommodate over 1,000 delegates with high speed internet access and electronic conferencing facilities.

Valuable assistance to business people visiting London can be obtained from the *London Chamber of Commerce and Industry, London First* and *London Tourist Board & Convention Bureau.*

Queen Elizabeth II Conference Centre

# EXCURSIONS

However interesting and rewarding, the metropolis' pavements can lose their charm, and fresh scenery is a useful restorative. A change, however short, is as good as a rest. London is, after all, by no means representative of the rest of England and visitors should try to see some of the many historically rich and culturally varied provincial towns.

Windsor Castle:
Garter Service Procession

## ❑ **BATH** (Avon)

| | |
|---|---|
| 🚗 | 167km |
| 🚆 | 82min (Paddington) |
| ☺ | 85,000 |
| *i* | ☎ (01225) 477 101 |
| ✈ | Bristol Lulsgate, 25km |

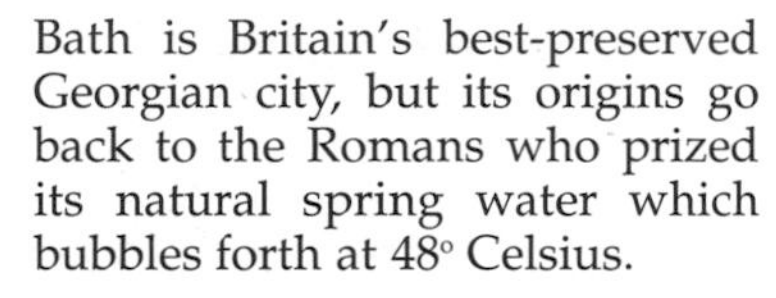

Bath is Britain's best-preserved Georgian city, but its origins go back to the Romans who prized its natural spring water which bubbles forth at 48° Celsius.

You can still sample its therapeutic virtues and its taste – by the glass – in the splendid Pump Room, looking down on the very attractive and instructive *Roman Baths Museum* (Abbey Churchyard ☎ 477 785 ☛).

The history of fashion over the last 400 years is brought alive at the *Museum of Costume and Assembly Rooms* (Bennett St ☎ 477 789 ☛). The fan-vaulted *Abbey* is a late medieval delight.

Roman Baths Museum

Museum of Costume

The *Bath Postal Museum* (8 Broad St ☎ 460 333 ☛) is housed on two floors of Bath's former Post Office. It was from here that the world's first postage stamp was sent on May 2nd, 1840. Only 4km away from Bath is **Claverton Manor** with its rich *American Museum* (☎ 460 503 ☛) devoted to 16–19thC domestic life in the USA.

Claverton Manor

❑ **BRIGHTON** (East Sussex)

🚗 85km
🚆 52min (Victoria)
☺ 152,700
*i* ☎ (01273) 292 592
✈ Gatwick, 22km

The small fishing village, then known as Brighthelmstone, rose to fame when the Prince Regent (later George IV) made it a fashionable seaside resort. The marvellous onion-domed *Royal Pavilion* (☎ 290 900 ☛), started in 1787 by Henry Holland, was rebuilt in 1815 by John Nash in the Mogul Indian style. *The Lanes* are the last remains of the medieval village with their fishermen's cottages converted into antique shops, cafés and restaurants. The new town, some of its squares dating back to the Regency, is still a favoured place to live, Brighton being the South Coast resort nearest to London.

Royal Pavilion

George IV

It has a large *Aquarium*, pedestrianised shopping streets and a modern *Marina* with moorings for 2,000 yachts. An *International Arts Festival* takes place usually in May, regarded as one of England's largest.

*Preston Manor* (☎ 292 770 ☛), not far from the city centre, is a delightful Edwardian gentry home. It contains notable collections of furniture, portraits and memorabilia.

Preston Manor

❑ **BRISTOL** (Avon)

🚗 182km
🚆 97min (Paddington)
☺ 411,500
*i* ☎ (0117) 926 0707
✈ Bristol Lusgate, 10km

SS Great Britain

This thriving ancient city-port has long been important to English trade. From here John Cabot sailed to reach Newfoundland in 1497. The *Cabot Tower*, one of Bristol's landmarks, commemorates his historic voyage. Apart from the well-endowed *City Museum and Art Gallery* (Queen's Rd ☎ 922 3571 ☞), there is the *Georgian House* (Gt George St ☎ 921 1362 ☞), a typical late 18thC merchant's house, and *Red Lodge* (Park Row ☎ 921 1360 ☞), containing the city's only surviving set of 16thC rooms.

The picturesque old *Llandoger Trow* Inn is said to have been the model for the 'Admiral Benbow' in R.L. Stevenson's *Treasure Island*. The *Maritime Heritage Centre* (Gasferry Rd ☎ 926 0680 ☛) contains the Hillhouse Collection, which illustrates ship-building in Bristol and includes the restored *SS Great Britain* (Great Western Dock, Gas Ferry Rd ☎ 929 1843), the world's first propeller-driven, transatlantic, iron ship, launched by Prince Albert in 1843. Another of Isambard Kingdom Brunel's great achievements, the *Clifton Suspension Bridge*, can be seen in nearby **Clifton**, soaring dramatically over the Avon Gorge. The bridge, started in 1836 but completed 18 years later for shortage of money, spans the river at a height of 82m.

Llandoger Trow

Clifton Suspension Bridge

❑ **CAMBRIDGE** (Cambridgeshire)

| | |
|---|---|
| 🚗 | 89km |
| ⥈ | 57min (Liverpool Street) |
| ☺ | 103,000 |
| *i* | ☎ (01223) 322 640 |
| ✈ | Stansted, 28km |

The Backs at King's College

The city is both the county town and, more famously, the home of one of the two oldest places of learning in the British Isles. The first scholars came here from Oxford in 1209 but it was from the 14thC onwards that the fame of the University spread abroad.

Of the 31 colleges, *Peterhouse* (established in 1284) is the oldest. *Christ's College* was founded by Margaret Beaufort, mother of Henry VII. Milton is reputed to have planted the mulberry tree in the Fellows' Garden. The Old Court of *Corpus Christi College* was the first enclosed college courtyard. The Chapel of *Emmanuel College* (where John Harvard was a pupil) was created by Wren who also designed the

## The University at work

The main role of the university is to teach, to promote research, to hold examinations and award degrees. In Cambridge this ceremony takes place at the 18thC Senate House.

Both Cambridge and Oxford are unique in that their various colleges are private self-governing bodies and jointly constitute the University. They house both undergraduates (as students are called) and a number of Fellows, who are graduates elected by the college and who pursue their own studies and research. Fellows teach undergraduates, singly or in groups of two or three, although undergraduates also attend University lectures outside the college. Each college selects its own undergraduates by examination, most of whom live in it for two of their usual three years residence at the university. Almost all are open to the public (some making a charge), except during the examinations period (May to mid-June).

Cambridge: Senate House by James Gibbs

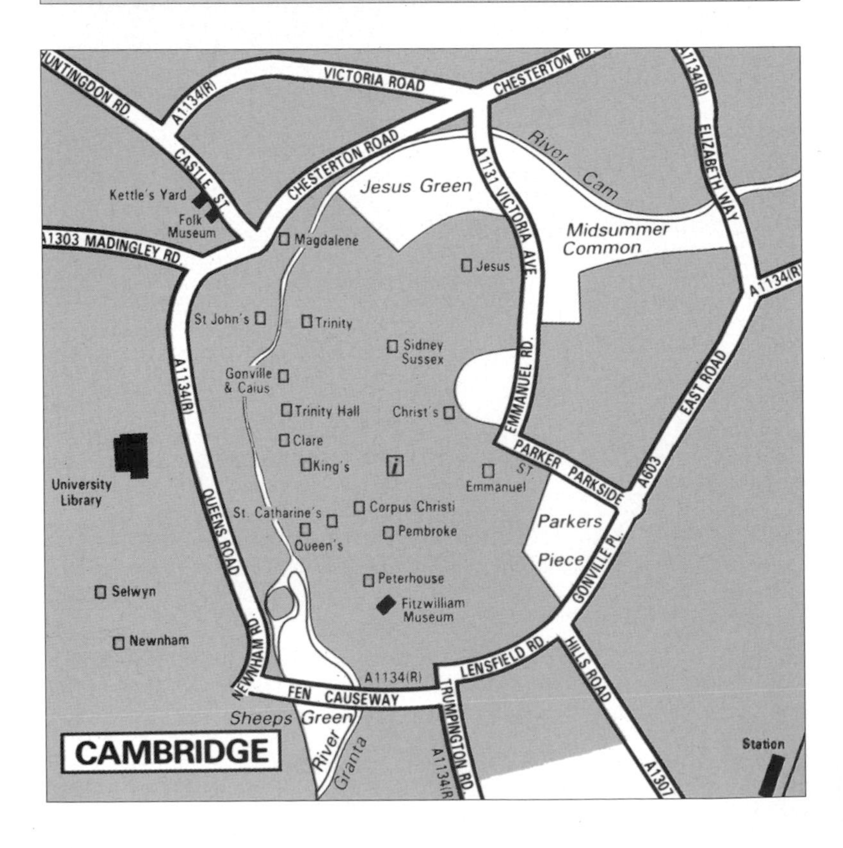

Library of *Trinity College*. This is the largest Cambridge college, with over 800 students, and among the many famous figures who once studied here were the physicist Isaac Newton and the poet Lord Byron.

The Chapel of *Jesus College* has windows designed by the Pre-Raphaelite artist Burne-Jones. *King's College* Chapel (1446–1515) (☎ 331 212 ☛) is a magnificent example of Perpendicular architecture. It contains Rubens's *Adoration of the Magi*. Its choir of undergraduates and schoolboys is famous the world over. The Pepys Library in *Magdalene College* houses some 3,000 of the books of the 17thC diarist Samuel Pepys in the original bookcases he designed to hold them.

The *Fitzwilliam Museum* (Trumpington St ☎ 332 900 ☞), part of the University, has exceptional collections. The neoclassic building, designed by George Basevi, was opened in 1848 and further extended between 1924 and 1975. It contains Egyptian, Greek and Roman antiquities; medieval and Renaissance objects of art; Oriental and Western pottery and porcelain; coins and medals; medieval manuscripts; paintings and drawings. There is also a notable library.

The *Backs*, the college gardens and lawns which slope towards the River Cam, where undergraduates pole their punts under the trees and bridges, epitomize the tranquillity and beauty of the university city.

At 24km to the north-west lies **Huntingdon** (*i* ☎ (01480) 388 588) where Oliver Cromwell, who was also a student at Cambridge, was born and is remembered in the *Cromwell Museum* (Grammar School Walk ☎ 375 830 ☞) while **Ely** (*i* ☎ (01353) 662 062) and its outstanding 12–14thC *Cathedral* with the massive octagonal lantern tower is 25km to the north east.

The imposing towers of Ely Cathedral

## ❑ CANTERBURY (Kent)

🚗 93km
⇄ 80min (Victoria)
☺ 36,300
*i* ☎ (01227) 766 567
✈ Gatwick, 46km

When the Romans arrived in AD 43 the town had already been in existence for 350 years. Its first major church, the cradle of Christianity in Saxon England, was built soon after the coming of St Augustine from Rome in 597. The present *Cathedral*, which is the Mother Church of the Anglicans, was begun in 1067. In 1170 the then Archbishop of Canterbury, Thomas Becket, was murdered here. The Cathedral became a shrine for devout pilgrims who came from all over Europe until 1535, when Henry VIII seized church property and dissolved the monasteries. Among the Cathedral's principal features are: the medieval stained glass, the Norman Crypt (the oldest part of the

Canterbury Cathedral

building), the Trinity Chapel, the 12thC Choir with its 14thC screen, and the elegantly simple nave. Stretches of the medieval walls and houses can still be seen in the lanes leading to Christ Church Gate. *West Gate*, the only surviving original gate, houses a museum (St Peter's St ☎ 452 747 ☛). Ruins of the 11thC *St Augustine's Abbey* (Monaster St ☎ 767 345) are among the most important ecclesiastical sites in England.

**Rochester** (*i* ☎ (01634) 843 666), half-way from London, with its Norman Cathedral (☎ 401 301) and Castle (☎ 402 276), has strong connections with Charles Dickens. The *Charles Dickens Centre* (Eastgate House, High St ☎ 844 176 ☛) brings the novelist's works to life through displays. Over 400 years of shipbuilding is brought to life at **Chatham** (☎ 823 800). **Leeds Castle** (12 km west of Canterbury, ☎ (01622) 765 400 ☛), built on an island in a lake surrounded by wood, is the quintessential fairy-tale moated castle.

❑ **OXFORD** (Oxfordshire)

| | |
|---|---|
| 🚗 | 90km |
| ⇄ | 55min (Paddington) |
| ☺ | 116,000 |
| *i* | ☎ (01865) 726 871 |
| ✈ | Kidlington, 11km |

At the junction of the rivers Thames and Cherwell, Oxford began to grow with the foundation of a nunnery in the 8thC. The University evolved gradually in the latter half of the 12thC with the migration of scholars from elsewhere including Paris.

The first colleges were *Merton, University College* and *Balliol*, all founded around the mid-13thC. Merton has the oldest library in England and the University's oldest quad (or quadrangle). The grandest of all is *Christ Church* (1525). Its chapel is the Cathedral of Oxford. *Somerville* (1879) is for women only. Mrs Gandhi of India and Mrs Thatcher of Britain were both undergraduates here. The *Sheldonian Theatre* (Broad

Oxford: aerial view with domed Radcliff Camera

St ☎ 277 299 ☞), designed by Christopher Wren, with a spectacular painted ceiling, is used for University ceremonies. The *Bodleian Library* (Broad St ☎ 277 000 ☞) is one of the world's oldest and most important. The domed *Radcliffe Camera*, designed by James Gibbs in 1737, is the first round library in Britain.

The *Ashmolean Museum* (Beaumont St ☎ 278 000 ☞) is rich in Egyptian, Greek and Roman antiquities. It has paintings by Uccello, Giorgione, Tiepolo and Claude, amongst others, and drawings by Michelangelo and Raphael, as well as a huge collection of 18thC Worcester porcelain and such historical curiosities as the lantern carried by Guy Fawkes when he attempted to blow up the Houses of Parliament in 1605. The *University Museum* (Parks Rd ☎ 272 950 ☞), an elaborate essay in Victorian Gothic architecture, houses huge scientific collections in zoology, entomology and geology. Ethnography, prehistoric archaeology

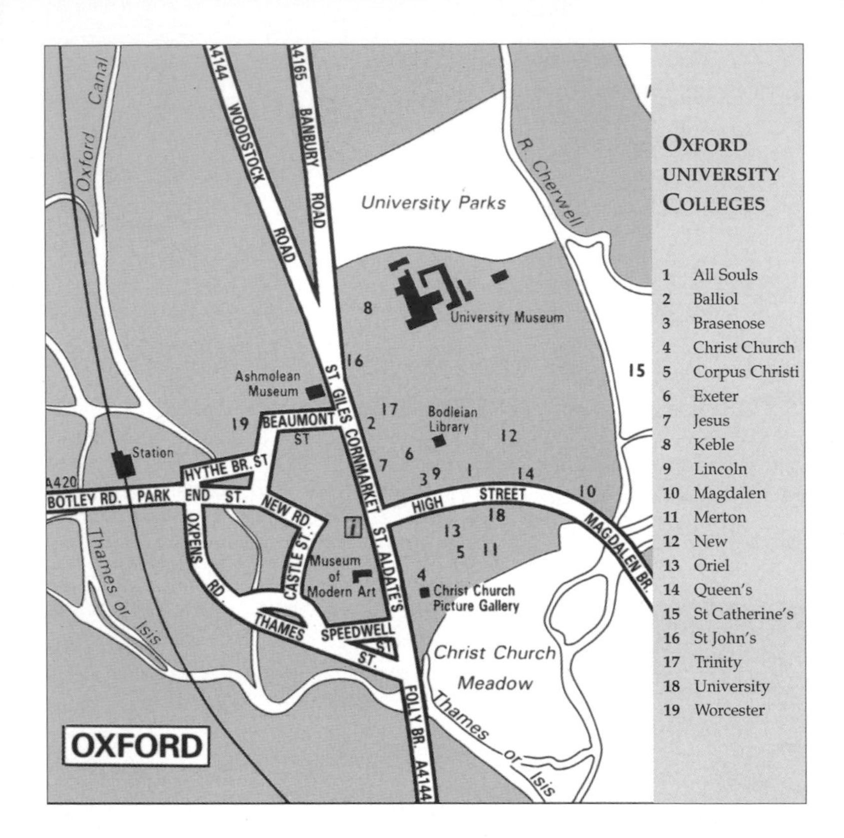


and a collection of musical instruments from all over the world and from all centuries are at the *Pitt Rivers Museum* (Park Rd ☎ 270 927 ☞). Old Master drawings, paintings from the 14thC to the mid-18thC, and 18thC English glass can be seen in the striking setting of the *Christ Church Picture Gallery* (Canterbury Quadrangle ☎ 276 172 ☛), while the *Museum of Modern Art* (30 Pembroke St ☎ 722 733 ☛) specializes in contemporary art. The town has a vigorous and prosperous shopping centre, a lot of it pedestrianised, and a wealth of specialist shops dealing particularly in books (new, second-hand, antiquarian). But much of Oxford's most characteristic charm lies out of doors, in the quiet withdrawn quadrangles, in the formal gardens of Trinity and the richly wooded deer park of Magdalen, and in Christ Church meadows.

**Blenheim Palace** (☎ (01993) 811 325 ☛), 12km north of Oxford, is a large baroque style mansion built as a gift from the nation to the first Duke of Marlborough for his victory over the French at Blenheim (1704, northwest of Augsburg). Collections include fine tapestries and sculptures. Winston Churchill, born in the Palace in 1874, is buried close by in the village of **Bladon**.

Blenheim Palace

## ❑ ST ALBANS (Hertfordshire)

🚗 30km
🚆 30min (St Pancras)
☺ 127,530
*i* ☎ (01727) 864 511
✈ Luton, 18km

St Albans: Cathedral and Abbey Church

Under the name of Verulamium this was one of the most important centres of the Roman Western Empire. The semicircular *Roman Theatre* (Bluehouse Hill ☎ 854 051 ☛) had seating for some 1,600. Some magnificent mosaics are at the *Verulamium Museum* (St Michael's St ☎ 781 810 ☛).

Verulamium Museum: Sea God Mosaic

In AD 303 the legionnaire Alban died saving a Christian fugitive and became Britain's first martyr. A Saxon church on the site of the shrine was developed by the Normans into the Abbey, which became a *Cathedral* (☎ 860 780 ☛)in 1877. Built of a variety of materials including Roman bricks it shows traces of several different styles. It has the longest nave in Europe, extended by 100m in the 13thC, and is notable for the massive piers adorned with medieval paintings.

*French Row* is a reminder of the French presence in the 13thC. In the Fleur de Lys Inn King John of France was held prisoner following the Battle of Poitiers in 1356.

**Hatfield House** (10km from St Alban's ☎ (01707) 262 823 ☛), a grand mansion in Jacobean fashion, was re-built in 1611 for Robert Cecil and is still occupied by his descendants. Among the treasures are two portraits of Elizabeth I, who during her childhood lived in the Old Palace, now partly demolished.

Hatfield House

## ❑ SALISBURY (Wiltshire)

| | |
|---|---|
| 🚗 | 134km |
| ⇄ | 84min (Waterloo) |
| ☺ | 36,000 |
| *i* | ☎ (01722) 334 956 |
| ✈ | Eastleigh, 21km |

The roots of Salisbury are to be found in Old Sarum, a few miles north of the present location, which was inhabited since the Iron Age. The present town is famous above all for its *Cathedral* (The Close ☎ 555 120 ☛), with the spire 122m high, immortalized by the painter John Constable. Stylistically, this is the purest of all England's great churches, completed, except for the spire, within a mere 38 years in 1258. There is no more perfect example of Early English Gothic architecture. The busy town retains some other important historic buildings, especially around the Cathedral, including the magnificent early 18thC *Mompesson House* (The Close ☎ 335 659 ☛). It contains a notable collection of over 370 English 18thC glasses. A secluded garden at the back of the house with a magnolia, a wisteria and a pergola provides a welcome shade in summer.

Salisbury Cathedral

About 16.5km away is **Stonehenge**, the famous Bronze Age site. This is Europe's most impressive prehistoric monument. Its huge stones, each weighing up to 50 tonnes, have stood on this windswept plain for over 4,000 years. Its origin is obscure; its mystery and magic are today as strong as ever.

Megalithic ruins at Stonehenge

## ❑ STRATFORD-UPON-AVON (Warwickshire)

| | |
|---|---|
| 🚗 | 150km |
| ⇌ | 120min (Paddington) |
| ☺ | 20,770 |
| *i* | ☎ (01789) 293 127 |
| ✈ | Birmingham International, 32km |

An ancient and prosperous market town, it was Shakespeare's birthplace and childhood home. He was born in 1564 at the house where his father carried out his trade as a glove-maker. He was educated at the local Grammar School, founded in 1483. He died in 1616 and is buried in the parish church, Holy Trinity, where he had been baptized. The house is now a fascinating museum of authentic relics and documents: *Shakespeare's Birthplace* (Henley St ☎ 204 016 ☛).

Shakespeare Birthday Celebrations (April)

The Royal Shakespeare Company (RSC) performs its annual season from March to December at the *Royal Shakespeare Theatre* (Waterside ☎ 296 655). The *RSC Collection* has important items.

*Anne Hathaway's Cottage* (☎ 204 016 ☛), where she lived before her marriage to Shakespeare, is at **Shottery**, very close to Stratford.

Royal Shakespeare Theatre on the river Avon

❑ **WINCHESTER** (Hampshire)

| | |
|---|---|
| 🚘 | 105km |
| ⇄ | 63min (Waterloo) |
| ☺ | 33,221 |
| *i* | ☎ (01962) 840 500 |
| ✈ | Eastleigh, 18km |

The capital of England up to Norman times, **Winchester** was a great centre of learning under King Alfred (871–901). Two of the five original city gates survive. *Westgate* (High St ☎ 848 269 ☛), once a prison, is now a small museum displaying a collection of armour and weapons. The *Cathedral* (☎ 857 225 ☛), built on the site of an earlier Saxon church, was begun in 1079 but not finished until 1404 and thus incorporates several different styles from massive Norman to graceful Perpendicular. Jane Austen (1775–1817) is buried here. The Norman crypt is the oldest of its kind in England. Treasures in the Library include the 12thC Winchester Bible. Adjoining the Cathedral are the 13thC Old Deanery and *Pilgrims' Hall*, a 14thC building with a hammer-beam roof where pilgrims lodged in the Middle Ages. Other historical sites are the 12thC *Wolvesey Castle*, where Mary Tudor spent her honeymoon with Philip of Spain, and the 13thC *Castle Hall*, where Walter Raleigh was tried and condemned to death in 1603. *Winchester College*, founded in 1382, is Britain's oldest public (ie independent) school, and one of the most distinguished. *St Cross Hospital*, founded in 1136 for the benefit of 13 poor men, is said to be the oldest surviving charity in Britain.

Winchester Cathedral

At **Chawton** (22km to the east of Winchester) is the red-brick cottage where Jane Austen lived and worked from 1809 until her death. The great naval harbour of **Portsmouth** (*i* ☎ (02392) 826 722) is 43km south-east of Winchester. An arsenal was first constructed here by Richard I at the end of the 12thC. *HMS Victory* (☎ 723 111 ☛), Lord Nelson's flagship at the Battle of Trafalgar, the *Mary Rose Ship Hall* (College Rd ☎ 872 931 ☛), with the hull of Henry VIII's favourite warship, the Mary Rose, recovered in 1982 from the Solent, and the *Royal Navy Museum* are potent reminders of Portsmouth's long naval history. The house where Charles Dickens was born is now the *Charles Dickens Birthplace Museum* (393 Old Commercial Rd ☎ 827 261 ☛).

A section of the Royal Armouries has been moved from the Tower of London* to the 19thC **Fort Nelson** (☎ (01329) 233 734 ☛), which overlooks Portsmouth Harbour.

❑ **WINDSOR** (Berkshire)

| | |
|---|---|
| 🚗 | 34km |
| ⇄ | 46min (Waterloo) |
| ☺ | 31,180 |
| *i* | ☎ (01753) 743 900 |
| ✈ | Heathrow, 12km |

The town, largely Victorian, is dominated by the ***Castle*** (☎ 869 898 ☛), founded by William the Conqueror and still used by the Royal family. The *Round Tower* was built in the reign of Henry II while the *Horseshoe Cloisters* are of 15thC origin. The *State Apartments* are the formal rooms used for Ceremonial, State and official occasions. They are rich with historical treasures: fine pictures and works of art, furniture, porcelain and armour. *Queen Mary's Dolls' House* is a masterpiece in miniature. *St George's Chapel* is an outstanding example of Perpendicular architecture with exquisite and intricate fan-vaulting and it is the burial place of royalty. The Choir contains the stalls and brasses of the Garter Knights. In June 1999 Prince Edward, the youngest son of Queen Elizabeth II, was married here to Miss Sophie Rhys-Jones. The *Albert Memorial*

Windsor Castle: Changing the Guard

*Chapel* was converted by Queen Victoria from a building erected originally by Henry VII into a shrine for the Prince Consort. Both are buried in the *Mausoleum* at Frogmore in the Home Park.

Across the Thames from Windsor is **Eton**, with its ancient High Street and the famous *College* (☎ 671 177), founded in 1440 by Henry VI and traditionally the school for the British governing class. A few km to the south are *Savill Garden* (Great Park ☎ 860 222 ☛), famous for flowering shrubs and trees, and *Virginia Water*, a large and much-loved area of woodland, exotic plants and artificial lake. **Runnymede** (☎ (01306) 742 809), on the edge of the Great Park, is a broad meadow, where in 1215 King John signed the Magna Carta, on which the American Constitution is based. The *Magna Carta Memorial*, built by the American Bar Association in the style of a classical temple, stands at the foot of Cooper's Hill. Half-way up the slope is the *John F. Kennedy Memorial*.

# PRACTICAL HINTS

❑ **ACCOMMODATION**. There is no official classification for hotels in England, Scotland and Wales. The BTA introduced a voluntary scheme based on one to five crown symbols. The AA and the RAC have similar classifications. The local Tourist Information Centre (TIC) provides information on accommodation in the area and can often make reservations.

❑ **ARRIVAL** (Passport/Visas/Customs). A valid passport is usually necessary to enter the UK. Those subject to immigration control (not EU citizens) have to fill in a landing card and the Immigration Officer may impose a time limit to the stay. Luggage must be made available for examination by Customs officers. Duty free allowances vary according to country of origin and length of stay in the UK. The penalties for landing an animal (pets included) without a licence are very severe.

❑ **BANKING & MONEY**. The pound is divided into 100 pence. Notes are issued to the value of £50, £20, £10 and £5. Coins are £5, £2, £1, 50p, 20p, 10p, 5p, 2p and 1p denominations. There are Bureaux de Change at all main ports, railway stations and airports and at most banks. Normal banking hours are Mon-Fri 0930–1630. Banks, like Western Union (☎ 0800 833 833), operate a quick money transfer to and from any country.

❑ **DISABLED ASSISTANCE**. Artsline (☎ 7388 2227) can give free advice on wheelchair access at arts and entertainment venues (theatres, museums, etc) in the capital. The service includes information available for deaf callers.

❑ **EMERGENCIES**. For Ambulance, Police and Fire Brigade dial ☎ **999**. Public transport services operate a **lost property** service. For LRT (Buses and Underground): 200 Baker St, London NW1; London Taxis: 15 Penton St, London N1.

❑ **ENTERTAINMENT**. The national press supplies details of performances for theatres, ballet, opera, etc. Ticket agencies will deal with bookings by post from overseas. When applying for tickets, requesting brochures or information, a stamped self-addressed envelope should be enclosed. Students can take advantage of special standby rates at certain theatres by showing proof of their status. In London reduced-price tickets can be obtained on the day of performance from the Half-Price Ticket Booth in Leicester Square WC2.

❑ **HOURS OF OPENING**. The opening times may change. It is advisable to check in advance. The majority of places of interest (buildings, museums, exhibitions, etc) are open from 1000 to 1800 (or later on some days), and closed on Christmas Day and major public holidays. Facilities (guides, floor plan, sound-track commentaries, cafés, restaurant, etc) are often made available. Churches are usually closed to the general public during services. Most gardens and parks close at dusk. Some properties have seasonal openings. Restaurants normally close after midnight. Some are shut on Sundays even if it is becoming commonplace for some ethnic restaurants to stay open throughout the week. For cinemas, theatres etc see daily newspapers.

❑ **SHOPPING & MEASUREMENTS**. Many large stores operate a personal export scheme whereby foreign visitors are exempt from paying

Value Added Tax (VAT) on their purchases. Most accept the major credit cards. Measurements are often given in both UK (Imperial) and metric units, and temperatures in both Fahrenheit and Celsius. Shops normally close at 1730, but there is a regular late-night opening (to 2000) once a week and many supermarkets stay open every evening until much later.

## Conversion Factors

| *Weight* | | *Capacity* | |
|---|---|---|---|
| 1lb | = 435g | 1 UK gallon | = 1.2 US gallon<br>4.5 litres |
| 1 ton | = 1,016kg | 1 US gallon | = 0.8 UK gallon |
| *Length* | | *Area* | |
| 1 foot | = 30cm | 1 square yard | = 0.836m² |
| 1 yard | = 91cm | 1 acre | = 4.046m² |
| 1 mile | = 1.6km | 2.5 acres | = 1 hectare |

❑ **TELEPHONE, MAIL & INTERNET**. The UK Area Telephone Code for London is (020). To operate a public **telephone** 50p and 20p coins are needed or in some cases a pre-paid card, obtainable from Post Offices, newsagents and other shops. For overseas collect calls, dial 155. To find a telephone number within Britain, dial Directory Enquiries on 192. Direct dialling to 190 countries is available from any telephone in Britain. The **Post Office** provides specialist services and direct links to 122 nations. There are **Internet** cafés and on-line facilities in various shops.

❑ **TOURIST INFORMATION**. The *Britain Visitor Centre* (1 Regent St, London SW1 ☎ 080 80 1000 000) answers queries on rail, air, coach travel, sightseeing, theatre tickets and accommodation, and provides essential literature. Around Britain there are over 700 Tourist Information Centres (TICs) which provide general guidance for their own areas and details about restaurants and accommodation. Please bear in mind that some TICs are shut in winter months or operate for fewer hours daily. The *London Tourist Board & Convention Bureau* (Glen Ho, Stag Pl SW1 ☎ 7932 2000) is a main source of information on the capital.

❑ **TRAVELLING & MOTORING**. The **Channel Tunnel** links Calais to Folkestone by rail with vehicle-carrying shuttles and express passenger trains (the Eurostar): Waterloo Railway Station is the London terminus. Heathrow and Gatwick handle the bulk of travel by **air**. *Heathrow* is linked by train to Paddington Station and by Underground and bus to central London and *Gatwick* by rail to Victoria Station. *London City Airport* is connected by Shuttle bus to Liverpool Street Station. *Stansted Airport* has a direct rail link to Liverpool Street Station. *Luton Airport* is accessible from King's Cross Station (Thames Link) and by coach.

The **Underground** system (otherwise known as the Tube) is the quickest way to move around London. On certain routes, the Underground trains leave for different destinations from the same platform. The network is divided into six fare zones. Zone 1 covers most of Central London. Make sure your ticket is valid for all the zones you will travel through in order to avoid a penalty. An alternative to the Underground is the **bus**, mostly painted red, one of the famous sights of London. When the Underground has closed, special Night Buses run from Trafalgar Square and the main theatre, cinema and restaurant areas in Central London into the suburbs until 0600. The **Docklands Light Railway** (DLR), connected to the bus, rail and Underground networks, links the City to the East of London, north and south of the Thames. Through the **Tramlink** Wimbledon, Croydon and Beckenham have been brought within easy reach of each other. The service integrates with the Underground (⊖ Wimbledon), bus and rail systems.

Fast Inter-City **trains** serve 90 business and leisure centres throughout Britain. There are passes which give the holder unlimited travel for a specified period. A Motorail service (car on train) is available to a few destinations. From London, trains depart from different stations according to the final destination (see diagram). **Coach** services cover most of the UK and overseas visitors can benefit from special terms.

Traffic travels on the left in the UK. Compulsory seat-belts, stringent measures against the abuse of alcohol, and the enforcement of speed limits have contributed to the improvement in road safety. **Taxis** can be hailed in the streets. When they are free the yellow sign with the word TAXI is lit at the front of the cab. AA (☎ 0800 887 766) and RAC (☎ 0800 082 8282) are the principal motoring organisations. Both offer special membership terms for overseas visitors. **Parking** is severely restricted. Meters, and a range of car parks, are available in city centres. Illegally-parked vehicles are subject to heavy fines, clamping or being towed away. Recovery of the vehicle can be costly and time-consuming.

❑ **WEATHER**. The AA Roadwatch (☎ 08705 500 600) provides information by telephone on weather conditions and traffic around Britain.

**LONDON & SURROUNDING COUNTIES**

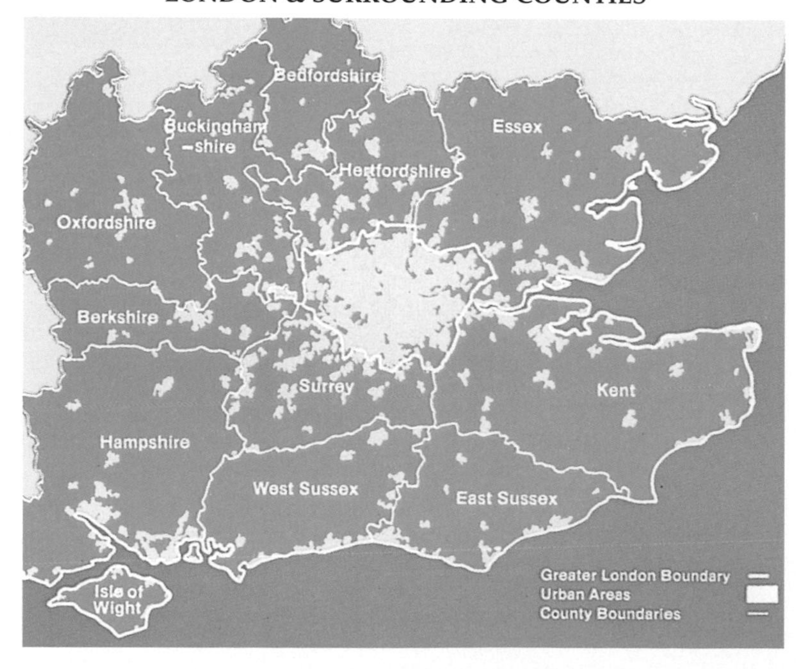

# MOTORWAYS & MAJOR ROADS

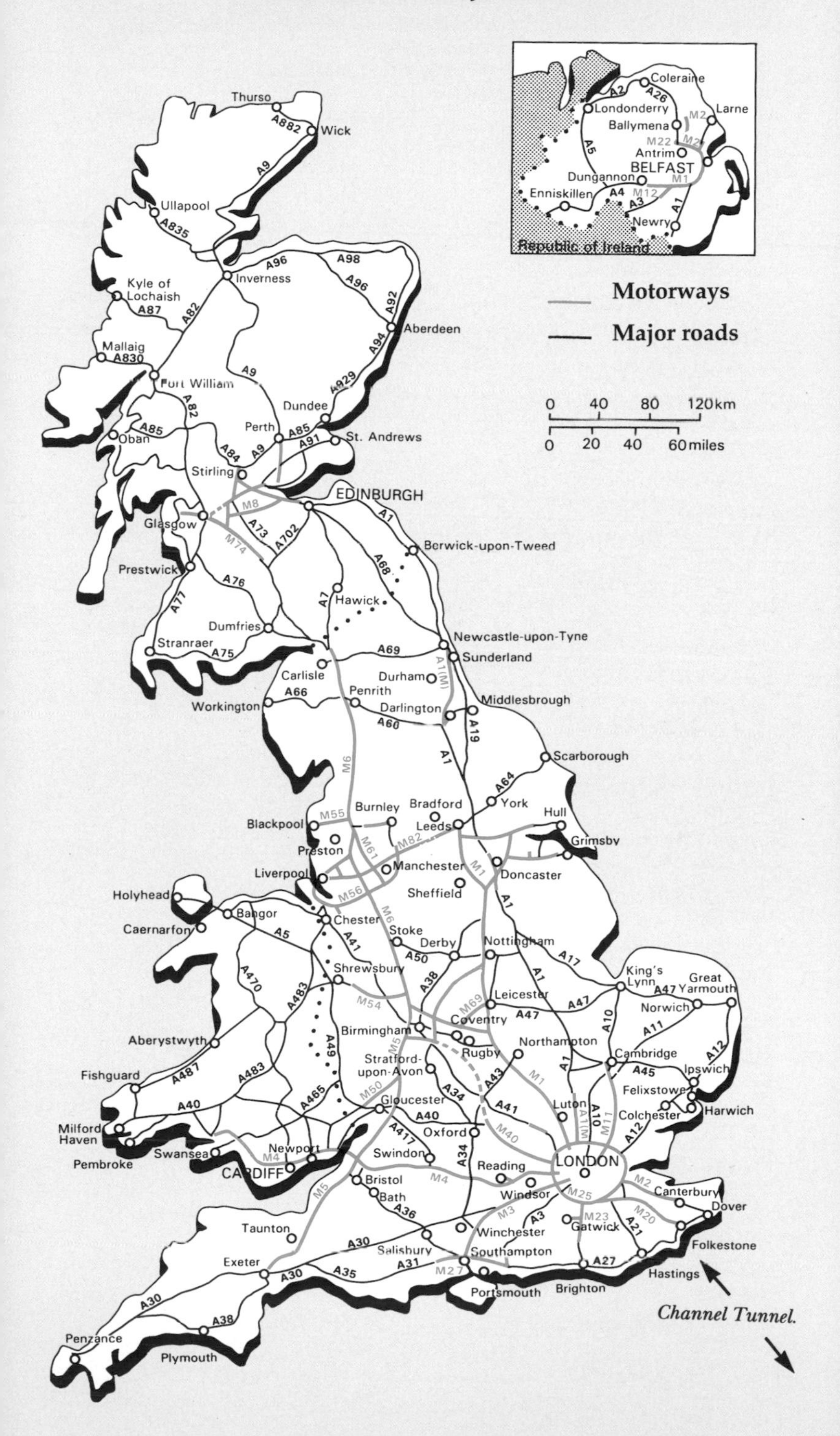

Area Telephone Code for London (020)

**AIRPORTS**

*Gutwick* (01293) 535 353

*Heathrow* 8759 4321

*London City* 7646 4000

*Luton* (01582) 405100

*Stansted* (01279) 680 500

*Heliport Battersea* 7228 0181

**CAR HIRE**

*Avis* 8 Balderton St W1 7917 6700

*Budget* 0800 181181

*Easy Rent-a-Car* 42 Gloucester Crescent NW1 7482 4050

*Enterprise Rent-A-Car* 466 Edgware Rd W2 7723 4800

*Hertz* 35 Edgware Rd W2 7402 4242

**EMBASSIES**

*Argentina* 65 Brook St W1 7318 1300

*Australia* Strand WC2 7379 4334

*Austria* 18 Belgrave Mews West SW1 7235 3731

*Belgium* 103 Eaton Sq SW1 7470 3700

*Canada* 5 Trafalgar Sq SW1 7258 6600

*China* 49 Portland Pl W1 7636 5197

*Denmark* 55 Sloane St SW1 7333 0200

*Finland* 38 Chesham Pl SW1 7838 6200

*France* 58 Knightsbridge SW1 7201 1000

*Germany* 23 Belgrave Sq SW1 7824 1300

*Greece* 1a Holland Park W11 7221 6467

*India* Aldwych WC2 7836 8484

*Ireland* 17 Grosvenor Pl SW1 7235 2171

*Israel* 2 Palace Green W8 7957 9500

*Italy* 14 Three Kings Yard W1 7312 2200

*Luxembourg* 27 Wilton Crescent SW1 7235 6961

*Netherlands* 38 Hyde Park Gate SW7 7590 3200

*New Zealand* Haymarket SW1 7930 8422

*Norway* 25 Belgrave Sq SW1 7591 5500

*Portugal* 11 Belgrave Sq SW1 7235 5331

*South Africa* Trafalgar Sq WC2 7451 7299

*Spain* 39 Chesham Pl SW1 7235 5555

*Sweden* 11 Montagu Pl W1 7917 6400

*Switzerland* 16–18 Montagu Pl W1 7616 6000

*United States of America* Grosvenor Sq W1 7499 6000

**HOTELS**

*Athenaeum* 116 Piccadilly W1 7499 3464

*Basil Street* 8 Basil St SW3 7581 3311

*Beaufort* 33 Beaufort Gdns SW3 7584 5252

*Berkeley* Wilton Pl SW1 7235 6000

*Blake's* 33 Roland Gdns SW7 7370 6701

*Britannia* Grosvenor Sq W1 7629 9400

*Brown's* Albemarle St W1 7493 6020

*Capital* 22-24 Basil St SW3 7589 5171

*Chesterfield* 35 Charles St W1 7491 2622

*Churchill* 30 Portman Sq W1 7486 5800

*Claridge's* Brook St W1 7629 8860

*Connaught* Carlos Pl W1 7499 7070

*Conrad* Chelsea Harbour SW10
7823 3000

*Dorchester* Park Lane W1
7629 8888

*Duke's* 35 St James's Pl SW1
7491 4840

*Durley House* 115 Sloane St SW1
7235 5537

*Durrants* George St W1
7935 8131

*Eleven Cadogan Gardens* 11 Cadogan Gdns SW3
7730 7000

*51 Buckingham Gate*
51 Buckingham Gate SW1
7769 7766

*47 Park Street* 47 Park St W1
7491 7282

*Forum* 97-109 Cromwell Rd SW7
7370 5757

*Four Seasons* Hamilton Pl W1
7499 0888

*Grafton* 130 Tottenham Court Rd W1
7388 4131

*Great Eastern Hotel*
40 Liverpool St EC2
7618 5000

*Grosvenor House* Park Lane W1
7499 6363

*Halkin* 5 Halkin St SW1
7333 1000

*Hampshire* Leicester Sq WC2
7839 9399

*Hazlitt's* 6 Frith St W1
7434 1771

*Hempel* 31 Craven Hill Gdns W2
7298 9000

*Hilton London Metropole*
Edgware Rd W2
7402 4141

*Hyatt Carlton Tower*
2 Cadogan Pl SW1
7235 5411

*Inter-Continental* 1 Hamilton Pl W1
7409 3131

*Kenilworth* 97 Gt Russell St WC1
7637 3477

*Kensington Hilton* 179 Holland Park Ave W11
7603 3355

*Landmark* 222 Marylebone Rd NW1
7631 8000

*Lanesborough* 1 Lanesborough Pl SW1
7259 5599

*Langham Hilton* 1 Portland Pl W1
7636 1000

*Lincoln House* 33 Gloucester Pl W1
7935 6238

*London Hilton* 22 Park Lane W1
7493 8000

*London Marriott* Grosvenor Sq W1
7493 1232

*Mandarin Oriental Hyde Park*
66 Knightsbridge SW1
7235 2000

*Marlborough* 9 Bloomsbury St WC1
7636 5601

*Mayfair* Stratton St W1
7629 7777

*Meridien (Le)* 21 Piccadilly W1
7734 8000

*Metropolitan* Old Park Lane W1
7447 1047

*Mountbatten* 20 Monmouth St WC2
7836 4300

*Number Sixteen* 16 Sumner Pl SW7
7589 5232

*One Aldwych* 1 Aldwych WC2
7300 1000

*Portman* 22 Portman Sq W1
7486 5844

*Portobello* 22 Stanley Gdns W11
7727 2777

*Ritz* 150 Piccadilly W1
7493 8181

*Royal Garden*
2 Kensington High St W8
7937 8000

*Royal Lancaster* Lancaster Ter W2
7262 6737

*St James Court*
45 Buckingham Gate SW1
7834 6655

*St Martin's Lane*
45 St Martin's Lane WC2
7300 5500

*Sanderson* Berners St W1
7300 1400

*Savoy (The)* Strand WC2
7836 4343

*Selfridge* Orchard St W1
7408 2080

*Sheraton Park Tower*
101 Knightsbridge SW1
7235 8050

*13 Half Moon Street*
13 Half Moon St W1
7409 0207

*Thistle Tower* St Katharine's Way E1
7481 2575

*Westbourne* 165 Westbourne
Grove W11
7243 6008

*Westbury* New Bond St W1
7629 7755

*White House* Albany St NW1
7387 1200

## ❑ RESTAURANTS

*Alastair Little* 49 Frith St W1
7734 5183

*Al Hamra* 31 Shepherd Market W1
7493 1954

*Anna's Place* 90 Mildmay Park N1
7249 9379

*Apollonia* 17a Percy St W1
7636 4140

*Ard Ri Dining Room*
88 Marylebone Lane W1
7935 9311

*Arirang* 31 Poland St W1
7437 6633

*Asuka* 209a Baker St NW1
7486 5026

*Atlantic (The)* 20 Glasshouse St W1
7734 4888

*Aubergine* 11 Park Walk SW10
7352 3449

*Aurora* Great Eastern Hotel EC2
7618 5000

*Axis* One Aldwych Hotel WC2
7300 0300

*Bagatelle* Wallace Collection W1
7563 9504

*Bank* 1 Kingsway WC2
7379 9797

*Belgo Noord* 72 Chalk Farm Rd NW1
7267 0718

*Bengal Clipper* Butlers Wharf SE1
7357 9001

*Benihana* 37 Sackville St W1
7494 2525

*Bentley's* 11 Swallow St W1
7734 4756

*Bibendum* 81 Fulham Rd SW3
7581 5817

*Bloom's* 7 Montague St WC1
7323 1717

*Bluebird* 350 Kings Rd SW3
7559 1000

*Blue Elephant*
4 Fulham Broadway SW6
7385 6595

*Boisdale* 15 Eccleston St SW1
7730 6922

*Bombay Brasserie*
Courtfield Close SW7
7370 4040

*Brasserie Rocque*
37 Broadgate Circle EC2
7338 7919

*Borshtch 'N' Tears*
45 Beauchamp Pl SW3
7589 5003

*Café Lazeez* 21 Dean St W1
7434 9393

*Café Royal* 68 Regent St W1
7439 6320

*Café Spice* 16 Prescott St E1
7488 9242

*Cambio de Tercio*
163 Old Brompton Rd SW5
7244 8970

*Canteen (The)* Chelsea
Harbour SW10
7351 7330

*Caravaggio* 107 Leadenhall St EC3
7626 6206

*Casa Giovanni* 106 Finchley Rd NW3
7435 4913

*Cecconi's* 5a Burlington Gdns W1
7434 1509

*Chaopraya* 22 St Christopher's Pl W1
7486 0777

*Chez Gérard* 31 Dover St W1
7499 8171

*China House* 160 Piccadilly W1
7499 6996

*Chiquito* 20 Leicester Sq WC2
7839 6925

*Churchill Arms* 119 Kensington
Church St W8
7792 1246

*Chutney Mary* 535 King's Rd SW10
7351 3113

*Cinnamon Club* Gt Smith St SW1
7222 2555

*City Rhodes* 1 New Street Sq EC2
7583 1313

*Clarke's* 124 Kensington
Church St W8
7221 9225

*Concordia Notte* 29 Craven Rd W2
7402 4985

*Coq d'Argent* 1 Poultry EC2
7395 5000

*Corney & Barrow* 109 Old Broad St EC2
7638 9308

*Criterion (The)* Piccadilly Circus W1
7925 0909

*Dan's* 119 Sydney St SW3
7352 2718

*Delfina* 50 Bermonsdey St EC1
7357 0244

*Don Pepe* 99 Frampton St NW8
7262 3834

*Emporio Armani*
191 Brompton Rd SW3
7823 8818

*English Garden* 10 Lincoln St SW3
7584 7272

*Fina Estampa* 150 Tooley St SE1
7403 1342

*Firebird* 23 Conduit St W1
7493 7000

*Fish* 149 Central St EC1
7253 4970

*Flounders* 19 Tavistock St WC2
7836 3925

*Fortnum & Mason* 181 Piccadilly W1
7734 8040

*Four Seasons* Hamilton Pl W1
7499 0888

*Fung Shing* 15 Lisle St WC2
7734 0284

*Gay Hussar* 2 Greek St W1
7437 0973

*Gaudi* 63 Clerkenwell Rd E1
7608 3220

*Gordon Ramsay*
68 Royal Hospital Rd SW3
7352 4441

*Gradwins* 1 Minster Court,
Monk Lane EC3
7444 0004

*Greenhouse* 27a Hays Mews W1
7499 3331

*Green Olive* 5 Warwick Pl W9
7289 2469

*Hard Rock Café*
150 Old Park Lane W1
7629 0382

*Harvey Nichols*
109 Knightsbridge SW1
7235 5250

*Imperial City Royal Exchange*
Cornhill EC3 7626 3437

*Incognico* 117 Shaftesbury Ave WC2
7836 8866

*Ivy* 1 West St WC2
7836 4751

*John Burton-Race*
Landmark Hotel NW1
7723 7800

*Kaya* 42 Albemarle St W1
7499 0622

*Khan's* 3 Harrington Rd SW7
7581 2900

*Kaspia* 18 Bruton Pl W1
7493 2612

*Ken Lo's Memories* 67 Ebury St SW1
7730 7734

*Kensington Place*
201 Kensington Church St W8
7727 3184

*Kitchen* 61 Gt Queen St WC2
7404 6114

*Lalibela* 137 Fortress Rd N5
7284 0600

*Langan's Bistro* 26 Devonshire St W1
7935 4531

*Langan's Brasserie* Stratton St W1
7493 6437

*Launceston Place*
1a Launceston Pl W8
7937 6912

*Le Caprice* Arlington St SW1
7629 2239

*Le Gavroche* 43 Upper Brook St W1
7408 0881

*Leith's* 41 Beak St W1
7287 2057

*L'Escargot* 48 Greek St W1
7437 2679

*Lemonia* 89 Regent's Park Rd NW1
7586 7454

*Lee Ho Fook* 15 Gerrard St W1
7439 4588

*L'Incontro* 87 Pimlico Rd SW1
7730 6327

*Lou Pescadou*
241 Old Brompton Rd SW5
7370 1057

*Luigi's* 15 Tavistock St WC2
7240 1795

*Mandalay* 444 Edgware Rd W2
7258 3696

*Mandola* 139 Westbourne Grove W11
7229 4734

*Manzi's* 2 Leicester St WC2
7734 0224

*Mao Tai* 58 New King's Rd SW6
7731 2524

*Maxwell's* 8-9 James St WC2
7836 0303

*Mezzo* 100 Wardour St W1
7314 4000

*Minogues* 80 Liverpool Rd N1
7354 4440

*Mirabelle* 56 Curzon St W1
7499 4636

*Mon Plaisir* 21 Monmouth St WC2
7836 7243

*Moshi Moshi* Liverpool
Street Station EC2
7247 3227

*Montpeliano* 13 Montpelier St SW7
7589 0032

*Neal Street* 26 Neal St WC2
7836 8368

*New Diamond* 23 Lisle St WC2
7437 2517

*Nico Central* 35 Gt Portland St W1
7436 8846

*Nobu* 19 Old Park Lane W1
7447 4747

*Noura* 16 Hobart Pl SW1
7235 9444

*Novelli* 30 Clerkenwell Green EC1
7251 6606

*Oak Room (The)*
Le Meridien Hotel W1
7437 0202

*Odins* 27 Devonshire St W1
7935 7296

*One-O-One*
Sheraton Park Tower Hotel SW1
7290 7101

*One Lombard Street* 1 Lombard St EC3
7929 6611

*Oriental (The)* Dorchester Hotel W1
7629 8888

*Oxo Tower* Barge House St SE1
7803 3888

*Ozer* 4 Langham Pl W1
7323 0505

*Petrus* 33 St James's SW1
7930 4272

*Piccola Venezia* 39 Thurloe Pl SW7
7589 3883

*Pied A Terre* 34 Charlotte St W1
7636 1178

*Pizza Metro* 64c Battersea Rise SW11
7228 3812

*Pizza on the Park*
11 Knightsbridge SW1
7235 5550

*Planet Hollywood* 13 Coventry St W1
7287 1000

*Poissonerie de l'Avenue*
82 Sloane Ave SW3
7589 2457

*Poons* 4 Leicester St WC2
7437 1528

*Potemkin* 144 Clerkenwell Rd EC1
7278 6661

*Prism* 147 Leadenhall St EC3
7256 3888

*Quaglino's* 16 Bury St SW1
7930 6767

*Real Greek* 15 Hoxton Market N1
7739 8212

*Rebato's* 169 South Lambeth Rd SW8
7735 6388

*Red Fort* 77 Dean St W1
7437 2115

*River Café* Rainville Rd W6
7381 8824

*Rules* 35 Maiden Lane WC2
7836 5314

*Rupee Room* 10 Copthall Ave EC2
7628 1555

*Salloos* 62 Kinnerton St SW1
7235 4444

*San Lorenzo* 22 Beauchamp Pl SW3
7584 1074

*Santini* 29 Ebury St SW1
7730 4094

*Savoy Grill* The Savoy WC2
7836 4343

*Scotts* 20 Mount St W1
7629 5248

*Searcy's* The Barbican, Silk St EC2
7588 3008

*Sheekey's* 28-32 St Martin's Ct WC2
7240 2565

*Shepherd's* Marsham Court,
Marsham St SW1
7834 9552

*Simpsons* 100 Strand WC2
7836 9112

*Soho Soho* 11 Frith Street W1
7494 3491

*Soufflé (Le)* Inter-Continental W1
7318 8577

*Spoon* Sanderson Hotel W1
7300 1444

*Square (The)* 6 Bruton St W1
7495 7100

*Sri Siam* 16 Old Compton St W1
7434 3544

*St Quentin's* 243 Brompton Rd SW3
7581 5131

*Stephen Bull* 5-7 Blandford St W1
7486 9696

*Suntory* 72 St James's St SW1
7409 0201

*Tamarind* 20 Queen Street W1
7629 3561

*Tante Claire (La)* Wilton Pl SW1
7823 2003

*Tatsuso* 32 Broadgate Circle EC2
7638 5863

*Terminus* Great Eastern Hotel EC2
7818 5000

*Terrace (The)* Dorchester Hotel W1
7629 8888

*Titanic* 81 Brewer St W1
7437 1912

*Topkapi* 25 Marylebone High St W1
7486 1872

*Toucan* 19 Carlisle St W1
7437 4123

*Twenty Four* 42 Old Broad St EC2
7877 2424

*Vegia Zena* 17 Princess Rd NW1
7483 0192

*Vertigo* 42 Old Broad St EC2
7877 7842

*Viet-Hoa* 72 Kingsland Rd E2
7729 8293

*Veeraswamy* Swallow St W1
7734 1401

*Wheeler's* 12a Duke of York St SW1
7930 2460

*Whittington's* 21 College Hill EC4
7248 5855

*Wiltons* 55 Jermyn St W1
7629 9955

*Zafferano* 15 Loundes St SW1
7235 5800

*Zaika* 257 Fulham Rd SW3
7351 7823

*Zilli Fish* 36 Brewer St W1
7734 8649

## ❑ SOS

- **Police / Fire Brigade / Ambulance** 999
- **Chemists** (late closing)

*Bliss* 5 Marble Arch W1
7723 6116

- **Helplines**

*Drugs* 0800 776 600

*Samaritans* 0845 790 9090

- **Hospitals**

*St Mary's* Praed St W2
7886 6666

*St Thomas'* Lambeth Palace Rd SE1
7928 9292

*University College* Gower St WC1
7387 9300

## ❑ USEFUL TELEPHONE NUMBERS

*Directory Enquiries* 192

*Operator* 100

- **International Calls**

*General Enquiries* 155

*Directories* 153

*International Codes* 00 –

Australia 61; Austria 43; Belgium 32; Canada 1; Denmark 45; Finland 358; France 33; Germany 49; Greece 30; Hong Kong 852; Ireland 353; Italy 39; Liechtenstein 423; Luxemburg 352; Netherlands 31; Norway 47; Portugal 351; Saudi Arabia 966; Spain 34; Sweden 46; Switzerland 41; USA 1.

## ❑ TRANSPORT

*General Information* (London)
7222 1234

*Buses* 7222 5600

*Docklands Light Railway* (DLR)
7363 9700

*Eurostar* 7922 6180

*National Express* (coaches)
0870 580 8080

*National Rail* ⇌ 0845 748 4950

*River Services* 7918 4753

*Underground* (⊖) 7222 5600

*Victoria Coach Station*
7730 3466

## ❑ TRAVEL AGENCIES

*American Express* Stag Pl SW1
7834 5555

*Thomas Cook* 45 Berkeley St W1
0870 566 6262

*Trinatours* 74 New Oxford St WC1
7436 4488

## ❑ VISITOR INFORMATION

*Britain Visitor Centre*
1 Regent St SW1 080 80 1000 000

*London Tourist Board & Convention Bureau* Glen Ho, Stag Pl SW1
7932 2000

# Underground Network

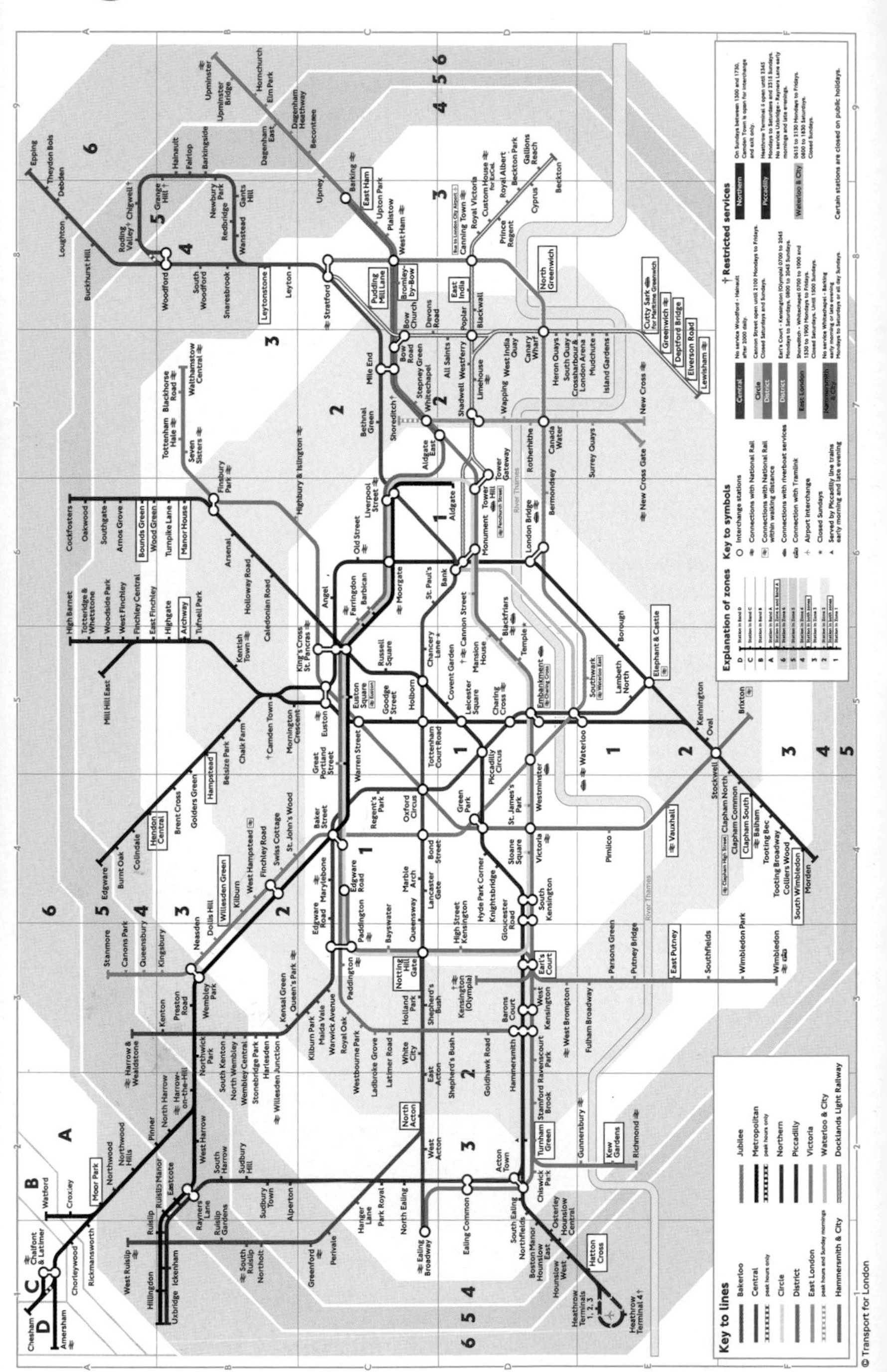

# Index to stations

| Grid | Station & facilities | Zone |
|---|---|---|
| D2 | Acton Town | 3 |
| D6 | Aldgate | 1 |
| D7 | Aldgate East | 1 |
| D7 | All Saints | 2 |
| B2 | Alperton 🚻 | 4 |
| A1 | Amersham P 🚲 🚻 | D |
| C6 | Angel | 1 |
| B5 | Archway | 2&3 |
| A6 | Arnos Grove P 🚲 | 4 |
| B6 | Arsenal | 2 |
| C4 | Baker Street 🚻 | 1 |
| F4 | Balham 🚲 | 3 |
| D6 | Bank 🚻 | 1 |
| C6 | Barbican | 1 |
| C8 | Barking 🚲 🚻 | 4 |
| B9 | Barkingside P 🚻 | 5 |
| D3 | Barons Court | 2 |
| C3 | Bayswater | 1 |
| D9 | Beckton 🚲 | 3 |
| D8 | Beckton Park 🚲 | 3 |
| C9 | Becontree 🚲 🚻 | 5 |
| B5 | Belsize Park | 2 |
| C7 | Bethnal Green | 2 |
| D5 | Blackfriars | 1 |
| B7 | Blackhorse Road P 🚲 | 3 |
| D8 | Blackwall 🚲 | 2 |
| C4 | Bond Street | 1 |
| E5 | Borough | 1 |
| D1 | Boston Manor 🚻 | 4 |
| A6 | Bounds Green 🚲 | 3&4 |
| C7 | Bow Church | 2 |
| C7 | Bow Road 🚲 | 2 |
| B4 | Brent Cross P 🚲 | 3 |
| F5 | Brixton 🚲 | 2 |
| C8 | Bromley-by-Bow | 2&3 |
| A8 | Buckhurst Hill P 🚲 🚻 | 5 |
| A4 | Burnt Oak P | 4 |
| B6 | Caledonian Road | 2 |
| B5 | Camden Town | 2 |
| D7 | Canada Water 🚲 🚻 | 2 |
| D7 | Canary Wharf | 2 |
| D8 | Canning Town 🚲 🚻 | 3 |
| D6 | Cannon Street † | 1 |
| A3 | Canons Park P 🚲 🚻 | 5 |
| A1 | Chalfont & Latimer P 🚲 🚻 | C |
| B5 | Chalk Farm | 2 |
| C5 | Chancery Lane ★ | 1 |
| D5 | Charing Cross 🚻 | 1 |
| A1 | Chesham P 🚲 🚻 | D |
| A8 | Chigwell † | 5 |
| D2 | Chiswick Park 🚲 | 3 |
| A1 | Chorleywood P 🚲 🚻 | B |
| F4 | Clapham Common 🚲 | 2 |
| F5 | Clapham North 🚲 | 2 |
| F4 | Clapham South 🚲 | 2&3 |
| A6 | Cockfosters P 🚲 🚻 | 5 |
| A4 | Colindale P 🚲 | 4 |
| F4 | Colliers Wood | 3 |
| D5 | Covent Garden | 1 |
| E7 | Crossharbour & London Arena | 2 |
| A2 | Croxley P 🚲 🚻 | A |
| D8 | Custom House 🚲 | 3 |
| E7 | Cutty Sark 🚲 | 2&3 |
| D8 | Cyprus 🚲 | 3 |
| B9 | Dagenham East 🚲 | 5 |
| B9 | Dagenham Heathway 🚻 | 5 |
| A8 | Debden P 🚲 | 6 |
| E7 | Deptford Bridge 🚲 | 2&3 |
| C7 | Devons Road | 2 |
| B3 | Dollis Hill 🚻 | 3 |
| C1 | Ealing Broadway 🚲 🚻 | 3 |
| D2 | Ealing Common | 3 |
| D3 | Earl's Court | 1&2 |
| C2 | East Acton | 2 |
| B2 | Eastcote P 🚻 | 5 |
| A5 | East Finchley P 🚲 | 3 |
| C8 | East Ham 🚲 | 3&4 |
| D8 | East India 🚲 | 2&3 |
| E3 | East Putney 🚲 | 2&3 |
| A4 | Edgware P 🚲 | 5 |
| C4 | Edgware Road (Bakerloo) | 1 |
| C4 | Edgware Road (Circle/District/H&C) | 1 |
| E5 | Elephant & Castle | 1&2 |
| B9 | Elm Park | 6 |
| E7 | Elverson Road 🚲 | 2&3 |
| D5 | Embankment | 1 |
| A9 | Epping P 🚲 🚻 | 6 |
| C5 | Euston 🚻 ℹ | 1 |
| C5 | Euston Square | 1 |
| B9 | Fairlop P 🚻 | 5 |
| C6 | Farringdon 🚻 | 1 |
| A5 | Finchley Central P 🚲 | 4 |
| B4 | Finchley Road | 2 |
| B6 | Finsbury Park 🚲 🚻 | 2 |
| E3 | Fulham Broadway | 2 |
| D9 | Gallions Reach 🚲 | 3 |
| B8 | Gants Hill P | 4 |
| D4 | Gloucester Road 🚲 🚻 | 1 |
| B5 | Golders Green | 3 |
| D3 | Goldhawk Road | 2 |
| C5 | Goodge Street | 1 |
| B9 | Grange Hill † 🚻 | 5 |
| C5 | Great Portland Street | 1 |
| C1 | Greenford P 🚲 🚻 | 4 |
| E7 | Greenwich 🚲 | 2&3 |
| D4 | Green Park 🚻 | 1 |
| E2 | Gunnersbury 🚲 | 3 |
| B9 | Hainault P 🚲 🚻 | 5 |
| D3 | Hammersmith 🚲 ℹ | 2 |
| B5 | Hampstead 🚻 | 2&3 |
| C2 | Hanger Lane 🚲 🚻 | 3 |
| B3 | Harlesden | 3 |
| A3 | Harrow & Wealdstone P | 5 |
| B2 | Harrow-on-the Hill P 🚲 🚻 | 5 |
| E1 | Hatton Cross P 🚲 | 5&6 |
| E1 | Heathrow Terminals 1, 2, 3 🚻 ℹ | 6 |
| E1 | Heathrow Terminal 4 🚻 ℹ | 6 |
| A4 | Hendon Central 🚻 | 3&4 |
| D7 | Heron Quays | 2 |
| A5 | High Barnet P 🚲 🚻 | 5 |
| B6 | Highbury & Islington 🚲 | 2 |
| B5 | Highgate P | 3 |
| D3 | High Street Kensington | 1 |
| A1 | Hillingdon P 🚲 | 6 |
| C5 | Holborn | 1 |
| C3 | Holland Park 🚲 | 2 |
| B6 | Holloway Road | 2 |
| B9 | Hornchurch P 🚲 | 6 |
| D1 | Hounslow Central 🚲 🚻 | 4 |
| D1 | Hounslow East P 🚻 | 4 |
| D1 | Hounslow West P 🚲 | 5 |
| D4 | Hyde Park Corner | 1 |
| B1 | Ickenham P 🚲 | 6 |
| E7 | Island Gardens 🚻 | 2 |
| E5 | Kennington 🚲 | 2 |
| B3 | Kensal Green | 2 |
| D3 | Kensington (Olympia) † 🚻 | 2 |
| B5 | Kentish Town | 2 |
| B3 | Kenton | 4 |
| E2 | Kew Gardens 🚲 🚻 | 3&4 |
| B4 | Kilburn 🚲 🚻 | 2 |
| C3 | Kilburn Park | 2 |
| B3 | Kingsbury 🚲 🚻 | 4 |
| C5 | King's Cross St. Pancras 🚲 🚻 ℹ | 1 |
| D4 | Knightsbridge | 1 |
| C3 | Ladbroke Grove 🚲 | 2 |
| E5 | Lambeth North 🚲 | 1 |
| C4 | Lancaster Gate | 1 |
| C3 | Latimer Road | 2 |
| D5 | Leicester Square | 1 |
| E7 | Lewisham 🚲 | 2&3 |
| B8 | Leyton 🚻 | 3 |
| B8 | Leytonstone 🚻 | 3&4 |
| D7 | Limehouse | 2 |
| C6 | Liverpool Street 🚲 🚻 ℹ | 1 |
| D6 | London Bridge 🚻 | 1 |
| A8 | Loughton P 🚲 | 6 |
| C3 | Maida Vale | 2 |
| B6 | Manor House | 2&3 |
| D5 | Mansion House | 1 |
| C4 | Marble Arch | 1 |
| C4 | Marylebone 🚲 🚻 | 1 |
| C7 | Mile End | 2 |
| A5 | Mill Hill East P | 4 |
| D6 | Monument | 1 |
| C6 | Moorgate | 1 |
| A2 | Moor Park P 🚲 🚻 | 6&A |
| F4 | Morden P 🚻 | 4 |
| B5 | Mornington Crescent | 2 |
| E7 | Mudchute | 2 |
| B3 | Neasden 🚻 | 3 |
| B9 | Newbury Park P 🚲 🚻 | 4 |
| E7 | New Cross 🚲 | 2 |
| E7 | New Cross Gate | 2 |
| C2 | North Acton | 2&3 |
| C2 | North Ealing P 🚲 🚻 | 3 |
| D2 | Northfields 🚲 🚻 | 3 |
| D8 | North Greenwich 🚲 🚻 | 2&3 |
| B2 | North Harrow 🚲 🚻 | 5 |
| B1 | Northolt 🚲 🚻 | 5 |
| B3 | North Wembley | 4 |
| B3 | Northwick Park 🚲 🚻 | 4 |
| A2 | Northwood P 🚲 🚻 | 6 |
| A2 | Northwood Hills 🚻 | 6 |
| C3 | Notting Hill Gate | 1&2 |
| A6 | Oakwood P 🚲 🚻 | 5 |
| C6 | Old Street | 1 |
| D3 | Olympia † 🚻 | 2 |
| D1 | Osterley P 🚲 🚻 | 4 |
| E5 | Oval | 2 |
| C4 | Oxford Circus ℹ | 1 |
| C3 | Paddington 🚻 | 1 |
| C2 | Park Royal 🚻 | 3 |
| E3 | Parsons Green 🚲 | 2 |
| C1 | Perivale P 🚲 🚻 | 4 |
| D5 | Piccadilly Circus 🚻 ℹ | 1 |
| E4 | Pimlico | 1 |
| A2 | Pinner P 🚲 🚻 | 5 |
| C8 | Plaistow 🚲 | 3 |
| D7 | Poplar 🚲 🚻 | 2 |
| B3 | Preston Road 🚻 | 4 |
| D8 | Prince Regent 🚲 | 3 |
| C8 | Pudding Mill Lane | 2&3 |
| E3 | Putney Bridge 🚲 | 2 |
| A3 | Queensbury P 🚲 🚻 | 4 |
| B3 | Queen's Park | 2 |
| C4 | Queensway | 1 |
| D3 | Ravenscourt Park 🚲 | 2 |
| B2 | Rayners Lane P 🚲 🚻 | 5 |
| B8 | Redbridge P 🚲 🚻 | 4 |
| C4 | Regent's Park | 1 |
| E2 | Richmond P 🚲 🚻 | 4 |
| A1 | Rickmansworth P 🚲 🚻 | A |
| A8 | Roding Valley † | 5 |
| D7 | Rotherhithe 🚲 | 2 |
| D8 | Royal Albert 🚲 | 3 |
| C3 | Royal Oak | 2 |
| D8 | Royal Victoria 🚲 | 3 |
| A1 | Ruislip P 🚲 🚻 | 6 |
| B1 | Ruislip Gardens P 🚻 | 5 |
| B2 | Ruislip Manor 🚻 | 6 |
| C5 | Russell Square | 1 |
| D4 | St. James's Park ℹ | 1 |
| B4 | St. John's Wood 🚲 🚻 | 2 |
| C6 | St. Paul's | 1 |
| B7 | Seven Sisters 🚲 🚻 | 3 |
| D7 | Shadwell | 2 |
| C3 | Shepherd's Bush (Central) | 2 |
| D3 | Shepherd's Bush (H&C) | 2 |
| C7 | Shoreditch † | 2 |
| D4 | Sloane Square | 1 |
| B8 | Snaresbrook P 🚲 🚻 | 4 |
| D2 | South Ealing | 3 |
| E3 | Southfields | 3 |
| A6 | Southgate | 4 |
| B2 | South Harrow P | 5 |
| D4 | South Kensington 🚻 | 1 |
| B3 | South Kenton | 4 |
| D7 | South Quay | 2 |
| B1 | South Ruislip P 🚲 | 5 |
| E5 | Southwark 🚲 | 1 |
| F4 | South Wimbledon | 3&4 |
| B8 | South Woodford 🚲 🚻 | 4 |
| D2 | Stamford Brook 🚲 🚻 | 2 |
| A3 | Stanmore P 🚲 🚻 | 5 |
| C7 | Stepney Green | 2 |
| E5 | Stockwell | 2 |
| B3 | Stonebridge Park | 3 |
| C8 | Stratford | 3 |
| B2 | Sudbury Hill 🚻 | 4 |
| B2 | Sudbury Town P 🚲 🚻 | 4 |
| E7 | Surrey Quays 🚲 | 2 |
| B4 | Swiss Cottage 🚲 | 2 |
| D5 | Temple ★ | 1 |
| A8 | Theydon Bois P 🚻 | 6 |
| F4 | Tooting Bec | 3 |
| F4 | Tooting Broadway | 3 |
| C5 | Tottenham Court Road | 1 |
| B7 | Tottenham Hale P 🚲 🚻 | 3 |
| A5 | Totteridge & Whetstone P 🚲 🚻 | 4 |
| D7 | Tower Gateway | 1 |
| D6 | Tower Hill | 1 |
| B5 | Tufnell Park | 2 |
| D2 | Turnham Green | 2/3 |
| B6 | Turnpike Lane | 3 |
| B9 | Upminster P 🚲 🚻 | 6 |
| B9 | Upminster Bridge | 6 |
| C9 | Upney 🚻 | 4 |
| C8 | Upton Park | 3 |
| B1 | Uxbridge 🚲 ℹ | 6 |
| E4 | Vauxhall | 1&2 |
| D4 | Victoria 🚻 ℹ | 1 |
| B7 | Walthamstow Central P 🚲 | 3 |
| B8 | Wanstead P | 4 |
| D7 | Wapping | 2 |
| C5 | Warren Street | 1 |
| C3 | Warwick Avenue | 2 |
| E5 | Waterloo 🚲 🚻 | 1 |
| A2 | Watford P 🚲 🚻 | B |
| B3 | Wembley Central 🚻 | 4 |
| B3 | Wembley Park P 🚲 🚻 | 4 |
| C2 | West Acton 🚲 🚻 | 3 |
| C3 | Westbourne Park | 2 |
| D3 | West Brompton ★ | 2 |
| D7 | Westferry | 2 |
| A5 | West Finchley 🚻 | 4 |
| C8 | West Ham | 3 |
| B4 | West Hampstead 🚻 | 2 |
| B2 | West Harrow 🚻 | 5 |
| D7 | West India Quay | 2 |
| D3 | West Kensington | 2 |
| D5 | Westminster | 1 |
| A1 | West Ruislip P 🚲 🚻 | 6 |
| C7 | Whitechapel 🚻 | 2 |
| C3 | White City 🚻 | 2 |
| B4 | Willesden Green 🚲 🚻 | 2&3 |
| B3 | Willesden Junction 🚲 🚻 | 3 |
| F3 | Wimbledon P 🚲 🚻 | 3 |
| F3 | Wimbledon Park | 3 |
| B8 | Woodford P 🚲 🚻 | 4 |
| A6 | Wood Green 🚲 | 3 |
| A5 | Woodside Park P 🚲 🚻 | 4 |

## Explanation of symbols

P Stations with car parks.

🚲 Stations with bicycle parking.

🚻 Stations with ladies and gents toilets on site or nearby.
You must have a valid ticket to use toilets in a Compulsory Ticket Area.

ℹ Stations with London Transport Travel Information Centre.

★ Closed Sundays.

† Restricted services.
See key to symbols on the other side of this leaflet.

Zones The Underground Network is divided into fare zones, details in the Underground and Bus fares within Greater London booklet. The Zone number is shown beside the station name.

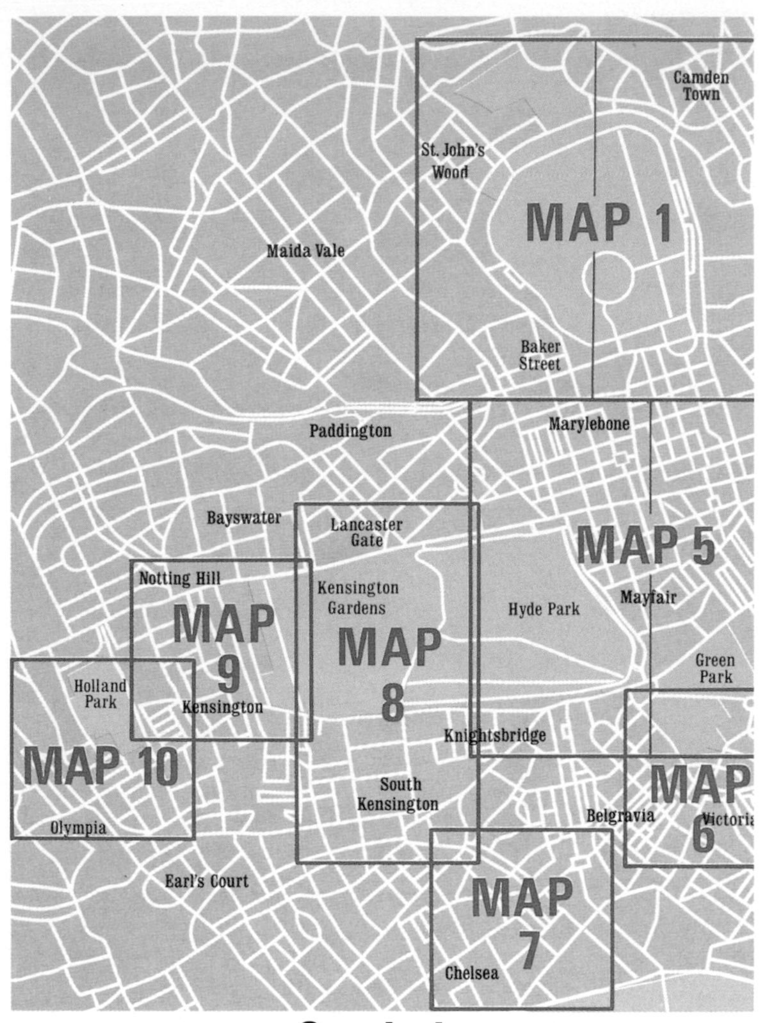


# Symbols

Principal Thoroughfare. . . . . . . . . . . . . . . STRAND

Place of Interest. . . . . . . . . . . . . . . . . . . . . .

Cinema or Theatre . . . . . . . . . . . . . . . . . . .

Street Market . . . . . . . . . . . . . . . . . . . . . . .

Underground Station. . . . . . . . . . . . . . . . . .

British Rail Station. . . . . . . . . . . . . . . . . . .

Information Centre. . . . . . . . . . . . . . . . . . . .

Embassy. . . . . . . . . . . . . . . . . . . . . . . . . . . . . .

Church . . . . . . . . . . . . . . . . . . . . . . . . . . . . .

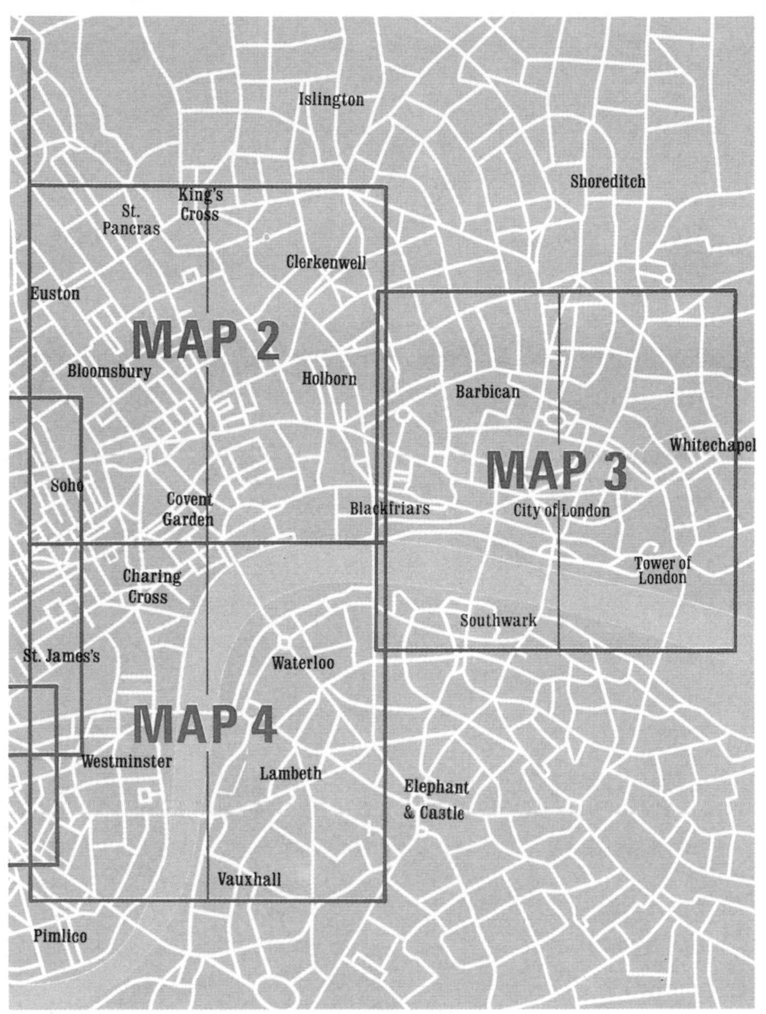


# Abbreviations

| | | | |
|---|---|---|---|
| AVE | AVENUE | PL | PLACE |
| BGS. | BUILDINGS | RD | ROAD |
| CRES | CRESCENT | SQ | SQUARE |
| GDNS | GARDENS | ST | STREET |
| GT | GREAT | TER | TERRACE |
| LA | LANE | UPR | UPPER |

YD . . . . . . . . YARD

**Scale** (for sectional maps)

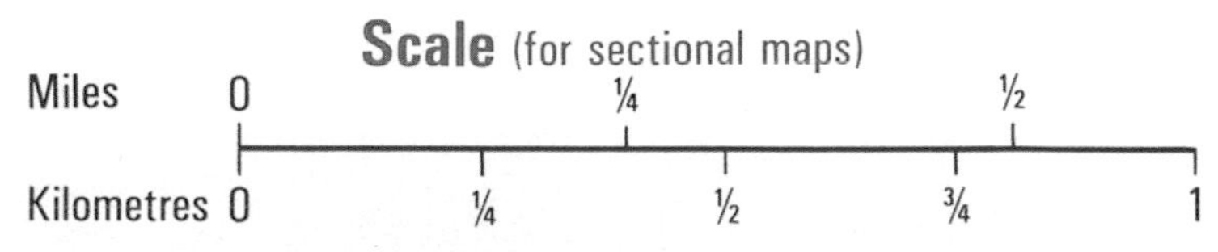

Miles 0 ¼ ½

Kilometres 0 ¼ ½ ¾ 1

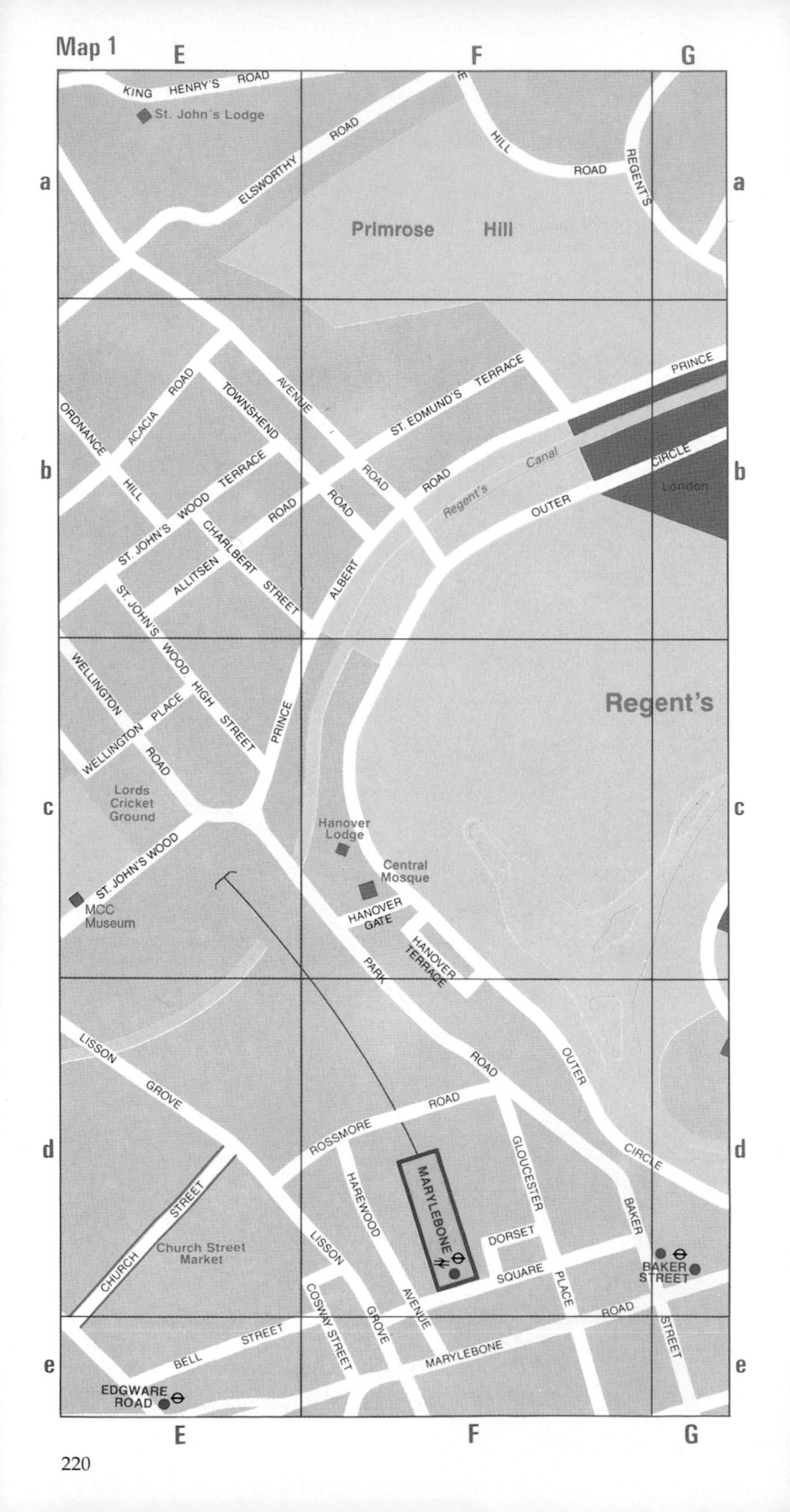
Map 1
E
F
G
a
b
c
d
e
KING HENRY'S ROAD
St. John's Lodge
ELSWORTHY ROAD
HILL ROAD
REGENT'S
Primrose Hill
PRINCE
CIRCLE
London
OUTER
ST. EDMUND'S TERRACE
AVENUE
ROAD
ACACIA ROAD
ORDNANCE HILL
TOWNSHEND ROAD
ST. JOHN'S WOOD TERRACE
CHARLBERT STREET
ALLITSEN ROAD
ALBERT ROAD
Regent's Canal
ST. JOHN'S WOOD HIGH STREET
WELLINGTON ROAD
WELLINGTON PLACE
PRINCE
Regent's
Lords Cricket Ground
ST. JOHN'S WOOD
MCC Museum
Hanover Lodge
Central Mosque
HANOVER GATE
HANOVER TERRACE
PARK ROAD
OUTER CIRCLE
LISSON GROVE
ROSSMORE ROAD
HAREWOOD
MARYLEBONE
GLOUCESTER PLACE
DORSET SQUARE
BAKER STREET
CHURCH STREET
Church Street Market
LISSON GROVE
COSWAY STREET
AVENUE
ROAD
MARYLEBONE
BELL STREET
EDGWARE ROAD

Map 1

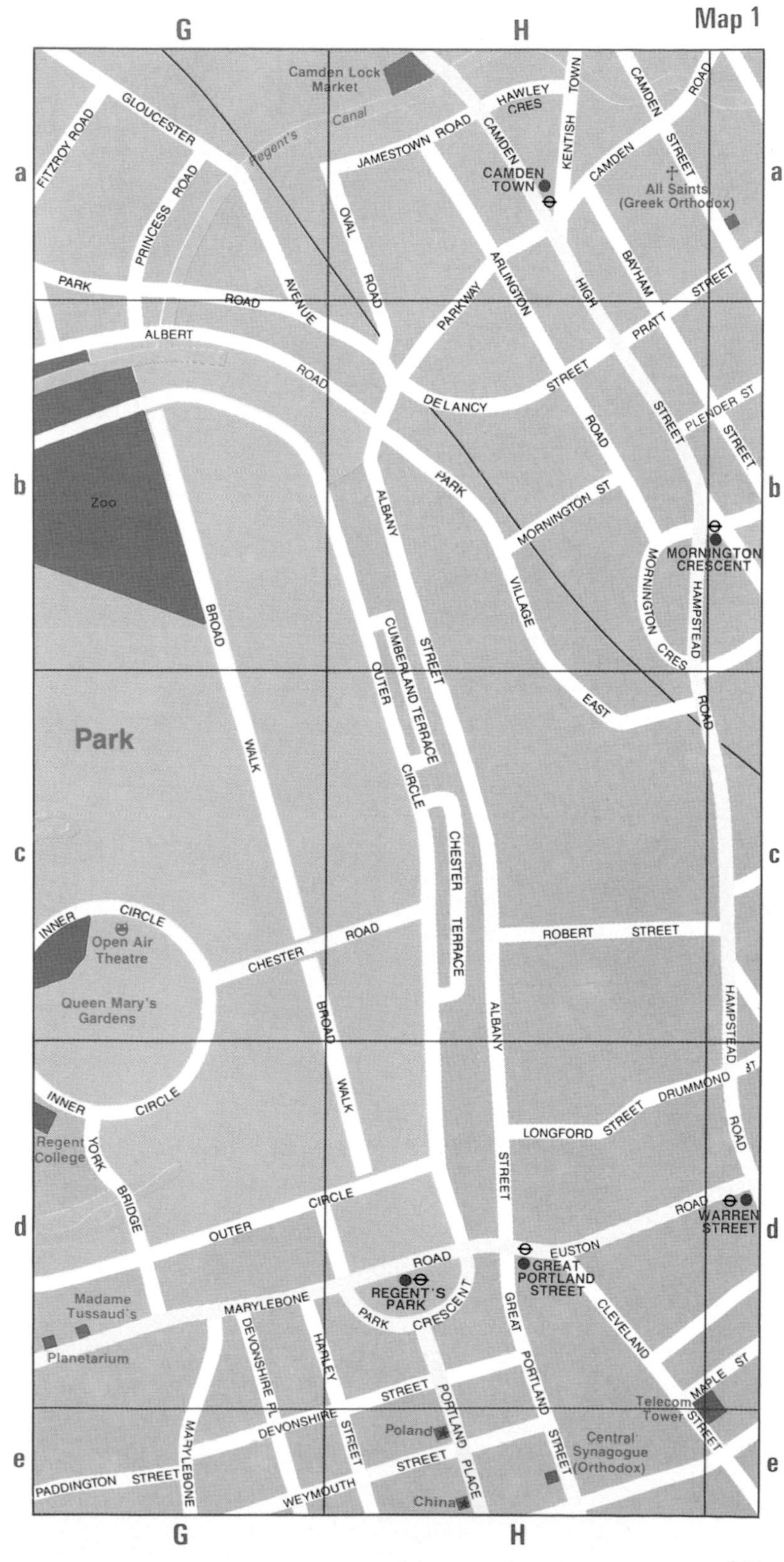
G
H
a
b
c
d
e
Camden Lock Market
Regent's Canal
Fitzroy Road
Gloucester
Princess Road
Park Road
Albert Road
Avenue
Oval Road
Jamestown Road
Hawley Cres
Camden
Kentish Town
Camden Town
Camden Road
Camden Street
All Saints (Greek Orthodox)
Bayham Street
High Street
Arlington Road
Parkway
Pratt Street
Delancy Street
Plender St
Park Village East
Mornington St
Mornington Crescent
Mornington Cres
Hampstead Road
Zoo
Broad Walk
Albany Street
Cumberland Terrace
Outer Circle
Chester Terrace
Park
Robert Street
Inner Circle
Open Air Theatre
Queen Mary's Gardens
Chester Road
Regent College
York Bridge
Drummond St
Longford Street
Warren Street
Euston Road
Great Portland Street
Regent's Park
Park Crescent
Madame Tussaud's
Planetarium
Marylebone Road
Devonshire Pl
Harley Street
Cleveland Street
Maple St
Telecom Tower
Devonshire Street
Portland Place
Poland
Central Synagogue (Orthodox)
Paddington Street
Marylebone
Weymouth Street
China

Map 2

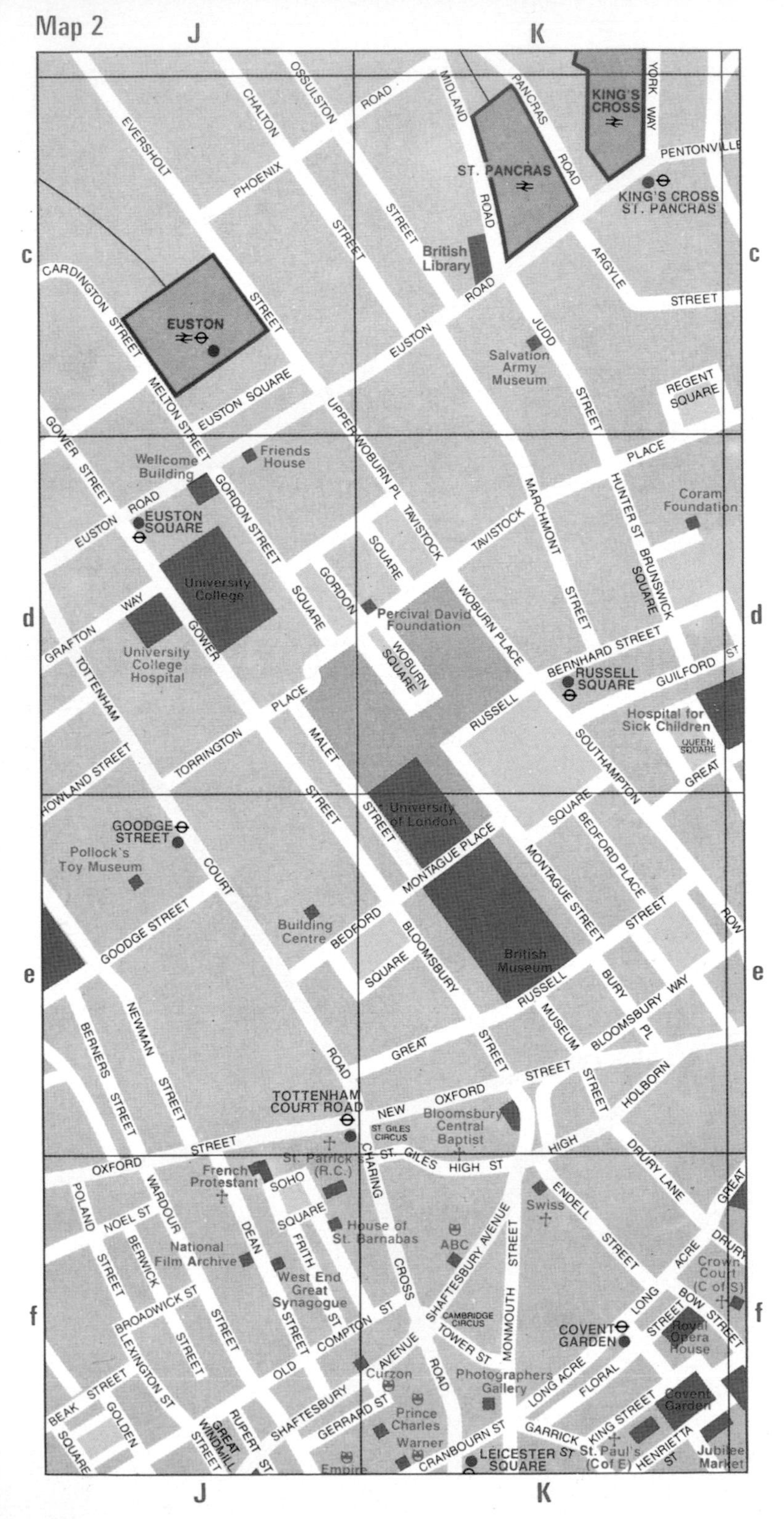
J
K
c
d
e
f
KING'S CROSS
ST. PANCRAS
KING'S CROSS ST. PANCRAS
British Library
EUSTON
Salvation Army Museum
REGENT SQUARE
Wellcome Building
Friends House
EUSTON SQUARE
Coram Foundation
University College
University College Hospital
Percival David Foundation
RUSSELL SQUARE
Hospital for Sick Children
QUEEN SQUARE
GOODGE STREET
Pollock's Toy Museum
University of London
Building Centre
British Museum
TOTTENHAM COURT ROAD
Bloomsbury Central Baptist
ST GILES CIRCUS
St. Patrick's (R.C.)
French Protestant
House of St. Barnabas
ABC
Swiss
National Film Archive
West End Great Synagogue
Crown Court (C of S)
CAMBRIDGE CIRCUS
COVENT GARDEN
Royal Opera House
Curzon
Photographers Gallery
Prince Charles
Covent Garden
Warner
Empire
LEICESTER SQUARE
St. Paul's (C of E)
Jubilee Market
EVERSHOLT
CHALTON
OSSULSTON
ROAD
MIDLAND ROAD
PANCRAS ROAD
YORK WAY
PENTONVILLE
PHOENIX
STREET
ARGYLE STREET
CARDINGTON STREET
EUSTON ROAD
JUDD STREET
EUSTON SQUARE
MELTON STREET
UPPER WOBURN PL
PLACE
GOWER STREET
GORDON STREET
TAVISTOCK SQUARE
TAVISTOCK PLACE
MARCHMONT STREET
HUNTER ST
BRUNSWICK SQUARE
GORDON SQUARE
WOBURN PLACE
GRAFTON WAY
GOWER
BERNHARD STREET
GUILFORD ST
TOTTENHAM
WOBURN SQUARE
PLACE
MALET STREET
RUSSELL
SOUTHAMPTON
HOWLAND STREET
TORRINGTON
GREAT
COURT
SQUARE
BEDFORD PLACE
MONTAGUE PLACE
MONTAGUE STREET
ROW
GOODGE STREET
BEDFORD
BLOOMSBURY
SQUARE
STREET
RUSSELL
BURY
BERNERS STREET
NEWMAN STREET
MUSEUM
BLOOMSBURY WAY
PL
ROAD
GREAT
STREET
STREET
OXFORD
HOLBORN
NEW
STREET
HIGH
DRURY LANE
CHARING
ST. GILES HIGH ST
OXFORD
SOHO
ENDELL STREET
GREAT
POLAND
WARDOUR
NOEL ST
SQUARE
DEAN
FRITH
SHAFTESBURY AVENUE
STREET
DRURY
BERWICK
CROSS
MONMOUTH
ACRE
STREET
LONG
BOW STREET
BROADWICK ST
STREET
ST
COMPTON ST
STREET
TOWER ST
LEXINGTON ST
OLD
AVENUE
ROAD
LONG ACRE
FLORAL
STREET
BEAK
GOLDEN SQUARE
GREAT WINDMILL STREET
RUPERT ST
SHAFTESBURY
GERRARD ST
CRANBOURN ST
GARRICK ST
KING STREET
HENRIETTA ST

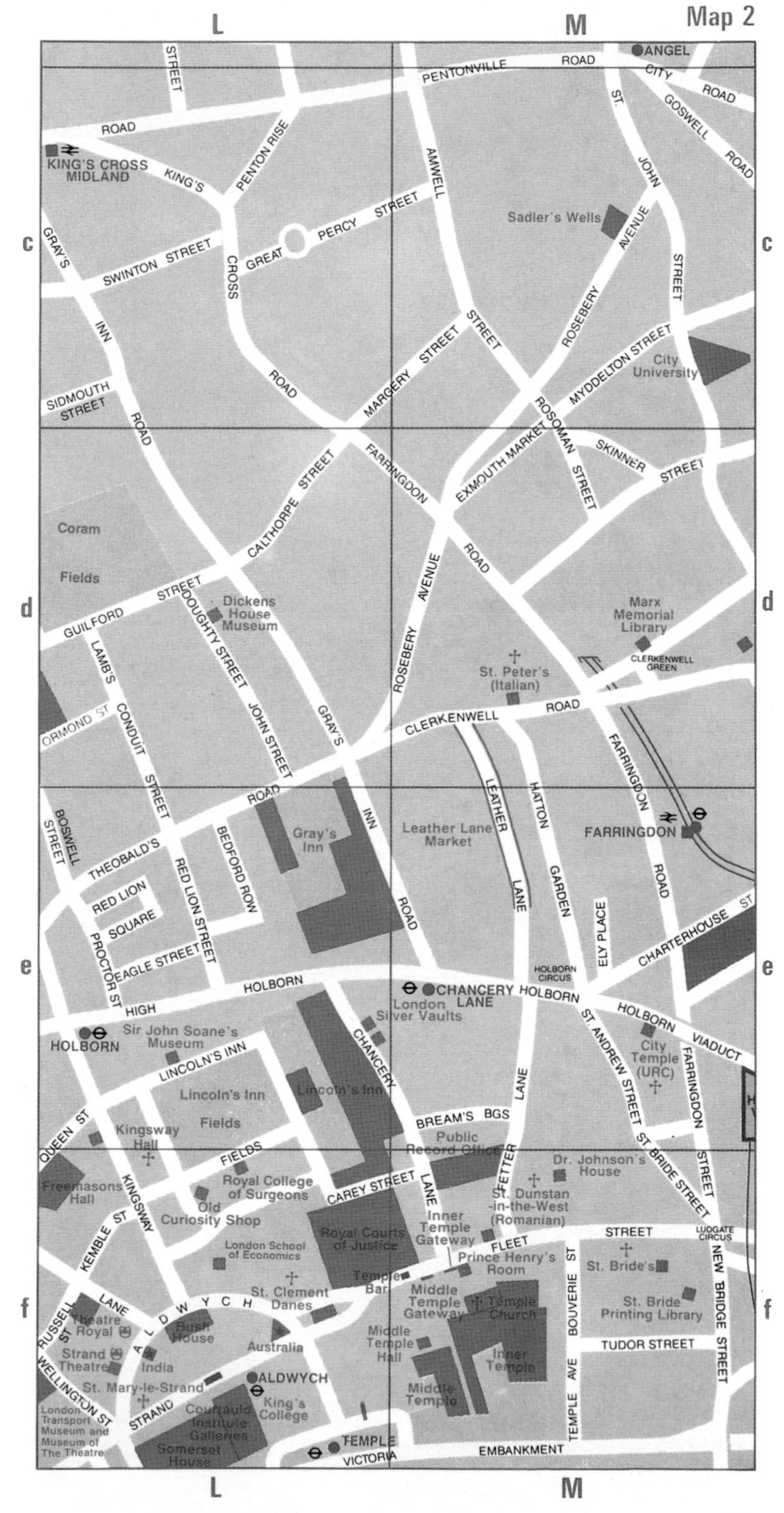
L
M
c
d
e
f
ANGEL
PENTONVILLE ROAD
CITY ROAD
GOSWELL ROAD
ST. JOHN STREET
KING'S CROSS MIDLAND
KING'S CROSS ROAD
PENTON RISE
AMWELL STREET
GREAT PERCY STREET
Sadler's Wells
AVENUE
GRAY'S INN ROAD
SWINTON STREET
CROSS
ROSEBERY AVENUE
MYDDELTON STREET
City University
SIDMOUTH STREET
MARGERY STREET
ROSOMAN STREET
EXMOUTH MARKET
SKINNER STREET
FARRINGDON ROAD
CALTHORPE STREET
Coram Fields
GUILFORD STREET
DOUGHTY STREET
Dickens House Museum
Marx Memorial Library
CLERKENWELL GREEN
St. Peter's (Italian)
LAMB'S CONDUIT STREET
ORMOND ST
JOHN STREET
CLERKENWELL ROAD
LEATHER LANE
HATTON GARDEN
BOSWELL STREET
THEOBALD'S ROAD
Gray's Inn
Leather Lane Market
FARRINGDON
RED LION SQUARE
RED LION STREET
BEDFORD ROW
ELY PLACE
CHARTERHOUSE ST
PROCTOR ST
EAGLE STREET
HOLBORN CIRCUS
HIGH HOLBORN
CHANCERY LANE
London Silver Vaults
HOLBORN VIADUCT
HOLBORN
Sir John Soane's Museum
LINCOLN'S INN FIELDS
Lincoln's Inn
Lincoln's Inn Fields
ST. ANDREW STREET
City Temple (URC)
FARRINGDON STREET
FETTER LANE
QUEEN ST
Kingsway Hall
BREAM'S BGS
Public Record Office
ST. BRIDE STREET
Dr. Johnson's House
Freemasons Hall
KINGSWAY
Royal College of Surgeons
CAREY STREET
St. Dunstan -in-the-West (Romanian)
Old Curiosity Shop
KEMBLE ST
Royal Courts of Justice
Inner Temple Gateway
FLEET STREET
LUDGATE CIRCUS
London School of Economics
Prince Henry's Room
BOUVERIE ST
St. Bride's
NEW BRIDGE STREET
Temple Bar
St. Clement Danes
Middle Temple Gateway
Temple Church
St. Bride Printing Library
RUSSELL ST
DRURY LANE
Theatre Royal
ALDWYCH
Bush House
Australia
Middle Temple Hall
TUDOR STREET
Strand Theatre
India
Inner Temple
TEMPLE AVE
WELLINGTON ST
St. Mary-le-Strand
ALDWYCH
King's College
Middle Temple
London Transport Museum and Museum of The Theatre
STRAND
Courtauld Institute Galleries
Somerset House
TEMPLE
VICTORIA EMBANKMENT

Map 3

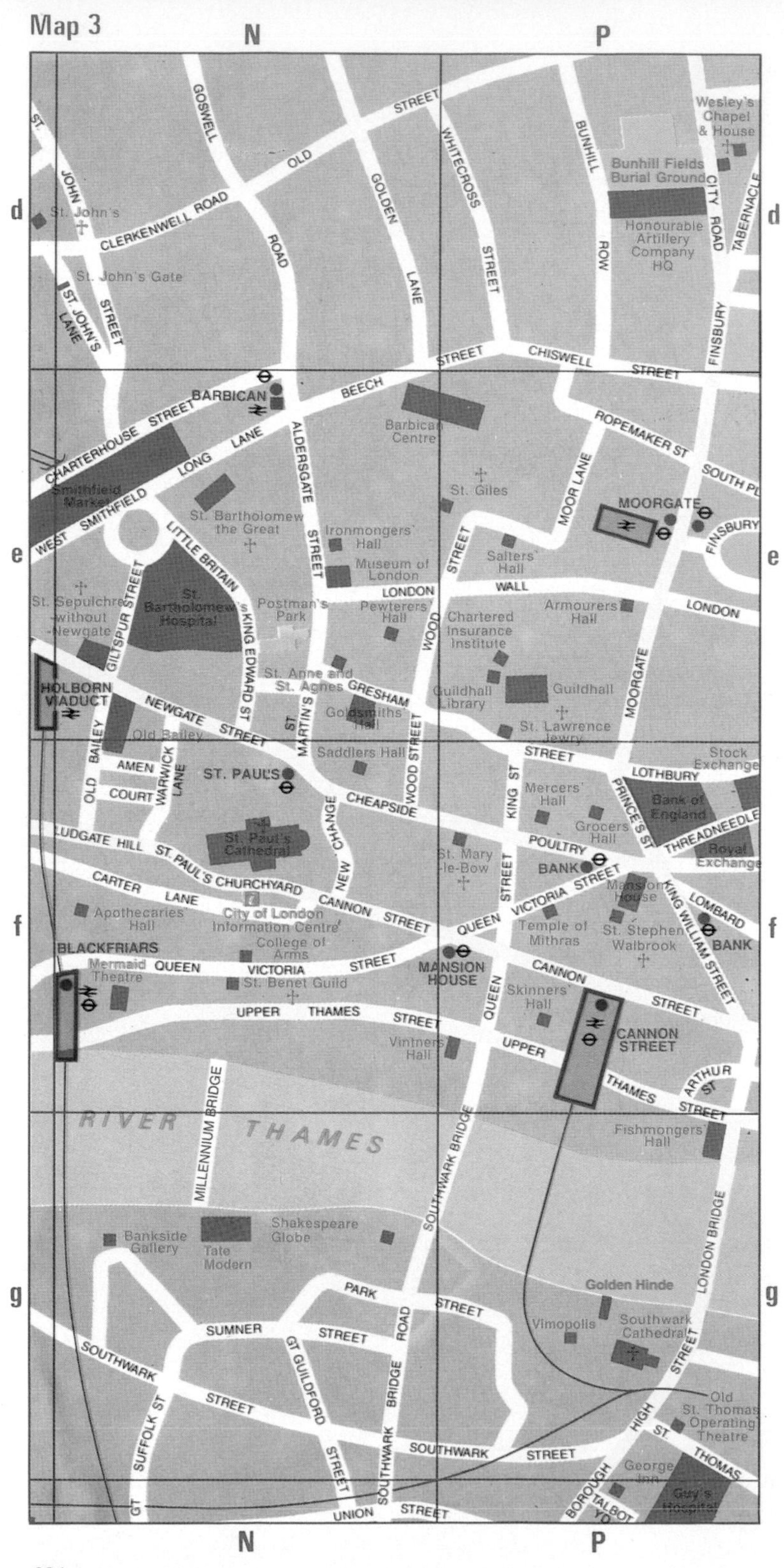
N
P
d
e
f
g
GOSWELL ROAD
OLD STREET
CLERKENWELL ROAD
ST. JOHN STREET
St. John's
St. John's Gate
ST. JOHN'S LANE
GOLDEN LANE
WHITECROSS STREET
BUNHILL ROW
Wesley's Chapel & House
Bunhill Fields Burial Ground
Honourable Artillery Company HQ
CITY ROAD
TABERNACLE
FINSBURY
CHISWELL STREET
BEECH STREET
BARBICAN
CHARTERHOUSE STREET
LONG LANE
ALDERSGATE STREET
Barbican Centre
ROPEMAKER ST
SOUTH PL
MOOR LANE
St. Giles
MOORGATE
FINSBURY
Smithfield Market
WEST SMITHFIELD
St. Bartholomew the Great
LITTLE BRITAIN
Ironmongers' Hall
Museum of London
Salters' Hall
WOOD STREET
LONDON WALL
LONDON
Armourers' Hall
St. Sepulchre without Newgate
GILTSPUR STREET
St. Bartholomew's Hospital
KING EDWARD ST
Postman's Park
Pewterers' Hall
Chartered Insurance Institute
MOORGATE
HOLBORN VIADUCT
NEWGATE STREET
St. Anne and St. Agnes
GRESHAM
Guildhall Library
Guildhall
Goldsmiths' Hall
St. Lawrence Jewry
OLD BAILEY
Old Bailey
ST. MARTIN'S
Saddlers Hall
WOOD STREET
STREET
Stock Exchange
AMEN COURT
WARWICK LANE
ST. PAUL'S
KING ST
Mercers' Hall
LOTHBURY
Bank of England
PRINCE'S ST
CHEAPSIDE
NEW CHANGE
Grocers' Hall
THREADNEEDLE
LUDGATE HILL
ST. PAUL'S CHURCHYARD
St. Paul's Cathedral
St. Mary -le-Bow
POULTRY
Royal Exchange
BANK
CARTER LANE
VICTORIA STREET
Mansion House
LOMBARD
KING WILLIAM STREET
Apothecaries' Hall
City of London Information Centre
CANNON STREET
QUEEN STREET
Temple of Mithras
St. Stephen Walbrook
BANK
College of Arms
BLACKFRIARS
Mermaid Theatre
QUEEN VICTORIA STREET
MANSION HOUSE
CANNON STREET
St. Benet Guild
Skinners' Hall
UPPER THAMES STREET
QUEEN
Vintners' Hall
UPPER THAMES STREET
CANNON STREET
ARTHUR ST
MILLENNIUM BRIDGE
RIVER THAMES
SOUTHWARK BRIDGE
Fishmongers' Hall
LONDON BRIDGE
Bankside Gallery
Tate Modern
Shakespeare Globe
Golden Hinde
PARK STREET
SUMNER STREET
ROAD
Vinopolis
Southwark Cathedral
SOUTHWARK STREET
GT GUILDFORD STREET
SOUTHWARK BRIDGE
Old St. Thomas Operating Theatre
HIGH STREET
ST. THOMAS
SUFFOLK ST
SOUTHWARK STREET
George Inn
GT
UNION STREET
BOROUGH
TALBOT YD
Guy's Hospital
N
P

# Map 3

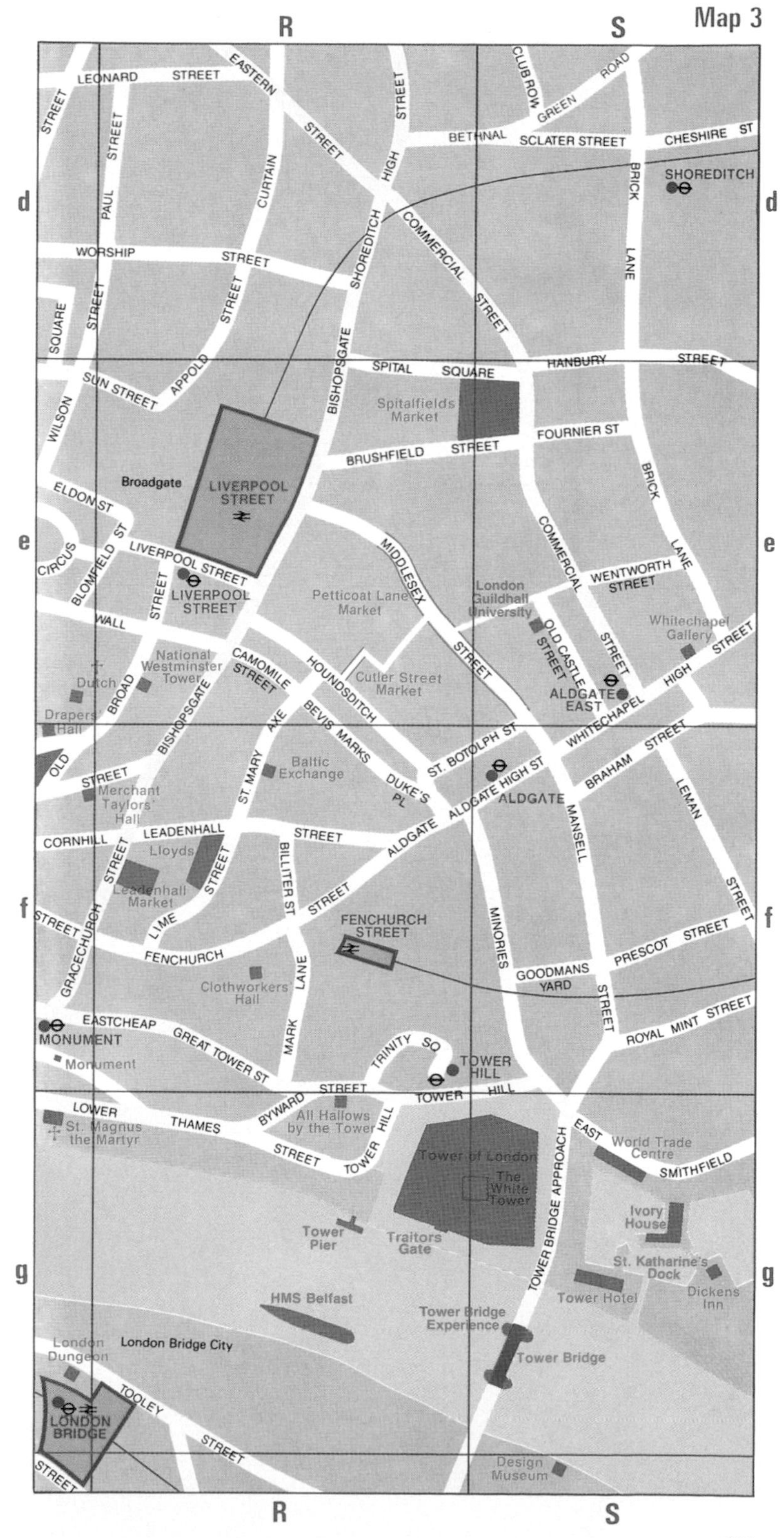
R
S
d
e
f
g
LEONARD STREET
EASTERN STREET
CLUB ROW
GREEN ROAD
BETHNAL
SCLATER STREET
CHESHIRE ST
HIGH STREET
SHOREDITCH
BRICK LANE
PAUL STREET
CURTAIN
WORSHIP STREET
COMMERCIAL STREET
SHOREDITCH
SQUARE
WILSON STREET
APPOLD STREET
BISHOPSGATE
SPITAL SQUARE
HANBURY STREET
SUN STREET
Spitalfields Market
FOURNIER ST
BRUSHFIELD STREET
Broadgate
LIVERPOOL STREET
ELDON ST
CIRCUS
BLOMFIELD ST
LIVERPOOL STREET
MIDDLESEX STREET
COMMERCIAL
WENTWORTH STREET
Petticoat Lane Market
London Guildhall University
WALL
National Westminster Tower
CAMOMILE STREET
HOUNDSDITCH
Cutler Street Market
OLD CASTLE STREET
Whitechapel Gallery
Dutch
BROAD
ALDGATE EAST
WHITECHAPEL HIGH STREET
Drapers' Hall
BISHOPSGATE
BEVIS MARKS
ST. BOTOLPH ST
OLD
STREET
ST. MARY AXE
Baltic Exchange
DUKE'S PL
ALDGATE HIGH ST
BRAHAM STREET
Merchant Taylors' Hall
ALDGATE
MANSELL
LEMAN
CORNHILL
LEADENHALL STREET
Lloyds
BILLITER ST
ALDGATE
Leadenhall Market
LIME STREET
STREET
FENCHURCH STREET
MINORIES
STREET
GRACECHURCH
FENCHURCH
PRESCOT STREET
GOODMANS YARD
Clothworkers' Hall
MARK LANE
EASTCHEAP
MONUMENT
GREAT TOWER ST
ROYAL MINT STREET
TRINITY SQ
Monument
TOWER HILL
BYWARD STREET
TOWER HILL
LOWER THAMES STREET
St. Magnus the Martyr
All Hallows by the Tower
EAST SMITHFIELD
World Trade Centre
Tower of London
The White Tower
TOWER BRIDGE APPROACH
Ivory House
Tower Pier
Traitors Gate
St. Katharine's Dock
HMS Belfast
Tower Hotel
Dickens Inn
Tower Bridge Experience
London Dungeon
London Bridge City
Tower Bridge
TOOLEY STREET
LONDON BRIDGE
STREET
Design Museum

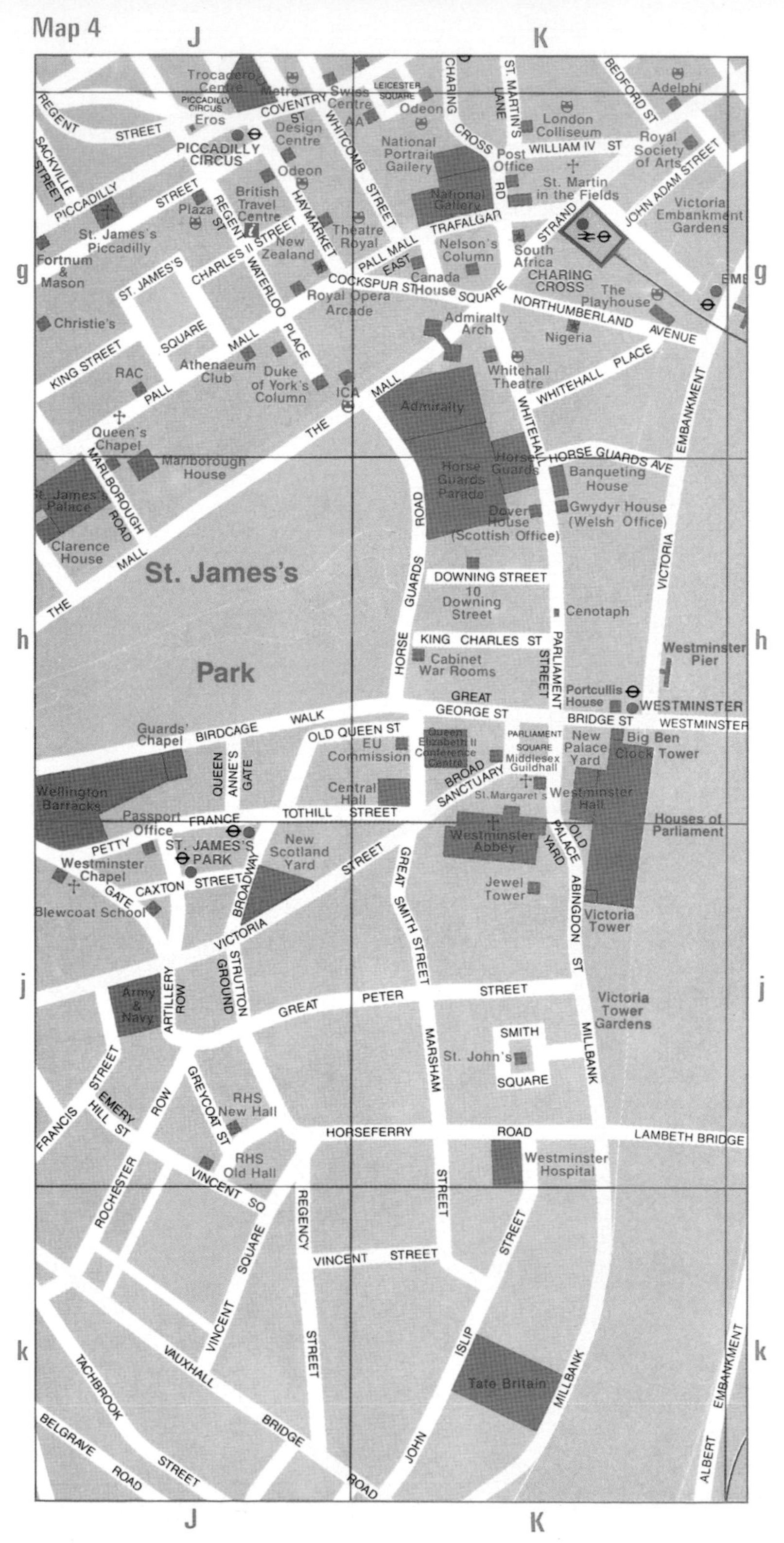
J
K
g
h
j
k
Trocadero Centre
Metro
Swiss Centre
LEICESTER SQUARE
Odeon
PICCADILLY CIRCUS
Eros
COVENTRY ST
Design Centre
AA
WHITCOMB STREET
CHARING CROSS RD
ST. MARTIN'S LANE
BEDFORD ST
Adelphi
London Colliseum
Royal Society of Arts
REGENT STREET
SACKVILLE STREET
PICCADILLY CIRCUS
National Portrait Gallery
Post Office
WILLIAM IV ST
JOHN ADAM STREET
St. Martin in the Fields
Odeon
PICCADILLY
St. James's Piccadilly
Plaza
REGENT ST
British Travel Centre
HAYMARKET
National Gallery
TRAFALGAR
STRAND
Victoria Embankment Gardens
Fortnum & Mason
ST. JAMES'S
CHARLES II STREET
New Zealand
Theatre Royal
PALL MALL EAST
Nelson's Column
South Africa
CHARING CROSS
WATERLOO PLACE
COCKSPUR ST
Canada House
SQUARE
The Playhouse
Royal Opera Arcade
NORTHUMBERLAND AVENUE
Christie's
Admiralty Arch
Nigeria
KING STREET
SQUARE
MALL
RAC
Athenaeum Club
Duke of York's Column
ICA
Whitehall Theatre
WHITEHALL PLACE
PALL
THE MALL
Admiralty
WHITEHALL
EMBANKMENT
Queen's Chapel
Marlborough House
Horse Guards
HORSE GUARDS AVE
Banqueting House
St. James's Palace
MARLBOROUGH ROAD
Horse Guards Parade
Dover House (Scottish Office)
Gwydyr House (Welsh Office)
Clarence House
THE MALL
St. James's Park
HORSE GUARDS ROAD
DOWNING STREET
10 Downing Street
Cenotaph
VICTORIA
KING CHARLES ST
PARLIAMENT STREET
Westminster Pier
Cabinet War Rooms
GREAT GEORGE ST
Portcullis House
WESTMINSTER
BRIDGE ST
WESTMINSTER
Guards' Chapel
BIRDCAGE WALK
OLD QUEEN ST
EU Commission
Queen Elizabeth II Conference Centre
PARLIAMENT SQUARE
Middlesex Guildhall
New Palace Yard
Big Ben Clock Tower
QUEEN ANNE'S GATE
BROAD SANCTUARY
Wellington Barracks
Central Hall
St. Margaret's
Westminster Hall
Passport Office
FRANCE
TOTHILL STREET
Houses of Parliament
PETTY
ST. JAMES'S PARK
New Scotland Yard
Westminster Abbey
OLD PALACE YARD
Westminster Chapel
GATE
CAXTON STREET
BROADWAY
STREET
GREAT SMITH STREET
Jewel Tower
ABINGDON ST
Blewcoat School
VICTORIA
Victoria Tower
ARTILLERY ROW
STRUTTON GROUND
Army & Navy
GREAT PETER STREET
Victoria Tower Gardens
MARSHAM STREET
SMITH SQUARE
St. John's
MILLBANK
FRANCIS STREET
EMERY HILL ST
ROW
GREYCOAT ST
RHS New Hall
HORSEFERRY ROAD
LAMBETH BRIDGE
RHS Old Hall
Westminster Hospital
ROCHESTER
VINCENT SQ
REGENCY STREET
JOHN ISLIP STREET
SQUARE
VINCENT STREET
VINCENT
Tate Britain
MILLBANK
EMBANKMENT
ALBERT
TACHBROOK
VAUXHALL BRIDGE ROAD
BELGRAVE ROAD
STREET
J
K

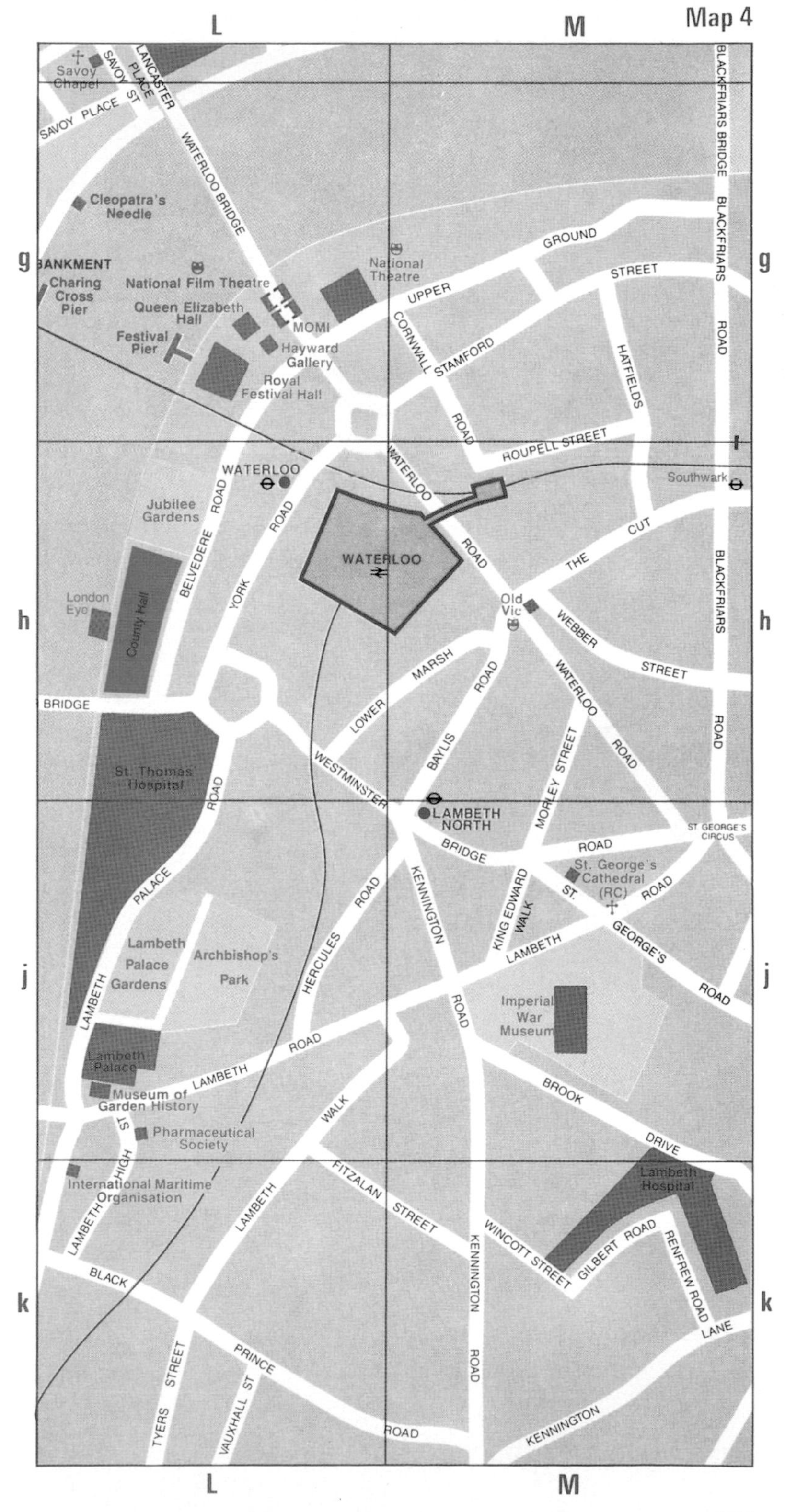
L
M
g
h
j
k
Savoy Chapel
SAVOY ST
SAVOY PLACE
LANCASTER PLACE
WATERLOO BRIDGE
BLACKFRIARS BRIDGE
Cleopatra's Needle
BANKMENT
Charing Cross Pier
National Film Theatre
Queen Elizabeth Hall
Festival Pier
MOMI
Hayward Gallery
Royal Festival Hall
National Theatre
UPPER GROUND
STREET
CORNWALL ROAD
STAMFORD STREET
HATFIELDS
BLACKFRIARS ROAD
HOUPELL STREET
WATERLOO
Southwark
Jubilee Gardens
BELVEDERE ROAD
YORK ROAD
WATERLOO ROAD
THE CUT
London Eye
County Hall
Old Vic
WEBBER STREET
BRIDGE
LOWER MARSH
BAYLIS ROAD
WATERLOO ROAD
St. Thomas Hospital
WESTMINSTER BRIDGE ROAD
MORLEY STREET
LAMBETH NORTH
ST GEORGE'S CIRCUS
PALACE ROAD
St. George's Cathedral (RC)
ST. GEORGE'S ROAD
KING EDWARD WALK
HERCULES ROAD
KENNINGTON ROAD
Lambeth Palace Gardens
Archbishop's Park
LAMBETH ROAD
Imperial War Museum
Lambeth Palace
Museum of Garden History
BROOK DRIVE
Pharmaceutical Society
LAMBETH WALK
International Maritime Organisation
LAMBETH HIGH ST
FITZALAN STREET
Lambeth Hospital
WINCOTT STREET
GILBERT ROAD
RENFREW ROAD
BLACK PRINCE ROAD
TYERS STREET
VAUXHALL ST
LANE
KENNINGTON LANE

Map 5

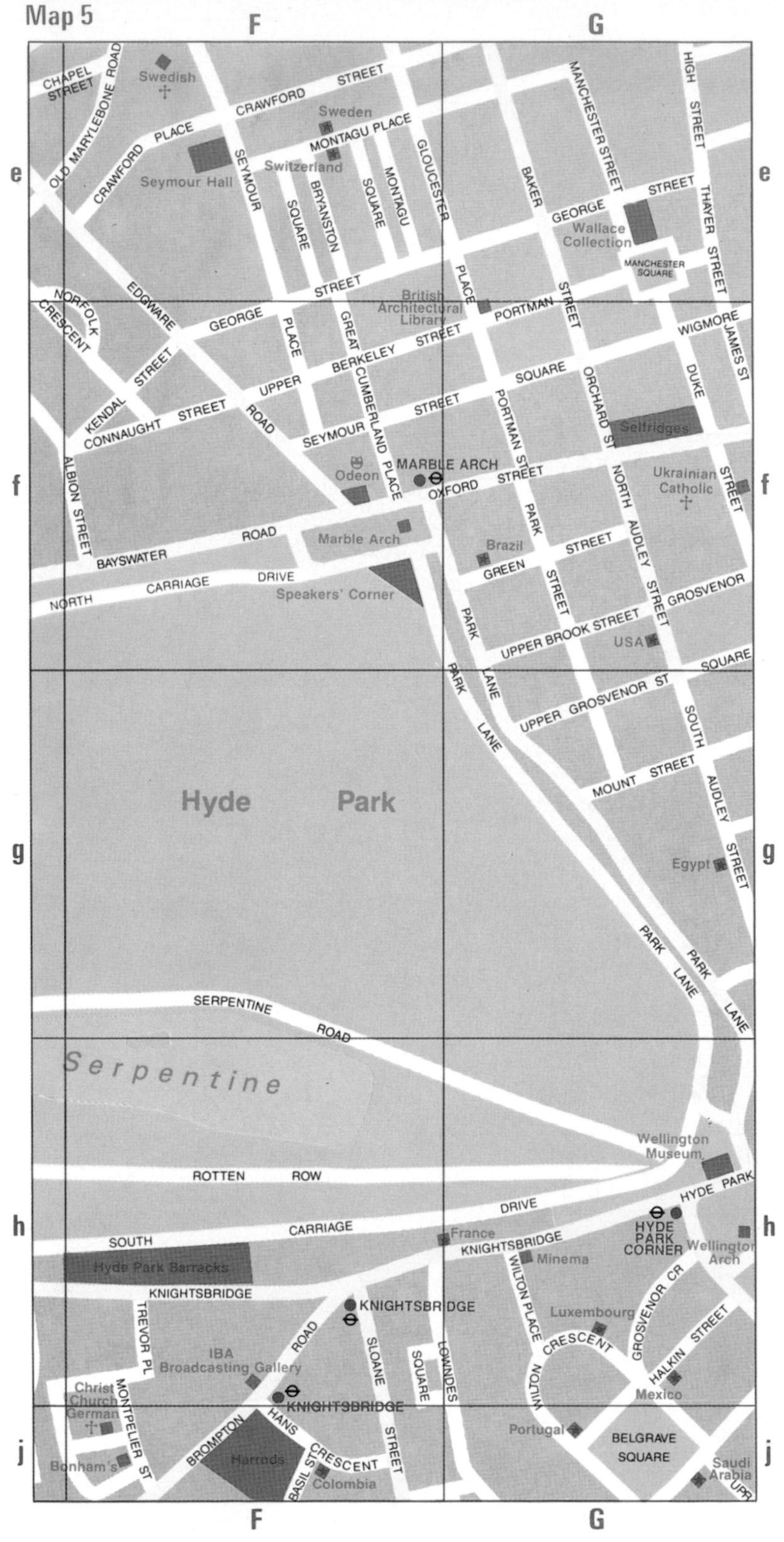

F
G
e
f
g
h
j
CHAPEL STREET
OLD MARYLEBONE ROAD
Swedish
CRAWFORD STREET
Sweden
CRAWFORD PLACE
MONTAGU PLACE
Seymour Hall
Switzerland
SEYMOUR
BRYANSTON SQUARE
MONTAGU SQUARE
GLOUCESTER PLACE
BAKER STREET
MANCHESTER STREET
HIGH STREET
THAYER STREET
GEORGE STREET
Wallace Collection
MANCHESTER SQUARE
NORFOLK CRESCENT
EDGWARE ROAD
GEORGE STREET
PLACE
GREAT CUMBERLAND PLACE
British Architectural Library
PORTMAN SQUARE
WIGMORE
JAMES ST
UPPER BERKELEY STREET
KENDAL STREET
CONNAUGHT STREET
SEYMOUR STREET
PORTMAN ST
ORCHARD ST
DUKE STREET
Selfridges
Odeon
MARBLE ARCH
OXFORD STREET
Ukrainian Catholic
ALBION STREET
NORTH AUDLEY STREET
BAYSWATER ROAD
Marble Arch
Brazil
GREEN STREET
PARK STREET
NORTH CARRIAGE DRIVE
Speakers' Corner
GROSVENOR SQUARE
UPPER BROOK STREET
USA
PARK LANE
UPPER GROSVENOR ST
SOUTH AUDLEY STREET
MOUNT STREET
Hyde Park
Egypt
SERPENTINE ROAD
Serpentine
Wellington Museum
ROTTEN ROW
HYDE PARK
SOUTH CARRIAGE DRIVE
HYDE PARK CORNER
France
KNIGHTSBRIDGE
Minema
Wellington Arch
Hyde Park Barracks
KNIGHTSBRIDGE
TREVOR PL
KNIGHTSBRIDGE
WILTON PLACE
GROSVENOR CR
Luxembourg
IBA Broadcasting Gallery
ROAD
SLOANE STREET
SQUARE
LOWNDES
CRESCENT
WILTON
HALKIN STREET
Christ Church German
MONTPELIER ST
Mexico
KNIGHTSBRIDGE
Portugal
BELGRAVE SQUARE
BROMPTON
HANS CRESCENT
Bonham's
Harrods
BASIL ST
Colombia
Saudi Arabia
UPR

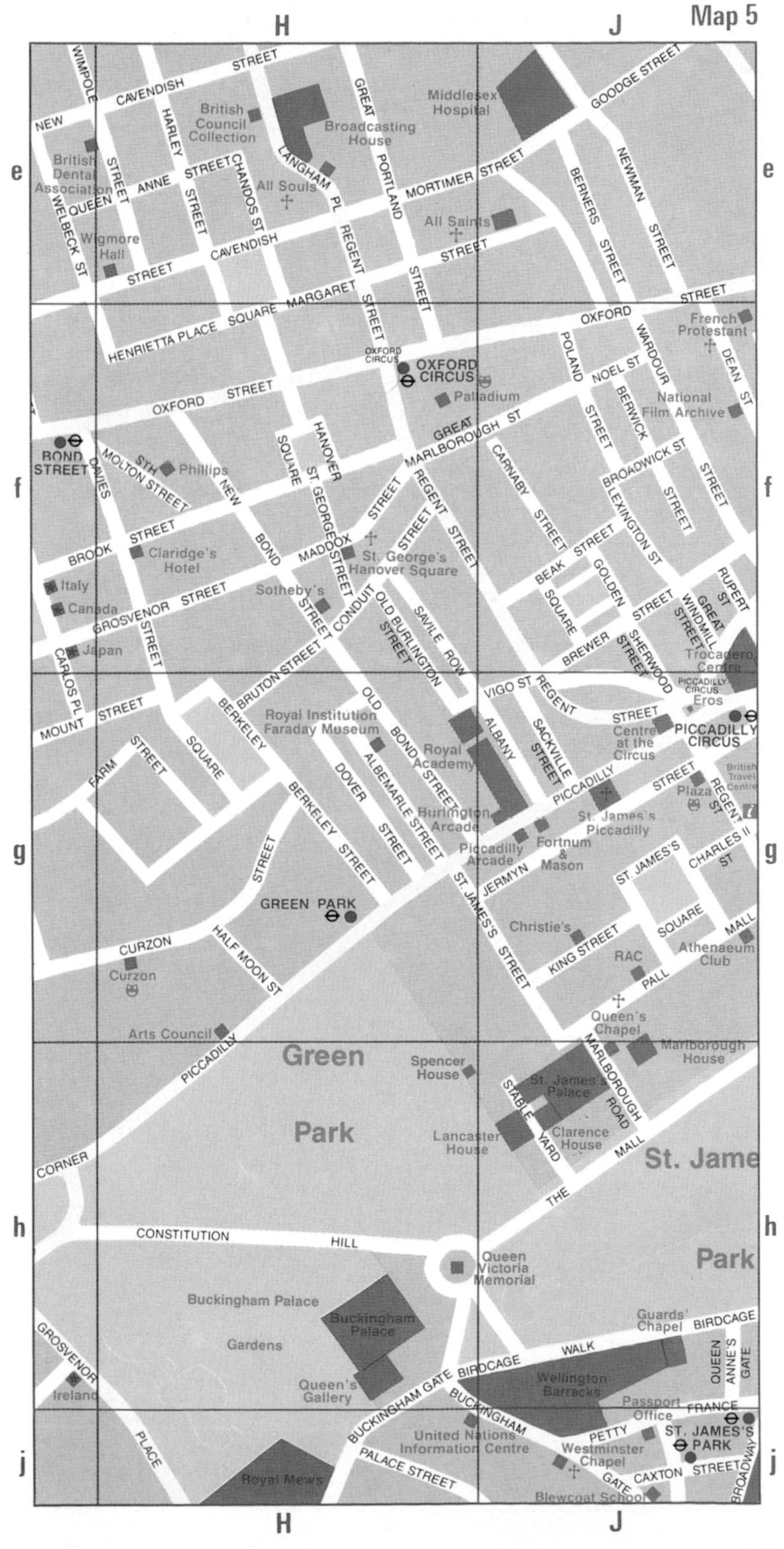
H
J
e
f
g
h
j
WIMPOLE
STREET
CAVENDISH
NEW
British Council Collection
Broadcasting House
Middlesex Hospital
GOODGE STREET
GREAT PORTLAND STREET
HARLEY STREET
British Dental Association
QUEEN ANNE STREET
CHANDOS ST
LANGHAM PL
All Souls
MORTIMER STREET
BERNERS STREET
NEWMAN STREET
WELBECK ST
Wigmore Hall
CAVENDISH STREET
REGENT STREET
All Saints
MARGARET STREET
HENRIETTA PLACE
CAVENDISH SQUARE
OXFORD STREET
French Protestant
POLAND STREET
WARDOUR STREET
DEAN ST
OXFORD CIRCUS
NOEL ST
Palladium
National Film Archive
BOND STREET
HANOVER SQUARE
GREAT MARLBOROUGH ST
BERWICK STREET
DAVIES
STH MOLTON STREET
Phillips
NEW BOND STREET
ST. GEORGE STREET
CARNABY STREET
BROADWICK ST
LEXINGTON ST
BROOK STREET
Claridge's Hotel
MADDOX STREET
St. George's Hanover Square
BEAK STREET
RUPERT ST
Italy
Canada
GROSVENOR STREET
Sotheby's
CONDUIT STREET
OLD BURLINGTON STREET
SAVILE ROW
GOLDEN SQUARE
GREAT WINDMILL STREET
Japan
CARLOS PL
BRUTON STREET
BREWER STREET
SHERWOOD STREET
Trocadero Centre
MOUNT STREET
BERKELEY SQUARE
Royal Institution Faraday Museum
OLD BOND STREET
VIGO ST
REGENT STREET
PICCADILLY CIRCUS
Eros
Centre at the Circus
FARM STREET
Royal Academy
ALBANY
SACKVILLE STREET
British Travel Centre
BERKELEY STREET
DOVER STREET
ALBEMARLE STREET
Burlington Arcade
PICCADILLY
Plaza
REGENT ST
St. James's Piccadilly
Piccadilly Arcade
Fortnum & Mason
ST. JAMES'S SQUARE
CHARLES II ST
GREEN PARK
JERMYN STREET
ST. JAMES'S STREET
Christie's
KING STREET
MALL
Athenaeum Club
CURZON STREET
HALF MOON ST
Curzon
RAC
PALL MALL
Queen's Chapel
Arts Council
Marlborough House
Green Park
Spencer House
St. James's Palace
STABLE YARD
MARLBOROUGH ROAD
Clarence House
Lancaster House
CORNER
THE MALL
St. James's Park
CONSTITUTION HILL
Queen Victoria Memorial
Buckingham Palace Gardens
Buckingham Palace
Guards' Chapel
BIRDCAGE WALK
QUEEN ANNE'S GATE
GROSVENOR PLACE
Queen's Gallery
Wellington Barracks
Ireland
BUCKINGHAM GATE
Passport Office
FRANCE
United Nations Information Centre
PETTY FRANCE
ST. JAMES'S PARK
Westminster Chapel
PALACE STREET
CAXTON STREET
BROADWAY
Royal Mews
Blewcoat School

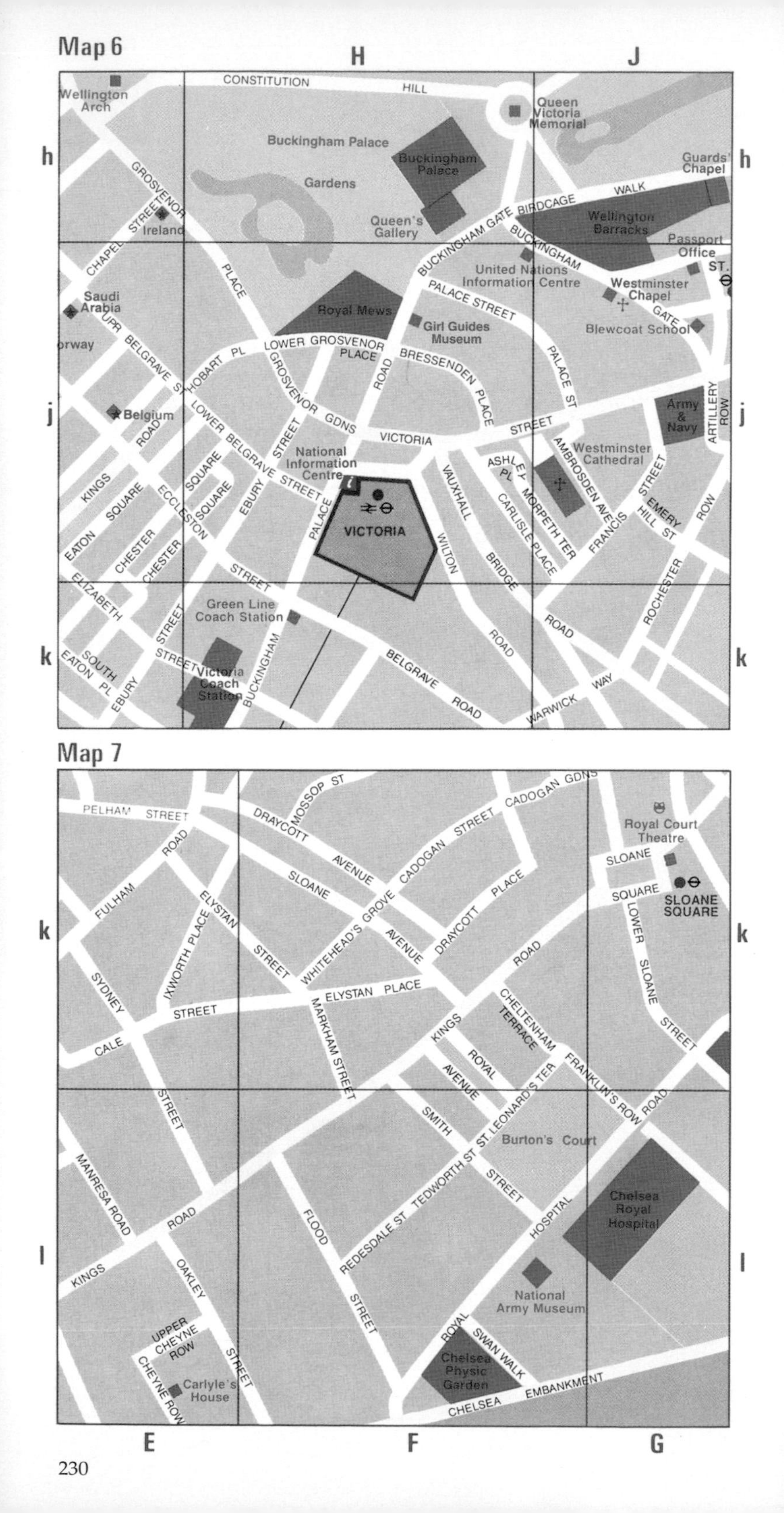
Map 6
H
J
h
j
k
CONSTITUTION
HILL
Wellington Arch
Queen Victoria Memorial
Buckingham Palace
Gardens
Buckingham Palace
Queen's Gallery
Guards' Chapel
WALK
BIRDCAGE
Wellington Barracks
GROSVENOR
CHAPEL STREET
Ireland
PLACE
BUCKINGHAM GATE
BUCKINGHAM
Passport Office
ST.
United Nations Information Centre
Westminster Chapel
GATE
Blewcoat School
Saudi Arabia
Royal Mews
PALACE STREET
Girl Guides Museum
UPR BELGRAVE ST
orway
HOBART PL
LOWER GROSVENOR PLACE
BRESSENDEN PLACE
PALACE ST
GROSVENOR GDNS
ROAD
ARTILLERY ROW
Army & Navy
Belgium
ROAD
LOWER BELGRAVE STREET
STREET
VICTORIA
STREET
Westminster Cathedral
National Information Centre
ASHLEY PL
AMBROSDEN AVE
KINGS
SQUARE
ECCLESTON
SQUARE
EBURY
VAUXHALL
CARLISLE PLACE
MORPETH TER
FRANCIS
STREET
EMERY HILL ST
ROW
EATON
SQUARE
CHESTER
CHESTER
PALACE
VICTORIA
WILTON
BRIDGE
ROCHESTER
STREET
ELIZABETH
Green Line Coach Station
ROAD
ROAD
STREET
STREET
BUCKINGHAM
EATON
SOUTH
PL
EBURY
Victoria Coach Station
BELGRAVE
ROAD
WARWICK
WAY
Map 7
k
l
E
F
G
PELHAM
STREET
MOSSOP ST
DRAYCOTT
CADOGAN GDNS
STREET
CADOGAN
Royal Court Theatre
SLOANE
ROAD
AVENUE
SLOANE
SQUARE
SLOANE SQUARE
FULHAM
ELYSTAN
CADOGAN
PLACE
DRAYCOTT
WHITEHEAD'S GROVE
AVENUE
LOWER
SLOANE
STREET
IXWORTH PLACE
STREET
ROAD
SYDNEY
STREET
ELYSTAN PLACE
MARKHAM STREET
CHELTENHAM TERRACE
CALE
KINGS
ROYAL
AVENUE
FRANKLIN'S ROW
ROAD
ST. LEONARD'S TER
STREET
SMITH
Burton's Court
MANRESA ROAD
TEDWORTH ST
STREET
Chelsea Royal Hospital
FLOOD
REDESDALE ST
HOSPITAL
ROAD
KINGS
OAKLEY
National Army Museum
STREET
UPPER CHEYNE ROW
ROYAL
SWAN WALK
Chelsea Physic Garden
STREET
CHEYNE ROW
Carlyle's House
CHELSEA
EMBANKMENT

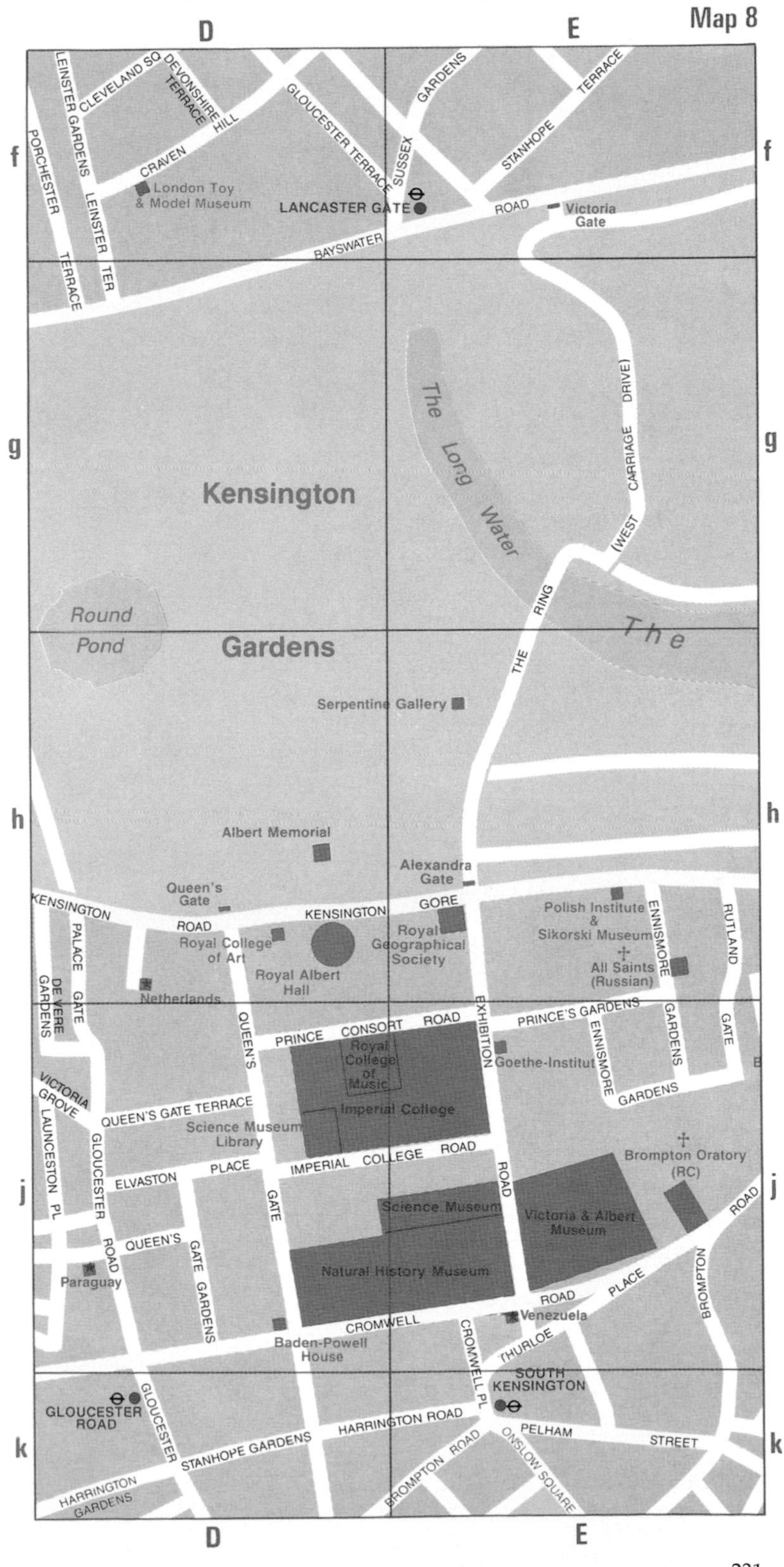
D
E
f
g
h
j
k
LEINSTER GARDENS
CLEVELAND SQ
DEVONSHIRE TERRACE
HILL
GLOUCESTER TERRACE
GARDENS
TERRACE
PORCHESTER
CRAVEN
SUSSEX
STANHOPE
London Toy & Model Museum
LANCASTER GATE
ROAD
Victoria Gate
LEINSTER
TERRACE
TER
BAYSWATER
The Long Water
(WEST CARRIAGE DRIVE)
Kensington
Round Pond
Gardens
The
THE RING
Serpentine Gallery
Albert Memorial
Alexandra Gate
Queen's Gate
KENSINGTON
ROAD
KENSINGTON
GORE
Polish Institute & Sikorski Museum
ENNISMORE
RUTLAND
Royal College of Art
Royal Geographical Society
All Saints (Russian)
PALACE
Royal Albert Hall
DE VERE GARDENS
GATE
Netherlands
EXHIBITION
QUEEN'S
PRINCE CONSORT ROAD
PRINCE'S GARDENS
Royal College of Music
Goethe-Institut
ENNISMORE
GARDENS
GATE
VICTORIA GROVE
QUEEN'S GATE TERRACE
Imperial College
GARDENS
Science Museum Library
Brompton Oratory (RC)
LAUNCESTON PL
GLOUCESTER
ELVASTON
PLACE
IMPERIAL COLLEGE ROAD
ROAD
GATE
Science Museum
Victoria & Albert Museum
ROAD
ROAD
QUEEN'S
GATE GARDENS
BROMPTON
Paraguay
Natural History Museum
ROAD
PLACE
CROMWELL
Venezuela
Baden-Powell House
CROMWELL PL
THURLOE
SOUTH KENSINGTON
GLOUCESTER ROAD
GLOUCESTER
HARRINGTON ROAD
PELHAM
STREET
STANHOPE GARDENS
BROMPTON ROAD
ONSLOW SQUARE
HARRINGTON GARDENS

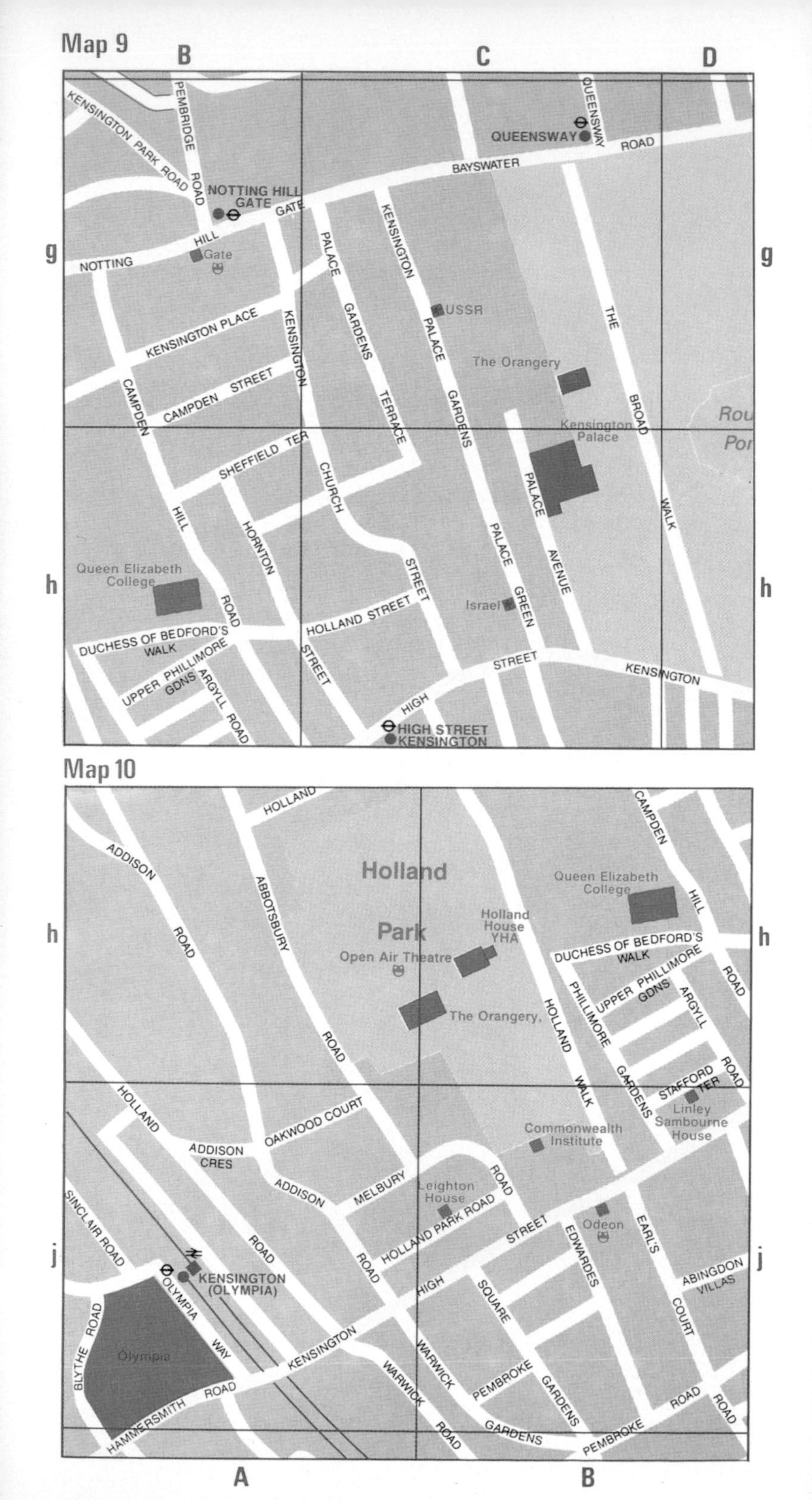
Map 9
B
C
D
g
h
KENSINGTON PARK ROAD
PEMBRIDGE ROAD
QUEENSWAY
QUEENSWAY
BAYSWATER ROAD
NOTTING HILL GATE
NOTTING HILL GATE
Gate
KENSINGTON PALACE GARDENS
PALACE GARDENS TERRACE
USSR
The Orangery
THE BROAD WALK
KENSINGTON PLACE
KENSINGTON CHURCH STREET
CAMPDEN STREET
CAMPDEN HILL ROAD
Kensington Palace
SHEFFIELD TER
HORNTON STREET
PALACE AVENUE
PALACE GREEN
Queen Elizabeth College
Israel
HOLLAND STREET
DUCHESS OF BEDFORD'S WALK
UPPER PHILLIMORE GDNS
ARGYLL ROAD
KENSINGTON HIGH STREET
HIGH STREET KENSINGTON
Map 10
A
B
h
j
HOLLAND
ADDISON ROAD
ABBOTSBURY ROAD
Holland Park
Holland House YHA
Open Air Theatre
The Orangery,
Queen Elizabeth College
CAMPDEN HILL ROAD
DUCHESS OF BEDFORD'S WALK
UPPER PHILLIMORE GDNS
ARGYLL ROAD
PHILLIMORE GARDENS
HOLLAND WALK
STAFFORD TER
Linley Sambourne House
Commonwealth Institute
HOLLAND ROAD
OAKWOOD COURT
ADDISON CRES
ADDISON ROAD
MELBURY ROAD
Leighton House
HOLLAND PARK ROAD
Odeon
EDWARDES SQUARE
EARL'S COURT ROAD
ABINGDON VILLAS
SINCLAIR ROAD
KENSINGTON (OLYMPIA)
OLYMPIA WAY
BLYTHE ROAD
Olympia
HAMMERSMITH ROAD
KENSINGTON HIGH STREET
WARWICK GARDENS
WARWICK ROAD
PEMBROKE GARDENS
PEMBROKE ROAD

# STREETS A-Z

## Addendum



## Postal Districts

# INDEX